SHAPESHIFTING
WITH OUR
ANIMAL COMPANIONS

———

"Dawn Brunke takes us on a magical mystery tour of the infinite shapes of consciousness. Shapeshifting with Our Animal Companions *gives fascinating, fresh outlooks exploring the vastness of life and death through the viewpoints of many animals and the author's refined spirituality and clear expression. Prepare to swim in an ocean of multidimensional possibilities."*

PENELOPE SMITH,
AUTHOR OF *ANIMAL TALK, WHEN ANIMALS SPEAK,*
AND *ANIMALS IN SPIRIT*

"This insightful, wise, and visionary book contains a rich tapestry of practical advice for those of us who yearn to deepen our knowing that the animal kingdom is a place of ardent tutors and mentors who can offer us keys to the greater human journeys. A compelling, world-class treasure."

SIMON BUXTON,
AUTHOR OF *THE SHAMANIC WAY OF THE BEE*

SHAPESHIFTING
WITH OUR
ANIMAL COMPANIONS

CONNECTING WITH
THE SPIRITUAL AWARENESS
OF ALL LIFE

———·———

Dawn Baumann Brunke

Bear & Company
Rochester, Vermont

Bear & Company
One Park Street
Rochester, Vermont 05767
www.BearandCompanyBooks.com

Bear & Company is a division of Inner Traditions International

Library of Congress Cataloging-in-Publication Data

Brunke, Dawn Baumann.
  Shapeshifting with our animal companions : connecting with the spiritual awareness of all life / Dawn Baumann Brunke.
    p. cm.
  Summary: "Journeys with animals for personal transformation and enlightenment"— Provided by publisher.
  Includes bibliographical references.
  ISBN 978-1-59143-083-4 (pbk.)
  1. Human-animal relationships—Religious aspects. 2. Animals—Religious aspects. 3. Metamorphosis—Miscellanea. I. Title.

BL439.B78 2008
133.8'9—dc22

                                                                                          2008008535

Printed and bound in the United States by Lake Book Manufacturing

10   9   8   7   6   5   4   3   2   1

Text design and layout by Virginia Scott Bowman
This book was typeset in Garamond Premiere Pro with Baskerville and Copperplate as display typefaces

To send correspondence to the author of this book, mail a first-class letter to the author c/o Inner Traditions • Bear & Company, One Park Street, Rochester, VT 05767, and we will forward the communication. For more information on her books or to contact her personally by e-mail, please visit the Animal Voices website at **www.animalvoices.net.**

Contents

PART 3

THE ART OF GREATER LIVING

Acknowledgments

Deepest thanks to all the beings of so many forms and species who offered their thoughts, insights, shared awareness and adventures, and unique presences, helping to make this book a reality.

Thanks to my mother Carol Baumann and good friend Phil Kotofski for excellent suggestions and unrelenting encouragement on early versions of the manuscript.

Thanks to all the great folks at Inner Traditions • Bear & Company who are not afraid to go beyond the ordinary and publish books that inspire us to be the extraordinary beings we are. Thanks to Jon Graham for his enthusiasm on this project, to Peri Champine for a lovely cover, and to Viriginia Scott Bowman for an engaging text design and layout. Thanks to Jeanie Levitan, Rob Meadows, and Ehud Sperling for all their work behind the scenes. Grateful thanks to editor Jamaica Burns and copy editor Vickie Trihy for their sensitivity, attention to detail, and finely tuned polishing of this book.

Thanks to Hal Zina Bennett, Simon Buxton, John Perkins, Rita Reynolds, Penelope Smith, and Tera Thomas for their very kind words of support.

Thanks to my husband, Bob, and daughter, Alyeska—you are both such a treasured source of caring, joy, and immense laughter in my life!

Thanks to Max and Riza, Tau, and the group for such a rich range of experiences. And extra special thanks to Barney and Zak, my very good pals—teachers and friends, confidants and instigators, clever guides and intrepid explorers of consciousness. This book would not be here today if it were not for you.

PART I

Apprentice to Change

1

—·—

Lessons in
Conscious Dying

It was midsummer in Alaska and I hadn't seen the star-filled night sky in several months. Sunlight blazed bright white off the snowy tip-tops of the mountains in the distance, and reflected a silvery sheen upon the tidal waters of the Knik Arm below. Closer to home, plump bumblebees buzzed in and out of the lilac tree, whose leafy green upper branches bulged against the railing of our second-story back porch.

I was looking for my dog Barney in the backyard. He had asked to be let out early in the morning and hadn't come in yet, even though it was nearing dinnertime.

I walked down the porch stairs, around the lilac, toward the wild patch of fireweed growing higher against our back fence each day. Folk legend has it that when the brilliant purple blooms reach the top of their stalk, summer will soon be over.

"Barney!" I called. "Barney!" Brushing past the chicken-wired garden, I entered the tangle of trees and shrubbery that provided wild space for the dogs. It was there—in a small clearing, behind the slate-roofed fish smoker we had built the year before—that I found him. Lying on his side, head tucked, legs curled, his body resting peacefully under the cool shadow of the smoker.

"Get up, Barn," I pleaded, nudging his front paw with the tip of my foot. He had grown so thin, so fragile. I knew he had gone there to die. It was just like him to choose a quiet way to release himself back into the earth. No big fuss, no big trauma. Simply breathe your last breath back into the soil and float yourself free into the sunshine.

It's easy to see this now—and to appreciate how peaceful such a death might have been—but back then I panicked. Despite all the talks we'd had, all the experiences we had shared, I wasn't ready. I ran inside and got my husband, wheedling him to carry Barney back inside.

As Bob hefted the limp body of my fine old buddy into his arms and headed toward the door, Barney rolled his head to look at me. His soulful brown eyes peeked through his overgrown white fur, fearlessly burrowing deep inside of me, connecting at that place where there is no room for lies. *Ah,* he remarked in passing, *we're going to do this your way, are we?*

IT BEGINS

Barney had been with me for eleven years. I adopted him as a two-year-old cocker spaniel/poodle/terrier mix from a shelter in Maryland. He was just being put into a cage as I walked into the room. Barks and yips and yowls reverberated against stark gray walls and metal bars. It was not a peaceful place, but the medium-sized white dog with the floppy ears sat quietly waiting. I knew as soon as I saw him—even before I felt that force of energy flowing between us, pulling me closer. I crouched beside the cage and as he turned to look at me, it was clear. He was the one I was looking for.

Barney was with me through a lot. He saw me through a variety of relationships and was my best friend on a month-long road trip exploring the ruggedly beautiful country of Nova Scotia. He hung out under the massage table I had in my home in Maryland, especially while I gave massages to clients. When I came home late after teaching evening classes in anatomy and kinesiology, I'd be greeted by his friendly face at the door, stub of a tail wagging wildly.

Most everyone liked Barney, and the most frequent adjective used to describe him was *cool*. "That's a cool dog," people would say, even if they didn't know him well. Indeed, Barney had a calm yet engaging presence. He *knew* things, and the way he expressed his knowing was undoubtedly cool. It was he who chose a particular someone to sidle up to at a party. Before long, that individual would be stroking his fur, quieting down, mellowing and centering in a way that visibly shifted something deep inside.

Barney traveled with me from Maryland to Wisconsin when I moved back to my home state. A few years later, after I married, he moved with me to the far north of the state. He loved our woodsy cottage home and would often visit a nearby resort to "fish." Patrolling the beach area for the perfect spot, Barney would stand tranquil as a seasoned fisherman; quiet and focused, paws planted firmly in the chilly, northern lake water, he watched small fish flutter by for hours at a time. Every so often he would suddenly plunge his whole head under the water to make a grab—mostly to no avail.

The only time Barney and I ever had a falling out was the day he disowned me. Coming out of a grocery store one Saturday morning, Bob and I passed two young girls guarding a huge cardboard box in the parking lot. "Puppies!" I cried, instantly reverting to my six-year-old self as I grabbed for one of the pups. It was a tiny, wriggling, tawny brown male—part cocker spaniel, part golden retriever, part samoyed. As soon as I held him, we all knew it was over. There was no way the warm, wriggling pup was going to leave my arms. It happened so fast, without conscious thought, and yet it felt inexplicably right . . .

Until we got into the truck, that is. Barney took one look and turned his head away from me. Moving over to Bob (whom he had never been especially close to), Barney refused to acknowledge me or the newcomer for the rest of the day. But the pup, whom we called Zak, had other plans. He tossed his toys in front of Barney like a

Barney

little kid trying to cajole a grouchy grandpa into play. When that didn't work, Zak jumped up and grabbed Barney's collar, attempting to walk him around the yard. It wasn't too long before Barney acquiesced, both to Zak and to me. Within a few days, we were good buds once again.

Barney and Zak helped to welcome my daughter, Alyeska, into the world. They were both gentle and considerate of the new baby. They became her first best playmate and, two years later, were part of our family caravan as we packed up our Suburban and trudged northwest-ward across the country, to Alaska.

Despite a lot of moving and uncertainty (no jobs, no house), Barney and Zak were dependable guardians and friends. Once we settled, they met the neighborhood dogs and established their own jobs in our home. Then, they set out to some deeper work with me.

I became the editor of a health, wellness, and spirituality magazine. One day, I came across an article written by a woman in Anchorage who talked with animals. Sparked by the idea, I interviewed the woman and learned there were other such "communicators" who, by means of quieting the mind, were able to tune into the thoughts, emotions, and consciousness of other beings and communicate back and forth, as in a real conversation.

I've always been interested in different ways of seeing the world and, in particular, how diverse cultures use language, the arts, and religion to talk about and understand spirit. So, the notion of seeing the world from an animal's point of view was deliciously intriguing. I contacted other communicators and wrote some articles, all the while relentlessly asking questions: What sorts of things did animals think about? What special knowledge or wisdom did they hold? What did they think of humans? If they could tell us what they most wanted us to know, what would it be?

Some of the communicators allowed me to interview animals through them. Thus, I asked questions of horses and llamas, dogs and cats, whales and dolphins. Even though I believed most all of the communicators were genuine and right-hearted in their talks, I still wondered how "real" this notion of talking to animals could be.

As I began writing a book on the subject, I shifted from journalist to explorer, skeptic to fascinated voyager. I bounced from disbelief to awe to sudden enlightenment—and then bumped right back to uncertainty. I began having my own experiences in connecting with animals. I understood what the communicators were telling me: it was like an inner switch turning on, reminding me of another way of being. I found that by closing my eyes, letting go of superficial chatter and focusing softly with an open heart, I could meet animals in a way in which our feelings, thoughts, and ideas were shared.

I was often surprised by how diverse and unusual their views were, especially in comparison to what I might have expected. It was all a process of relaxing and having fun, of being open enough to see the world in a new, different—and often much more vibrant—way.

I also found a knack for translating into words the sensations, images, and sensory ideas that washed through my consciousness as I connected at deeper levels with animals. Now, don't get me wrong—at times it was a bumpy ride. I doubted myself, told myself I had an overactive imagination or was guilty of projecting. While most communicators shared similar stories of self-doubt, especially in the early stages of remembering this ability we all have, I still found it difficult to accept some of the remarkable information that was shared in my conversations.

Luckily, Barney and Zak were happy to help. They most often intervened when I least expected anything—a good plan to shake me from the confines of my old, limiting beliefs into the open fields of expanded awareness. Still the closet skeptic, I asked for proofs that what I heard from animals was "true." Time and again, I was told things that I could not have known, things that were later verified by the animal's person. It's a funny game we humans play—not trusting our experiences until others confirm them for us.

Gradually, though, I came to accept the process. It was Barney who became my main teacher and guide, my encouraging friend and supportive confidant. He often pushed me—gently, as only a caring, clever, unassuming dog can do—to go beyond my self-imposed belief systems and the social paradigms enforced by language, culture, education, family, and peers. Barney asked me to dig deep and search for knots that held or blinded me to certain areas. And he instructed me, time and again, to "open to experience—the Grand Teacher," as he was so fond of saying.

Barney also called me on my fears, asking me to be present and consider the deeper roots of why I was so eager to turn away from a particular idea or experience. I never knew Barney to be a coy or evasive being. Rather, he put his cards on the table and encouraged others to meet themselves in the same way—eyes clear, mind alert, heart open—boldly, lovingly, in the mirror of self.

THIS MOST AMAZING JOURNEY

Let us begin with a short introduction to the topic of death, said Barney early one morning as he plopped below my desk, pushing my foot with his muzzle. Barney and I had a deal. If he lay under my desk, it was a sign that we were to have a chat.

It would be best to think of this subject as a transition or journey rather than as a finality or ending, he continued. *The journey is like a shaking off, just as a dog shakes water easily and naturally from its fur when wet.*

There are many avenues by which we could proceed. I would like to point out from the beginning that there is one major road to death, or transformation of bodily form, though there are numerous side paths that one can take along the way.

I am now preparing for my ending in this body of Barney the dog. It is like turning a page, closing a book, moving from one room to another, momentarily turning attention away from Barney the dog so as to focus on another aspect of being.

Ah, there is so much to discuss! That is why I would like to leave you now with the image of a road toward death. It is the major path to one's end in this particular space/time/being configuration. But, while on that road, we will take numerous side treks in order to more fully discuss and appreciate this most amazing journey.

This is where we stopped that first morning, a mere six weeks before I found him preparing to die behind the fish smoker, and his death a few days later. Although Barney and I had enjoyed many profound conversations over several years (during which time I came to realize that animals are not only sentient but wise, humorous, and talented beings with unique purposes for being upon this planet), these conversations—what I would come to think of as the Death

Talks—were special. Nearly every morning in the days that followed, we would speak about a good many subjects: the transition from life to death, reincarnation, karmic projections and illusions, and—one of Barney's favorite topics—the value and wonder of shapeshifting.

It seemed hard to confront so much so deeply when there was such precious little time left. Barney's eyesight was failing, he was growing thinner, and he had a disturbing way of occasionally staring off into space and shaking for several seconds at a time. Yet, in other ways, he seemed perfectly happy and healthy. He still ran like a puppy when I took him to the mountains, and never did turn away from a bowl of food.

Our first task, then, was to plunge in deeply just exactly where we were. And this, Barney told me, was facing death, square in the eyes.

WHAT'S WRONG WITH DEATH?

The word *death* comes to us from the Old English, though its roots go back much further than that. As far back as the most ancient parts of us can remember, we have known death. Most often, the word is associated with the permanent cessation of all bodily functions. Our heart stops, our lungs cease, our brain withers away: we die. In short, death is the end of life as we know it. Scary stuff for us humans, who want to plan and know and be in control of every last little detail.

Some people don't like to use the word *death*. They may say things like *passed away, crossed over, departed.* Although these phrases hold their own truths, it seems a funny human-thing to create euphemisms, as if that will somehow help us to sidestep the process. Yet, the very act of creating and using euphemisms reveals how deeply taboo—and thus fear inducing—this subject is for so many people.

Some may argue that death sounds so final, as if we absolutely cease to exist when we die. What about the soul? What about our vital essence? We don't really end with death, do we?

Parts of us—the very cells of our blood and skin and entire body—

are continually in the process of dying, just as other cells are continually being created. In this sense, death is a natural part of the process of living. Even if after death we do go on to another world—an alternate universe, a heaven, a hell, an ever-present continuum of consciousness—bodily death is still part of our life cycle on this earth. We may call it other things, but death is as integral to our current version of life as is birth. What's wrong with death?

I wish to talk about my own death, a personal path, for now, Barney began the following morning.

Others have seen this coming and have reflected it to you, yet you still do not wish to see. I understand. This is how it is for many, many beings. The shrouding of death from consciousness is a built-in defense mechanism, one that comes with a certain degree of grace or consciousness comfort. It is for this reason that it remains a mystery for many beings. Death is here, and yet it is not seen, hidden away deep within the being's knowingness.

My own death is not too far away, though I still have some time. I accepted my death many lifetimes ago and it is no longer a trauma for me. I am spending time with you on this subject since it interests you, and I am willing to share these teachings with others, since it may interest and help them as well.

One of the first things to observe is your relationship with death. How do you think about death and feel it in your body? Is it with a gasp of fear or a laugh of defense? Is it held with tension or lovingly, hand in hand?

The way you think-feel about death greatly influences the way death occurs, though I do not mean this to be a hard-and-fast rule. That is the trouble with some humans—your intellect can be developed to overpower your emotions. Sometimes this works in your favor; at other times it does not. I will say from the outset that as I give information in the following pages, it is important to note that this is from my perspective and my many lifetimes of learning, experiencing, and teaching about death. I do not wish for any one sentence to be taken as a hard-and-fast rule. It is better for your inner ear to listen, to grasp the wholeness of what I say, and use what fits best for you at this particular time.

You might ask me, What do you see or feel when you confront death? For myself, it is simply a passing into another mode of being. Many have said this before. Perhaps it would do well to take this into your consciousness at a very deep level: it is simply a movement to another mode of being—much like moving from one room to another within your house, or from one state to another. It is really nothing more than that: a moving.

I have a heaviness in my heart around all the fear that is associated with death. I have worked with death and with those beings making the transition for many lifetimes, and so I am familiar with this 'heavy door' syndrome. Do you feel it in your heart, Dawn?

"Yes," I admitted. "I can feel that heaviness. And I also sense how I want to keep the door closed. I don't even know why anymore."

It is because you fear the unknown. That is not so out of the ordinary. It is normal—and even encouraged in your society—to fear the unknown. At some level, this is a healthy thing. It prevents you from trespassing in places you ought not to go. At other times, however, it is much more of an obstacle. You know that Zak often talks about doors—his preferred metaphor is the sliding glass door. That is because he operates from a much more expanded viewpoint of always seeing the next room. For him, there is no mystery associated with moving and that is why his personality is rather fearless, don't you think?

Yes, sharp-witted Zak was indeed an intrepid explorer. "He is funny that way," I agreed, grateful for a small laugh and mild reverie.

WHAT HAPPENS?

So, how shall we proceed? asked Barney after a pause.

"Why don't we start with what you most want us to know."

Hmmm. Sometimes you use that question as a shield. Do you know that?

I felt my face flush. How was it that this dog could see through me so easily? "Yes, I know what you are getting at," I admitted at last.

"Sometimes I feel it is easier to be given information rather than searching for it myself."

And so, let us begin with you. What is it that you would most like to know about death?

"Oh, good question!" My curiosity jumbled forward. "I guess my biggest emotional fear is leaving the people I love. I wonder if the 'beyond' is going to be more fun than this world or if I will really miss it. But mostly the emotional ties I have to my family are what pulls at my heart and makes me not want to leave."

And your question is?

I laughed. Barney had a way of pulling me out of reveries just as skillfully as he nudged me into pondering the deeper questions of life, and death.

"What happens? I guess that is everyone's question, isn't it? Where do we go when we leave this world? Do we still have consciousness? Do we forget those on Earth or are we still connected with them? What happens?"

Most everyone knows in their heart and deep within their being the answers to these questions. Most beings have journeyed into death many, many times before.

Let us return to the metaphor of moving from room to room. Just because you leave one room does not mean you forget it. You simply are engaged in whatever you are now seeing and feeling, though the reality and memory of that other room still survives. This is how it is with death to some degree, at least at certain stages.

There are those who do not want to leave the room of the living. The emotional ties are too strong and they feel—mostly based on mistaken beliefs—that they cannot or should not leave. This leads to a slow transition and is not often very productive. Most beings, however, are fairly quick in leaving their bodies and moving on.

There are many wonders out-of-body, many different dimensional levels to explore. You might compare it to moving to another country— once there, you are excited by the newness and the different ways of the people and their land, their marketplaces, their art and language and culture. Death is a passage to another country—and there is very much to explore!

There are 'schools' one can attend. Some beings learn about healing emotional ties and releasing old personalities. Some choose to have personal guides, almost like taking a tour. In truth, there are as many versions to this experience as there are beings—which is to say, an infinite variety. That is why I remind you that your relationship to death is Paramount. It is your movie, after all!

I smiled as I wrote down Barney's words, his thoughts flowing through me like wild birds gliding across a calm, blue sky.

Does this help answer your question some? Barney asked.

"Yes, it goes along with what I have felt, too."

Well, you needn't fear that this is your 'projection.' You have had many lifetimes in which you also have assisted with the death process, so it is fairly easy to transmit this information through you. We will discuss projections again, however, and how they figure not only in this life but also in the death experience.

As we wrapped up our conversation that morning, Barney and I went on to discuss his physical form, which was showing further signs of wear. His eyesight was growing dimmer and his joints were getting creaky, though Barney assured me he could still see and appreciated the massage and herbal formulas I used to supplement his food.

Beneath the surface, I sensed we were moving into a sacred space of learning. I could feel it. There was a deeper quality to our exchange, a keen sensing that *this* was the culmination of why Barney and I had come together in this life—for me to hear these words, feel these feelings, open to these experiences. And thus I asked myself once again: Who was this amazing being who lived inside the white furry body of my dog Barney?

2

———

Facing Fear

When I first opened to the idea of talking to animals, I wasn't afraid. Other people did this—I was simply an observer, a reporter. But, as I continued to ask questions, pondering how this communication thing worked, I felt my inner world responding. Part of me was stirring, and I grew nervous and excited at the same time. Deep down, something had been triggered—an ancient memory? a dormant skill?—and that something called to me, quietly, yet persistent and tempting. Well, this is not surprising; this is often how deeper awakenings begin. For as we recognize—and gradually come to accept—that our thoughts and feelings, dreams and awareness are engaged at deeper levels, our surface consciousness begins to wake up to something we always knew but couldn't quite recall.

The very first time I heard an animal speak within my mind, a thrill ran through my body. I felt myself tingling—energy quickening, thoughts evaporating—in a strange, still moment out of time. There, on the other side of my window: a gathering of birds upon a bush. Window, bird, bush—it is not so much the surface thing that calls to us, but the deeper energy of life force, the deeper call of relationship. It is as if you finally realize that an invitation has been extended to you all along. And, one day, you accept.

I felt the deeper presence of the birds open to me that day.[1] And I to them. It was simple and surprisingly obvious: a coming together of worlds that had never truly been apart—a sudden clarity that we were not just woman and birds, but deeply connected beings. My body gave a little shiver as a too-long silenced self swooped up to consciousness. A part of me came home.

It wasn't until I thought about the experience that fear set in. My brain began objecting, raising doubts, worries, and all sorts of suspicions. My thoughts wanted to squelch down that initial feeling of communion, of heart-opening connection. Part of me wanted to make it unreal. But why? *(Safer that way.)* And who was in charge of thinking the worried thoughts? *(Clever ego!)*

As time went on, I began to notice that one of my favorite ways to avoid opening—both to new ideas or deeper levels of understanding—was to stay busy on the surface. For many of us, it seems easier this way; much less hassle to explain away events and encounters that don't fit with reality-as-we-know-it. We almost can't help it, for we're trained to rely on logic, linear thought, and explanation rather than fully experience the rich mystery of life beyond the ordinary. Society helps to reinforce this notion, pushing us to "do" (and do it quickly!) rather than allowing ourselves time to "be." Through conversations with animals (who tend to be experts in be-ing), I began seeing ever more clearly that the social push to rush-rush-rush was simply a huge admonition to keep us from looking deep, into ourselves. *(What are we so scared of, anyway?)*

As Barney once noted, that desire to hurry up and go onto something else is a defense, an anxious way of avoiding the deeper nature of self by clinging to the surface. Or, as he put it, *it is as if you are swimming in deep water, but constantly grabbing for more life preservers, when the answer to your situation is to dive deep and behold the majesty of the undersea world. You busy yourself with 'to do' lists, when all you need really do is let go, sink down into yourself, into the greater reality; trust the workings of the universe, the beauty and humor of interconnections, and allow yourself the luxury of meeting all in a deeper flow of time.*

Sounds easy, doesn't it? But putting this into practice means first facing what we fear the most: all those shadowy layers of self.

FEAR OF RABBITS

When Barney and I began talking the following morning, he began with a short summary:

A simple metaphor used by humans is that the world of the living is like one part of a house, closed off from the rest of the house by a door. That door is death. You fear the door because very few who go through that door come back to tell others what is beyond it. So, what is beyond the door is surely to be feared. Conjectures abound. Myths and stories and tales of all sorts surround the door and what lies beyond the door.

Humans sometimes say this is natural. Perhaps it is natural for the way your species has developed to this point in time, but it is not the only possibility with which you could view the door and that which lies beyond. There are many ways besides stories and conjectures to discern what the door actually is and what lies beyond it.

In my experience, I find the door is really about your own projection. Many civilizations, cultures, and societies have chosen not to see that particular gateway as a door, but as a bridge or tunnel or pathway. With these views, there is the possibility of moving to and fro. The passageway is open and seen and clear, with no need for a door. So, this is the first projection. Do you understand?

"You are saying that it is a Western human projection to view death as a one-way deal; that, metaphorically speaking, it is we who 'shut the door' on communication and relationship with those who have died. Is that it?"

Yes, that is closer. You are fairly open, Dawn, but you all too easily buy into the idea that death is something separate from life. And it is not.

Can you remember our life together as people who lived close to the land? There was a small white rabbit you were once fond of—do you recall? Do you remember what I taught you then about speaking with the spirits of the dead? You still carry the fear of death, and one of the ways it shows now is through fear of rabbits.

It is times like these when I am shaken to the core. I gave a little gasp at the computer, followed by a shudder of astonishment. What Barney said was true, though it was a truth I had never been so conscious of until this moment. It was an odd fear, too, one that didn't make sense to me and, because it seemed so silly, I would often push the feeling away. Although on the surface I didn't recognize a fear about rabbits, I was often squeamish when someone offered one for me to hold.

That comes from a 'past life' in which you as a young girl had become very close to a white rabbit, Barney pressed on. *It was killed, and when you saw this you could not bring yourself to touch this rabbit. (Do you see the pattern beginning here?) You felt the rabbit had changed, was completely different because its body had been killed in a violent way. So you began to believe that death is something that changes one irreversibly. That event held a pulling away for you—an emotional outpouring of grief that led you to focus on the body rather than spirit. Even when you reconnected with your rabbit in spirit, you questioned whether it was 'real.' This is another pattern that affects you in the now. You still retain a persistent questioning of whether your connection and communications are real. On the mental level, you may understand the game plan. But at the emotional level, there is still the hold. You are aware of this in your body?*

"Yes," I admitted, knowing full well this was a prime example of Barney's persuasive ability to get me to face fear. To do this successfully, honesty to self is required. Why bother trekking after shadow material if you aren't going to be honest with yourself, after all?*

---

*Shadow material is formed of those dark, repressed issues that we tend to deny in ourselves, though nimbly project onto others. Carl Jung suggested that shadow material offers a gateway to the unconscious. When meeting the shadow, we are forced to face our inner fears—even those fears we aren't consciously aware of.

"I can feel it high in my stomach," I acknowledged. "It is a tightening, like I am trying to hold something in. And as I feel into it, I sense a lot of sorrow and rage and bitterness and anger."

So we will breathe this out and give voice and expression to your grief.

Barney paused, allowing me a small reprieve.

Let us open to transformation. Let us return ourselves to that moment in time and re-vision it—that is, turn our vision to see again and shape again this moment that holds so much.

Begin by describing the scene, by remembering that personality and the essence of the feelings you held. The idea will be to re-vision the ending in such a way that your connection with the spirit world is left intact. Think of this as a repair mission—and I mean that in every sense of the word. It is to repair what was broken, and also to re-pair you with other aspects of yourself. Let us begin.

As I closed my eyes and felt for this forgotten self, I saw myself in another time: me, but not me. It is a curious mixture of consciousness, for I am both me, observing the memory, and she—a young girl, alone in a forest. As the girl, I am looking for my rabbit and I find her pinned to a tree. She is hanging there, loose and limp, tacked to the tree by a knife in her throat. Dark red blood seeps from her neck, down her fur. I don't want to believe it's her, but I know it is. Who would have done this? I feel so betrayed.

Let's talk to the rabbit. Sit down and calm yourself and ask her what happened.

As I watch the girl drop to the ground, knees folded neatly beneath her body, I hear her voice mix with my own, "Bun, what happened? What happened to you, sweet rabbit?" There is a pause and then—through the girl's mind, into my own—we see the rabbit eating grasses in the woods. It is a tranquil scene, the rabbit feeding quietly under sun-dappled trees, when out of nowhere—a strike to her neck. A man with dark boots, marching through the forest; he not looking, she not hearing until it is too late. The thud of his boot coming down—sharp, hard, breaking her neck. And, a few moments later, a carriage running over her, reinforcing the break. They are a group of people coming through the forest. First, the man, then the carriage, and then, following behind, another man walking. He sees that rabbit body, picks it up, pins her to a tree with his knife, then walks on. The rabbit says she is not sure why he did that, though he was acting compassionately.

Maybe he was doing it so you would find her?

"That could be true. I suppose," the girl and I answer together, still joined in consciousness, as we consider the possibility.

Ask her if it was a painful death. Was she ready to go?

"It was like a crack from out of the sky," says the rabbit. "One moment here and the next out of the body . . . hopping across the sky." No pain and, besides, she had nothing much left to do. She tells us she is going back to her home, which isn't so much heaven as another planet. She says she came to give us a connection, a reminder, for we knew each other before. She says she was "just a little visitor" and now she is reminding us of that, showing herself as who she really is: a silvery span of light leaping across the night sky. Like a rabbit!

I felt a small remembering playing around the edges of my mind, though it stayed vague and out of focus. "I'm still a bit lost here, Barney," I said at last.

Such stories hold an energetic key for those who require emotional release. That is, you are drawn to—or pulled into—the stories that still 'hold' for you. You have not completely released that which holds you to this 'past' story; you have not fully discovered the treasure that is stored within your story.

Before I wondered too much about what release—or discovery— might entail, Barney continued, *Hold the images of the slain rabbit and the star rabbit together. That is part of the re-pairing also. Can you do that?*

The two images came together: the small white rabbit in the sun-speckled forest, the vision like a tiny bubble of beauty; and the night sky rabbit—a huge expanse of silvery essence leaping upward from Earth, into the sky, spanning the stars. Although the spirit rabbit revealed a much larger energy than the tiny body below, they were no different; the two really were connected. "Ahh!" I said aloud.

So, why did you lose sight of that connection? If you really knew that, then why would the slain rabbit upset you so?

"Something about how it was done, I guess. The man?"

Yes. The outside force. That is another one of your threads, and this, too, is tied to the incident in this past-scenario story. Who is the man? What does he represent, and why are you angry with him rather than the first man who accidentally stepped on the rabbit?

Good question, I thought. Why would the man who picked up the rabbit be an issue when he had nothing to do with her death? But, as soon as I asked the question, I knew.

"I am mad at him for the way he pinned her to the tree. It seems crude and strange and . . . Oh!"—and as is so often the case when we shift from that logical, linear view of the world we most often inhabit to a deeper, richer expanse of synchronous connections and multileveled meanings—a sudden stream of knowing flowed through me. "That man was also of another place! And even though he barely remembered it, he felt a need to honor that rabbit, which is to offer it up to Spirit, and that is how they did it in his place, his home. Not usually with a knife in the throat, but that was all he had. And I knew this man from before!"

And then there was more: another avalanche of associations, bits of vision, pieces of memory, fragments of feeling—a second immersion into that vast universe of elegant, unexpected connections.

Like a story within a story within a story, I saw the man was part of a warrior society, a people with rigid ideas of right and wrong, yet great passion as well. I saw yet another version of us (the girl, myself) tied to a pole: a woman next to two others similarly tied, the three of us surrounded by a circle of angry warriors. "They are throwing spears at us; that is how they kill their own, those who have betrayed this society. In that life, I was the wife of that man—the one who nailed the rabbit to the tree. I see him there; he is not throwing a spear and there is still love, but he does not prevent my death."

The vision was so multilayered that my words seemed like jagged rocks, not even close to expressing the fullness of what I was feeling.

"So the rabbit was a reminder of that?" I asked at last. "The man nailed the rabbit to the tree because it would also remind me of that life?" Although I marveled at how the connections interplayed—fitting so exactly, exquisitely, one atop another—another part of me balked. "I don't think he knew that consciously," I said to Barney.

Interesting how it is all interrelated, isn't it?

Before I could object, another surge quickened through me, drawing me back into the story. "There is something about the throat: the knife in the throat of the rabbit—not in the heart or in the body but in the throat—why did the man do it that way? It's about 'speaking one's truth.' I voiced my truth in the warrior society and that was why I was killed. And even at death, I wasn't so much afraid as angry, because I would have liked to live longer with that man. I had certain ideas about how we might live, but he was very into the ways of the tribe. And I sense that warrior life was just one, among many, about speaking my truth."

Hmm. I sat with that and wondered aloud. "So, all this is about hidden signs? About secret memories linking one being to another, one self to another, and back again? We're sending each other coded messages across time, between lives? Is that what you're saying? That we store pieces of ourselves in the stories of our lives? That our life events hold a kind of secret, hidden language? We are coding each other, telling stories within stories, in order to remember ourselves?"

But Barney didn't answer. *Do you still have the fear about the rabbit?* he asked.

"I can take the body down and clean it off now. I can hold it. I have the idea to offer its meat to the animals of the forest and use the skin as a memory, to wear the rabbit's skin as a tribute. Maybe it will help me remember the rabbit being of the night sky—like a talisman, a potent gateway to that memory."

What about the man?

"I can thank him for calling my attention to the rabbit, for leading me to my memory. And I can see how the rabbit was right, how maybe it was an act of love."

Will you have the love to leave him signs as well? asked Barney. *Many have left you signs, just as you have left signs for others. Now is the time to become more conscious of this—to see more clearly these coded memories left by and for other aspects of self, other relationships of the 'past' and 'future.' It is truly a time to 're-member' on a more conscious level.*

As in so many of our experiences together, my mind was confused, yet my being was expanded.

And so, said Barney with a satisfied enthusiasm, *Let us begin with death. Let us clear the pathways, sweep the gateways, lower the bridges, and—open up those doors!*

A smile snuck up my face and I laughed with wonder.

That is all for now, said Barney. *A long session, but you needed the experiential piece to see how it works. We are still clearing your vision, in a manner of speaking. As we clear more, it will be easier for you to transform into other beings and experience other ways of seeing. And as you continue to do this on all levels, we will be ready to do some more interesting voyaging.*

SHAPESHIFTING FEAR

The more I pondered the rabbit story and the interrelated pieces of that puzzle, the more rabbits came to mind. I saw images of rabbits on television, in magazines, as floating cloud formations in the sky. Rabbit energy was playing with me while my thoughts scrambled to make sense of things.

The idea of sending signs to other selves resonated within me.

Perhaps we do play memory games of hide-and-seek with our many selves, storing our stories across a continuum of lives, leaving reminders to ourselves and others in different times, stashing clues in the framework of different lands and cultures.

And could it be our old friend Fear who acts as guardian to these treasures? Steadily he tests us, making sure we are ready to become our own locksmiths of consciousness, challenging us to "re-pair" ourselves with all those forgotten selves we haven't yet fully re-membered into our greater being.

One night I had a dream of walking through a very large, unusual house. I was having fun exploring the many rooms when I heard a party in a kitchen on the second floor. As the partygoers called to me and I walked across the threshold, I felt a crunch. There, below my feet: a life-sized ice sculpture of a rabbit, broken at its neck.

On waking, I squirmed at the deeper implications of the dream and rabbit. Even though I didn't know what it meant, I felt a second wave of resistance.

It was Zak who proposed another way of meeting fear. Rather than look to what I supposed I feared, he suggested I describe the feeling of fear itself.

"Right now I can feel it in my mouth, almost like I have to gag or throw up," I told him. "Like I am keeping something in and not wanting to give it up."

Could it be your old hold on reality? he asked in such a way that I began laughing—not only with pleasure at being with Zak, but at the obvious answer to the question.

"Laughing out loud helps," I observed after a moment, and Zak laughed with me, as good dog buddies so often do.

Yes, he agreed. *It is a movement outward and onward—that rush of expansive energy! Laughter is a key way for you to release. For others, tears or talking or physical movement may be easier. There are many different ways to release and open. For you, however, it is often laughter and humor, especially when it is a simultaneous laughing at yourself and*

Dawn and Zak

the situation. Do you feel how that old fear—or, that old you—becomes transformed?

"I really do!" I exclaimed. "It's like that inner heaviness is changing into something light—as if the fear is a big brick wall and laughter transforms it into something light and thin and fluffy-flowing, like a sheet airing out in a breeze. It's like holding in rotten eggs and then laughing out an airy meringue!"

I sat with the image for awhile. And then a thought occurred: "So, maybe the quality of fear—or whatever belief or opinion is being held like the brick wall—actually changes as well?"

A good question, said Zak. *Has the quality itself changed, or has your perception?*

"Actually, it feels like both have shifted."

Yes, and this is important to see. On an intellectual level, you might have answered that it is 'all a matter of perspective.' And from one point of view that is true: it is merely perspective which changes how we view reality. But in reality—this reality we are playing with at this particular time and space—it was both that changed. What you were holding was heavy and old and probably bad-smelling. What you released was changed by virtue of 'you' shifting the form of 'you.' And here we come to another teaching of shapeshifting.

This is difficult for some to comprehend, because at one level shapeshifting is about changing form in a certain reality. But the very act of changing form also alters one's reality. So, not only is form shifting, but reality is shifting as this occurs.

Let us say you continued to hold the old reality—the fear and heaviness of nervous energy. At that moment, you hold both form and reality in a certain way. However, by the act of shifting your form—which you accomplished by laughing—you also shifted reality itself. It is as if you walked beyond a doorway. For you, the key was a certain frequency of laughter. It is what unlocked the door for you. And thus you walk into a new version of reality at a different level of being. A new you.

New me or not, part of me was still perplexed. "I don't know where this is taking us, Zak," I said after a bit.

Only that each shift in form is also a shift of reality. This is a core teaching, though you may not understand it until you have experienced it several times. Many animals are ready to journey with you into an ever-deepening experience of shifting form. From there, you may desire to encounter other realities. But let us begin with what you know. Just be open. Breathe. And remember to keep your center. Do that and you will be fine.

3

—·—

A New Set of Eyes

As Barney and I continued our daily talks, both he and Zak encouraged me to hang out with different animals, to ask questions and delve more deeply into shared consciousness. It was a beginning, they said, a small gathering of experiential keyholes into diverse ways of seeing the world. We were already working with the concept of shapeshifting, and Barney used a variety of these experiences both to educate and to cheer me on.

Things were moving along until I became ill. I couldn't sleep, and a fever danced in and out of my body. It was one of those minor, anomalous illnesses that no outer doctor can help you with, for the symptoms jumped erratically—head, lungs, sinus, back. Besides, I suspected it was mostly dis-ease over all the integration that was going on within me. As such, there was nothing to "fix;" rather, a simple need to slow down, rest, and allow assimilation to occur.

One day while relaxing on the couch, I closed my eyes for a few moments and felt Barney sit by my side. As I rested my hand on his head, an image of horizontal lines and the word *bandwidth* came to mind. Just then Barney barked: a single woof followed by silence. Then, the sound of another dog's bark from outside. Silence. Barney's bark again; a pause; then the dog's bark, and so on. It was remarkable in that it was a single bark each time—not the more typical rush to the win-

Barney's bark

dow and bark-bark-bark exchange with canine passers-by. More notable, however, was that I also "saw" the sound of each bark play upon the bandwidth of horizontal lines within my mind. It occurred to me—in that lovely, lightheaded way of fever—that if I could travel into each bark I would see something about each dog, that the unique sound and energy of each bark offered a portal to another way of seeing. So too, it occurred to me, was this vision an apt metaphor for shapeshifting.

There you go, said Barney. *Much of the experiential learning regarding shapeshifting is about shifting one's velocity to match another's 'bandwidth.' You are very focused with your own preferred method of vision and seeing. To shapeshift requires a new set of eyes, a new mode of perceiving. But first the old must go. This corresponds with the shifts of your body as it releases old matter, old holds and patterns, old habits, and old ways of being. These must first be cleared in order that you can take in the new.*

As you release the old, you become less dependent on habitual ways of perceiving the world. Moving toward a more conscious form of dying—as well as shapeshifting—requires that you 'unlearn' some of your body's habits of perceiving the world. Thus, the 'shift' in shapeshift is about exploring other bandwidths, other dimensions, other perspectives and other ways of being.

Lack of sleep is a boon to you, as it makes it easier to release control and simply feel and experience this mode of blending. In fact, initial shapeshifting experiences may seem like a blending—a gradual shifting to plant or animal form wherein you can feel that being's bandwidth. Complete or more accomplished shapeshifting entails more conscious awareness, but students often begin by gleaning the basic patterns of others as they hop along the vibrational continuum. Does this set things in perspective?

I opened my eyes and smiled. "Yes, that helps. So, what's your best advice for releasing the old and making way for a cleaner perception of the new?"

Pay attention to the footnotes of life—the symbols, signs, and inner meanings that speak to you. Open to the bandwidth of synchronicity and enjoy the experience of coming to know other forms of being, all of which are, of course, richly diverse, creative expressions of our essential oneness.

FLIPPING THROUGH METAPHORS

It sounded like simple advice. And it was in line with what Barney so often advised: just be open to experience. But sometimes experience is not so easily experienced.

As the days went on, my body felt better. But still something was not quite right. The world seemed altered, out of focus. I was easily distracted, annoyed. It was like being in a land of remarkable new colors and forms, yet unable to really take it in. This too, I had a hunch, was a form of resistance, a crafty way to defend against experience itself.

One morning I complained to Zak. "What to do?" I sighed.

It is true that experience and expanding awareness are required here, he replied. *It is as if you are up in a small airplane with a teacher, being shown the wonders of vision from a new perspective. But, unless you do the work to learn how to fly (the plane or your consciousness), you are wholly dependent on the teacher to take you up again.*

Perhaps what is needed now is some ground time—to learn more of the basics from a settled and grounded position within yourself. Even though your aims are experiential, it may be best to start small, one step at a time.

Another way to look at merging with another is through the lessening of perceived energetic boundaries. This is perhaps the best beginning: To enter into a small relationship with animals you meet. To greet them and begin to open to them, expecting nothing, asking nothing. If they are open to this exchange, you will sense an agreement and your energies will touch. It is the equivalent of a handshake on the energetic level. Begin with the basics. From there, you build other experiences.

The energy you are experiencing in terms of being irritated and overwhelmed is because you are indulging in possibilities rather than focusing on your center and beginning to truly experience. It is the ego's defense. Best to see that first: to confront that fear of the ego and begin to work with it in common pursuit.

The feeling of fear is part of ego's job—to protect you. Your ego is becoming ever more refined about its plan to 'save' you. My advice is to work with ego on this, engage it with what it loves: intellect, thought, description. This is your ego love. So, feed it this information for a time. It may then be more open to working with you as you begin to explore other modes of perception.

It sounded like an interesting plan: rather than squelch or starve the ego, offer it some food, sit down and have a talk; become friends and collaborators over tea and scones.

Zak also suggested some practical work in discerning the unique signatures of energy as expressed not only from the various chakras (energy centers in the body), but also from within each chakra itself. As an example, Zak instructed me to open from the *hara* (the stomach region, slightly above the third chakra or will center) and focus on merging with him from that level. As I centered my consciousness on this level, I could feel a quickly moving energetic flow that looked like a shimmering round tube connecting us. This "tube" we would come to call the "connection portal."

Zak asked me to describe the portal—it seemed dark yet vibrant. He encouraged me to open to its other possibilities, to allow myself to see its different aspects. Was it always dark? Or, did it take on different colors, different textures: clear, blue, sparkly, smooth? What about sound? What was the tone of the energy? How did it "feel" in my body? By engaging the energy—by meeting it and becoming more aware of it—could I also move with it? Could I feel the flow of its distinctive dance? Could I sense it becoming larger? Wider? Stronger? As I did this—with pleasure at how much fun it was to shift into different hues and patterns and movements—Zak reminded me that this was a metaphoric interpretation of energy. Others might experience it in different ways, and we would all experience variances in the energy of our chakras (and how that energy would feel in meeting the energy of others) at various times, depending on the circumstances.

Flip through your metaphors, advised Zak. *Begin to see and feel and know the energy in as many different ways as possible. To get stuck in one metaphor is to get stuck in form. That is what we are trying to unlearn. Continue to practice this with every being who is open to such an exchange. It is an exercise in getting to know the feel of energy and developing your skills and learning more in the process. Allow the energy to guide you.*

WALKING THE PATH

And so it was that I began to see a pattern in the way assorted pieces of experiential knowing were coming into play, one into and around another. Deep learning is rarely a logical 1, 2, 3, affair. Rather, it is an infusion of awareness as deeper aspects of self rise up and surface aspects of self reach down. Worlds collide as differently known stratums of perceptions and insights meet and merge. It's an earthquake of shifting awareness, a collision and concurrence of consciousness—the early formation of an entirely different being than the one we were before.

While meeting and merging with other animals, I made the acquaintance of a cat named Queen, who was consciously preparing to die. I found her energy expansive and her insights profound. In one of my morning talks with Barney, I related Queen's experience of "walking the path of death." Queen showed this to me as an actual path through green foliage, past tall trees and thick bushes. I sensed this was a place she visited during her many catnaps throughout the day. I could feel her paws upon the earth, the warm sunlight playing upon her fur, the smells: rich, loamy dirt; distinct odors of different plants; the air itself.

Queen explained that she was walking on this path, a little way at a time, to meet death. As I understood it, she would go only so far, and then come back into her body to ground this "meeting" in a more physically mindful way. Later, she would walk the path again, a bit further, and then back, to take that into her body, and so on. Queen related that in the past she had an apprehension of death. Now, she was using this approach, this path, as an opportunity to grow.

There are many who are working with death in a more conscious way these days, Barney commented. *Of course, in what you think of as 'the past,' most everyone worked with death in a conscious way. That cycle of awareness is now returning.*

Queen's work with transitioning awareness from 'life' to 'death' is a meditative exercise that many can follow, whether or not they are close to death. Do you recall that I once spoke of there being many side paths on the road to death?

"Yes, when Queen mentioned the path, I remembered your metaphor."

In truth, there are many points or opportunities within every life where death may occur. Some have more than others do. Equally, there are other points at which other opportunities are present. If you looked at the road map of your life possibilities you would find that some of the cities are required stops, while others offer side trips—experiences that you may or may not choose to visit. This is one dimension of the map. Another dimension reveals that each road has an alternate route—or several alternate routes. Some offer vistas of death or out-of-body adventures, of shapeshifting and other types of so-called psychic awareness.

The meditative experience into death is a side trip that may be taken at any time. It is 'timeless' in this sense, for it exists on the inner roadmap as an option to learn more. As Queen explained, it offers a visionary journey that may bring one closer to consciously transitioning from the physical body to another form of spirit body.

The scenery will depend upon how you see the world. Many choose a forest path—especially many small animals, for we are comfortable with the forest. Others use mountains or deserts, or out-of-body adventures— anything that your psyche deems worthy in fitting the patterned manner in which you perceive death.

For those who are working on a conscious appreciation of death— and especially on transitioning with consciousness intact—this exercise is very helpful. One simply begins the journey ahead of 'time' and becomes acquainted with the scenery and signposts of your path to death. One can only travel so far, though most find that it is quite a ways and there is much to learn along the way.

I also suggest this exercise for those who are interested in learning about shapeshifting, for as we've discussed, shapeshifting involves a certain relearning in the body and many small deaths along the way. You will discover much about your inner roadmap as well as become aware of particular skills that will be of value to you, especially with shapeshifting.

THE CROSSOVER

We will begin by filling in a few blanks today, began Barney one morning a few days later, and it suddenly occurred to me that we were not so much speaking here and there, in bits and pieces, but actually having one long, multilayered conversation. This was something I would continue to experience, not only with Barney but with a great many other animals and beings. In short, I was becoming aware of an underlying continuity that was not dependent upon the passage of time as we ordinarily know it. Call it a growing familiarity with tapping in to a stream of consciousness in which time is nonexistent; one is free to come and go and still continue the same conversation as if no time has passed at all.

Let us first look at the notion of reincarnation, said Barney. *On a larger scale, this is simply a form of shapeshifting. From this viewpoint, the connection between bodily forms is achieved with spiritual consciousness—which is a different vibratory level of what you are used to as everyday consciousness. We could also call it* soul, *or* atman, *or even* Buddha-nature, *though these all 'hold' the concept in slightly different forms.*

Let us call this soul consciousness essence *for this talk. All essence is* one, *though the way in which each essence learns and experiences reality at slower moving vibratory levels is different. Though, of course, to explain this in terms of duality, we are necessarily shifting meaning already—another reason why experience itself is a much better teacher in this regard.*

Upon death, an individual essence 'wakes up' (a bit) to another form of reality and 'remembers' (to some degree) its other options of form. Some think that death is a huge awakening, as if All That Is is suddenly known. It is not my experience that this is the case. Rather, it is as if each essence 'awakens' according to its own level of awareness. It is true that, generally speaking, being without form allows for a faster learning since one already has the advantage of seeing/feeling/being essence and not being so caught up in the illusions of form. However, illusions still exist.

Many essences choose to express themselves as a light body. Certainly this is helpful to some degree, as essence is comfortable with the physical earth body and seeks to find another, but there is also a degree of humor here, for there is no real need for form. One can just as easily move as light or sound or any other energetic vibration. It is much easier to shape-shift in this realm, yet you would be surprised that it is not practiced more often—that essence so frequently chooses to mimic the old body. Old habits from physical form die hard, I suppose we could say.

After a period of learning, clearing old ties, releasing what can be let go of, and so forth, one may begin to strategize about another life and, thus, look to form. What is the best form (body) in which to reenter the physical world? There are many to choose from, and again, this is only limited by one's level of awareness. Some do not choose to see beyond their own 'tribe,' so to speak. Others get very imaginative.

In the end, one's choice of form is directly related to one's choice as regards teaching and learning. There is often a dual nature of awareness that incarnates, for Earth is a planet of high duality, and so one part goes in to teach and another to learn. Often they work in concert, and that crossover is a very interesting space in which one has direct access to the multidimensional world of spirit. At that point, one has a sense of one's essence. It is at that point where physical shapeshifting can occur, and where miracles are possible.

Barney took a pause. *Do you have a question here?*

Only one? I wondered. "Are you saying that it is only at the cross-over of teaching and learning that you have access to this? Or could it be any point at which you are doing two things at once?"

Intent is key. For example, talking on the phone while working at your computer does not have the power of intent I am talking about. To some degree, you are simply using part of yourself on the phone and part of yourself on the computer. But you are not consciously aware of underlying connections.

What I mean when I speak of this teaching and learning intersection is a state in which you are consciously aware that you are both serving others and others are serving you. This is often the beginning of consciously opening to the multi-nature of incarnation. It is as if you are aware of essence speaking through you as well as essence speaking to you. Of course, from a larger perspective it is always you talking to you, though that is hard to grasp in a physical modality. Do you understand?

"Well, maybe it is like this right now. When I focus my attention on what we are doing, I am aware of a deeper force speaking through me—and I'm also aware of a part of me which is listening, just as I listen to your words and type them on the computer."

Exactly so. It is a crossover in which you are aware of the crossover. You are aware for a moment not only of you, but also of me and of the underlying force or energy or essence which moves through both of us. If you stay with that—if you release yourself into that—you will begin to feel that energy of 'you' and 'me' and 'underlying force' not as separate or as a division but as one continuous flowing movement. In discerning that flow of movement, you open to the nexus of our communication. Moreover, you are that. You begin to feel yourself as that movement; you come to know yourself as part of that flow, and you become that—which is, of course, none other than you!

My brain was beginning to hurt.

It is often easier to do this with animals because we tend to be more aware of this essential connection. But the challenge is to do it with those of your own kind. That is why 'form' is such a huge illusion for humans. Look at your society and see how you have built form into such an important illusion: how you look, in what type of house you live, how much money you make, what you do, and so on and so on—every little thing becoming such a huge concern . . . So much energy put into these illusive forms!

"Sounds like you are laughing about this, Barney," I said.

Laughing in a good way. For the focus on illusion can also be creative. I have lived some lives as a human, though mostly in a tribal society where form is not as important. Then again, don't think for a moment that tribal societies don't also value form; it is simply used in another way. So, I do know of the pull of form and how it can hoodwink one so completely that it both shields one from knowing and keeps one from discovering the treasure underneath.

Why do you think it is that all treasures are buried or hidden away?

It is a reminder to dig deep, to find the key. Look to early myths and fairytales when learning how to find the treasure. The treasure is compared to wealth because—again—that is the power of the illusive form! True wealth has more to do with connections than it does with sitting alone in a room of gold. Even money works this way—it only has power through exchange, though there are so many who want to keep it for themselves, hoarding it. Why? Fear, once again! Fear of death, fear of releasing form—when the real joke is that you can only grow and learn and experience joy by dropping form, by experiencing many forms and by reveling in the joy and beauty and fun of form until at last you get bored with that and decide to play with form in yet another way—to work with non-form—and that is another discussion.

And with that, Barney sent me off to meet experience, the Grand Teacher, once again.

4

———

Endless Variations and Infinite Perspectives

While my thoughts played with the notion of the crossover point and all that it entailed, a series of merging experiences came, fast and furious. They most often occurred unexpectedly and, in the beginning, were short-lived.

Once, while sitting low to the water in a flat-bottomed boat, chugging down a narrow inlet slough, I relaxed into a very calm state. Luckily, I was not driving, simply along for the ride. The sky arched intensely blue overhead, with only the thinnest wisps of clouds curling around the distant mountains. Sunlight sparkled upon skiffs of water and splashed in silvery sheets against the dark, silty shore. It was a glorious day, and I felt joy in the wild, wingy dances of the birds: soaring eagles, plunging gulls, and swooping long-legged cranes.

Dazzled by sun and wind, birds and sky, my boundaries of self expanded and diffused. As a large flock of ducks rose nearby, I felt myself sailing upward, settling into a dense yet agile and constantly changing vibratory field. There I was: within the larger body of the flock—a body not of flesh or feather, but of interconnected awareness. It was altogether unlike anything I knew, though in the moment I simply felt it, enjoying the curious way this space curled around me, through me. It was a consciousness in which wind and feather, air and flight intermeshed. There was a moment of knowing myself not only as part of the flock, but as the flock itself, as if I were directly plugged into the "knowing" of the ducks—simultaneously aware of individual and group, feeling the flow, riding the flow—knowing the flow—of flock mind. And in that moment, brilliantly clear and immensely huge, I understood for the first time how each duck could come and go, clicking into the larger body or not—a choice that clearly lay beyond the scope of instinct.

Suddenly, I was back. It was becoming strangely familiar—this unpredictable, still-clumsy way of visiting other forms of consciousness. For a moment I had been fully aware and present within the knowing of the birds. And yet, for me, merging was still an in-and-out affair— away and beyond the confines of "me" and then back again, ground- ing the information, translating it into and through my own way of knowing. It reminded me of Queen's walk with death—though this was more a walk with life.

At home that evening, I asked Barney about the "shift" in shape- shifting. I knew the focus was trying on a variety of perspectives in order to experience other versions of the world, but how far—how deep—could one actually travel into and know the consciousness of another? And where exactly was the meeting or crossover point in which perspectives met and merged?

Perspective is a combination of one's software—that is, one's unique sensing apparatus for seeing, touching, tasting, and so on, along with one's brain circuitry in how one interprets and perceives the world—and the existence of nature both as it is and as it is perceived, answered Barney, apparently wearing his Mr. Scientist hat. *There are many subtleties involved here, but on a basic level, you need to keep in mind that your human perception of nature and another animal's per- ception of nature are two different things. They may, however, coincide in some ways—a meeting place of those experiences which are in your world and those in the experiential world of the animal, myself for example.*

What I mean to explain is that there are numerous versions of nature existing simultaneously. Some things do not exist for me in the way they exist for you, and vice versa. This will become more apparent as you begin to work with other beings and see through their eyes. In all cases, remember to deepen, to center. You can do this at any time, in any and every moment.

It became a mandate of sorts, for as the next few days unfolded, my talks with animals took on a decidedly multi-perspective quality. Snippets of vision from the animals' points of view were entwined with memories and images pulled from my own repertoire; I felt the translation of my words infused with their thoughts, feelings, and sensations. And yet there was more—this meeting place of consciousness was not just the telepathic connection I was used to in connecting with animals, but something deeper, something altogether more intrinsic to relationship itself. The first experiential tendrils of the crossover were snaking through my awareness.

In addition, it was amusing to find the underlying focus of shapeshifting at the core of the talks, whether or not I said anything about it. It made a kind of sense to me, however, for once engaged at deeper levels, there is no need to "say" anything as thoughts become ripples, our curiosities and inquiries bobbing like bright little floats upon the ocean of shared awareness.

The following three talks occurred in succession over several days. They came easily each morning as I sat at my desk, in front of my computer. I didn't ask who I might speak to; rather, I simply opened awareness and the mystery guest was present. As I would come to see, the talk-experiences not only revealed three different ways of seeing the world—three different takes on the "shift" in shapeshifting—but also essential pieces of learning that would help to form a larger vision of being.

PERSPECTIVES OF
THE PENGUIN PEOPLE

We are the Spirit of Penguins, began the group voice, embellishing its words with the distinctive black and white coloring of penguins in movement. *We show you images of penguins jumping from a land of ice into the open sea. And, we show ourselves traveling through those waters very quickly—a type of 'flying' for us.*

These images have to do with transformations and the ability of all beings to meld with their environment, to adapt a way of being that is in league with who they are and what they wish to accomplish. We reveal ourselves flying through water as a metaphor for being or becoming in a different way, so as to see from another perspective and gain more fluidity in shifting perspectives. Not to get lost in any one perspective, but to see from that vantage point and integrate the vision with your own. It is in this manner that we wish to talk about shapeshifting, or the art of transformation.

We speak for southern sea-traveling mammals and birds at this point, for all of us have shifted in a common focus. There is a twisting of the earth poles and many animals have taken on the opportunity to work with (and learn more about) shifting magnetics via the use of their bodies and consciousness. We speak of a grid pattern that has moved out of alignment. It is seeking a new alignment, and these animals are working to bring both versions into further clarity.

"Do you mean as in two Earths?" I asked, wondering if this corresponded to the idea some humans had proposed that certain Earth changes may involve two or more versions of Earth present at a single time.

That is exactly what we mean, said the Penguin People. *We see Earth becoming two, or manifesting in a way in which different aspects of her being will become conscious for a brief period of human time. You will have a choice as to which vibrational level of Earth/consciousness you choose. This shift coincides with (or is aided by) various astronomical events as well as by certain experiments occurring under the earth, and by the consciousness growth of those who live on the planet. In short, Earth and all her inhabitants are in the course of becoming more conscious. We know this is not news to you, nor to many others, but it is upon this growth in consciousness that we focus now.*

To return to the image of penguins flying through water: this is the metaphor of what life will become for many of Earth's inhabitants. It will be about learning how to work and live and exist in 'new waters' (though we do not mean waters literally), learning to adapt to new situations while still holding sight of the land, the icebergs of home. For some time there will be a movement back and forth. Animals who live in two environments (land and sea, air and water, or air and land) will be very helpful here, either as guides or simply as animals to observe and learn from in that manner.

There is much about the relationship of duality in unity that has yet to be explored and explained. Duality is not a problem when attempting to reach unity, for duality is the gateway to unity. We penguins live both in the water and on 'land' (ice). One is not better than the other. We have learned how to see both as parts of the continuum of oneness. That is a physical example of how the two are the gateway to becoming and being in the flow of one.

Our advice is to see this—feel this—at deeper layers in your everyday life. It will help you with shapeshifting as you observe the oneness within all, especially when you attempt to become or ride with another.

Seek to become more familiar and comfortable with a variety of perspectives. That is our lesson for today: to see from the point of view of others—humans as well as animals. If you open in that way to learning, you will come to appreciate far more than what we can convey in simple talk.

HOLOGRAPHIC WISDOM

Indeed, I did feel a keen sense of appreciation for the penguins' perspective and the depth of insight they offered. So, too, I felt a growing tug to listen rather than ask questions, to feel rather than evaluate, to simply be aware and watch the unfolding. And so it happened the very next morning that we dove into water once again:

We are the Spirits of the Fish on Land, they began. *By that, we mean the fish who swim in lakes and rivers. Our kind is related to our brothers and sisters in the sea, though we hold our oceanic memories in another way. We also hold a different vibration in relating with people and animals on the land.*

We are here today briefly to remind you that when you eat fish you clue in to a remembering of our watery beginnings. This planet was founded mainly in or with water, and it was from the sea that we all arose. Our kind brings nourishment as well as memory to you. Some of our kind is dying to waken you to the fact that what you eat relates directly to you, that if you poison the waters, you truly poison yourself. Others bring particular memories of common understanding and awakening.

Our kind relates to humans and animals through the interchange of knowledge and nourishment. By eating us, you make us a part of you (and you of us, is another way of seeing this), and some of our knowledge and wisdom is awakened in you. We do not mean this merely metaphorically (though there is also that level), but physically—biologically, physiologically—as well.

When you eat fish, you partake of our wisdom and knowledge. Do take care how you pull us from the water, how you prepare us, and with what intention you partake of our being. The deeper you explore this notion of interconnection, the more you will see the great circles and grand designs within the web.

For example, we are now showing you our scales. They are used in some metaphors in your language, such as having the 'scales fall from your eyes.' Scales are a kind of protection, a covering—our 'skin,' though scales are also like your pointillist paintings, each dot or scale a part of the whole. Fish are more about holographic wisdom and knowledge—and especially about how that knowledge is transferred to humans—than you are presently aware.

That is, we are not just about interrelating with humans but about expressing the brilliant nature of our role in the web of life, especially as relating to exchange—such as by eating. We partake of other fish at times, or of plants or other life, and we know others will partake of us. Some humans use the expression 'cold as a fish' and relate that to emotions. Do you see how that is your projection upon us—a defense against the depth of our understanding of life, which you perceive as so far different from your own?

We are eager to help humans learn more about interconnections, and perhaps there are things you will have to share with us, to teach us. It may not be something you think of as a teaching, but simply sharing information can often yield interesting associations, new ideas and, thus, different avenues of creative expression—all the way from the personal to the evolutionary.

As the Fish People signed off, I felt a gentle nudge, a parting invitation to open my "underwater eyes." Although I was not sure exactly what this meant, I went along with the request and, with physical eyes closed, opened my underwater eyes. In doing so, I was treated to a stunning montage of fish! There were fish of all sorts, though it was the eyes that were highlighted: most with the distinctive black center and perfectly round ring of surrounding color. Some eyes were small and darkly bright, others flat and shimmering; some were convex and bulging, others rimmed in gold or covered with an opaque silver sheen reflecting light from above—all unblinking, wide open.

I laughed in admiration for the Fish People, for their good-humored wink of encouragement and confirmation. And, I wondered where we'd go from here.

ANCIENT WAYS

A day later I had the answer. Once again closing my eyes to deepen in connection, I felt a light, soaring sensation. As I would discover, not only was it a hint of soaring through the air but through a temporal twist of time.

We come to you today from the air: Birds of wide, white wings. We are not well known in your time, but come from an ancient order. We wish to speak about resurrection of the world heart. In some ways, this is an opening of the past so as to better embrace the future. Let us explain.

Our kind is about lifting and opening, about giving up old patterns so as to be open to the filtering down of the new. Our energy descends onto the earth in this time of change. We sweep across the land and offer our wisdom—our 'new-old' perspective to those who are open and wish to be filled. Our energy is light and barely visible, like fairy dust that shifts and sifts over all, covering everything in a veil of white light. Our energy is readily dissolvable, taken in by the hair and skin. Understand that it is a very fine, yet physical substance that falls from the sky (from our wings and our being) and can then be absorbed into your being. It is as the moth's spirit dust. And, in the same way, it is about wisdom and eternity.

I knew exactly what the Birds of the Wide White Wings were referring to, for their message carried a multitiered array of images, ideas, and impressions. The "veil of white light" was a kind of etheric snow—something both visible and not visible, depending on one's perspective. The "moth's spirit dust" was connected with a moth who had appeared on my office window for several days while I was writing my first book. The moth had led me to experience a moment of synchronicity in which I slid an old copy of Carlos Casteneda's *Tales of Power* from my book shelf, only to see on the cover a drawing of a large moth surrounded by its shimmering light body. I then opened the book to the exact page where don Juan told Carlos that it was time to talk about moths. "The moths are heralds or, better yet, the guardians of eternity," don Juan told Carlos. "The moths carry a dust on their wings . . . that dust is the dust of knowledge." When Carlos asked what knowledge had to do with dust on the wings of moths, don Juan explained, "Knowledge comes floating like specks of gold dust, the same dust that covers the wings of moths." "But how can the dust on their wings be knowledge?" asked Carlos. "You'll see," said the enigmatic don Juan.[1]

The memory made me laugh, for "you'll see" seemed to be an all too common occurrence in such adventures of consciousness. Fragments of things I had once not fully understood were reappearing—now, many years later, in conversations or events—with fuller symbolic import and deeper meaning. Like the moth's dust, an "old" connection was now presented as a "new" inspiration, or as the birds called it, a "new-old" perspective.

The birds continued: *To tie back into resurrection, the taking in of our 'essence' or 'dust' allows for the rebirth of a deadened, sluggish, or sleepy spirit. It rejuvenates, refreshes, and allows all to re-member with other times as well as other beings. A common, united purpose is needed here, on this earth, and it is that pathway of purpose to which we speak.*

This is a slight deviation on your notion of shapeshifting, but we offer the information to help reveal the many ways that spirit works. In fact, our 'dust' is a shapeshifting of sorts, for it is the transformation of spiritual essence into a form that can be taken in by the many. Other animals have spoken to you about partaking of common energy or spirit through eating their bodies. Our way is another: ingesting essence through your skin and hair and being. It is a more ancient way, as we have said; one that has not been seen on earth very often in the present, just as our kind is not well known.

We are similar to an angelic order, though that is not our classification. We are of an old animal order who work with the earth during times of change. We answer the call when change is needed to flow seamlessly with the ways of nature. We answer the call for the need of specialized circumstances, designed for the unfolding of planetary evolution. And, with that, the Birds of the Wide White Wings were gone.

INCARNATIONAL OPTIONS
AND OPPORTUNITIES

Let us continue, said Barney the morning after my set of talks. *What have you observed from your connections with the penguins and fish and birds?*

"That there are many ways we might take in knowledge or deeper wisdom or 'coded information': by observing it, by sharing it, by eating it, by ingesting it through the skin, or by water or air, and so on."

Yes. And there is more than that.

I paused to consider, allowing the energy from the talks to form a larger picture. "The value of diversity?" I ventured. "Especially within the framework of multidimensionality?" As I spoke, I felt the flow of a deeper connecting thread. "So, underlying energy manifests in particular ways—or on particular levels—precisely because those ways are best suited for each situation?"

Now you're on to something! Let us consider this in more detail from the perspective of spirit.

In preparation for incarnation, your spirit-being is presented with a wide range of choices. You may start with just a few basics: the desire to learn, to experience, to evolve, to create, and so forth. These might be thought of as driving forces, or energetic variables.

From these variables, you construct a scenario: species, bodily system, geography of land interactions, availability and openness to guiding information (from spirit guides, angels, and other teachers), and so on. Layer upon layer, you construct the basics of a life program. In doing so, you—as spirit-being—choose which circumstance, form, and setting will best fit your need.

Once incarnated, there are ever more choices and opportunities. There are truly no 'right' or 'wrong' choices. Rather, there are a variety of paths as well as the choice to follow one path over another, or one through another— or to choose several paths. The more creative may add subprograms of alternate awarenesses, or interdimensional meetings between a group of selves.

For example, some spirit-beings incarnate in multiplicity—as alternate versions of the same self—so they can choose all paths simultaneously. This specialized form of incarnation is just another version or choice in which to live. Attention in these incarnations is placed on synthesis. Sometimes these individuals seem not to care where their choices lead. Why? Because at some level they are aware that they are a multiplicity, and that all paths will be covered, thus allowing a very rich diversity of experience.

Another example is to simultaneously incarnate into a variety of selves. That is, your spirit-being could choose to be several selves in different forms—such as different species—at the same time. Often the focus here is a meeting or 'coincidence' in which two or more of the selves interact in one reality of the here and now. This may lead to a gestalt in which each self awakens to its larger awareness, thus allowing for a more conscious creation of life.

This is a multilayered lesson, so let us be clear before proceeding.

"So far you have given two examples: in one, a spirit-being chooses many versions of the same self? Is that it? These alternate selves all begin the same, with the same start in life, but take different life paths in order to see where each path goes?"

That is one way of seeing it. You could also view this as multiple planes of reality played out simultaneously. As you note, the same 'start' or beginning position is taken at birth, though the wheres and hows each personality-self chooses will vary from one life path to another.

"Uh huh." I had a vision of multiple planes of life stacked one atop another, each a possible version of the same life. "So, the second example is more about spirit-being taking on several forms—like you said, different species, or maybe even different planes of existence—and then meeting in some way?"

Yes, this is so. And you are thinking of past lives and future lives—this is another variation in which alternate lives are played out in different segments of a time-based continuum. Difficult to understand if you hold a rigid view of time and space as you are used to thinking about them.

Even as you find with humans living on the earth, however, after a long period of sophisticated or complex programming for a series of lives, as one nears the end of this type of planning, we see a return to basics, to simplicity. There are even those spirit-beings who choose 'autoprogram.' Masters who desire to remain aware without any knowledge of what circumstances will present often choose this. That, also, is a unique programming.

The old truth that 'all is here and now' is the seeded core of understanding this. The examples I give are patterns of variation, ways to 'play out' different aspects of spirit-being. Even to individuate as a 'spirit-being' is to hold a level of illusion, for in truth there is only one essence. Though to separate out and engage in game playing of any sort is a celebration of form and, at times, a deepening of essence.

I share this information to shake up some old ways of thinking and remind you that there are infinite perspectives in life. The more you learn about shapeshifting and ways of connecting with other forms and species, the more you will see—and perhaps more deeply appreciate—the unlimited array of form, thought, creation, incarnation, and experience.

When you choose to shapeshift, it is as if you enter a bubble of space-time-form configuration. And, as noted, there are endless variations of this. You may choose to 'ride along' with another being, or to become that being, or to become a new being. I am describing many threads to you, many paths. As you explore some in more detail, you will begin to sense the larger picture of how this grand tapestry all flows together.

5

Open Doorways

Although our talks continued nearly every day, along with a range of deepening experiences, Barney was slowing down, eating less, and taking more time to sleep. "Is there anything more I can do?" I asked him early one morning. "Are you planning to leave soon? How can I help?"

Many questions! exclaimed Barney, with an edge of humor. *It is true I am slowing my vibration on one level, though that allows for an increase on another level. The need for my 'sleep' time is actually a form of meditation or centering in another space. I am working on other levels now, along with the reality we are engaged in.*

It is true I am thinking of leaving the body behind, but there is still time left for us to finish our discussions. You are now briefly thinking about why I waited until 'the last minute' to have these discussions, but another part of you also knows that this is the exquisite nature of timing and the unfolding of events in this dimension. If I had given you this information before, would you have been able to hear it? And, if you had, then why would I need to stay? This is not to say that I am here solely for you, but perhaps you get my drift about our relationship—much of our time together has led to this.

Barney paused, peering deep into a space that I could not see. After a few moments, I heard his familiar sigh. He turned his head, glancing up at me from below the desk, and continued.

As for myself, I am an old dog. More than that, I am an old soul on Earth. I have spent many lifetimes on Earth and am very familiar and comfortable in the ways of Earth. To fully understand this, it might help to open the doors a little, to go back in time and review what is encoded on Earth.

Earth was originally set up as a polarity system. That is—using terms of duality—manifestation was set to occur from physically 'lower' organisms evolving into 'higher' or more complex organisms, and also by 'higher' or finer aspects of spirit moving into denser, 'lower' forms of physicality. Thus, manifestation on Earth is a simultaneous coming together of high and low, left and right, male and female, light and dark. The nexus of the two is the core of manifestation on this dimensional level.

In many ways, death is simply stepping out of that nexus, out of that framework, and moving to another level of being—one wherein the framework of polarity or opposition is no longer dominant.

However, many humans find the polarity framework useful for teaching. Good and evil, heaven and hell still provide a powerful framework for many, and that is why you will see death explained in these polarity terms within many religious traditions, from Christianity to Tibetan Buddhism. These teachings are ways of coping with understanding the initial death experience.

KARMIC PROJECTIONS

A few minutes after our talk ended that morning, I glanced up at my book shelves and had the notion to flip through an old copy of W. Y. Evans-Wentz's third edition of *The Tibetan Book of the Dead* (subtitled *The After-Death Experiences on the Bardo Plane, according to Lama Kazi Dawa-Samdup's English Rendering*).[1] I hadn't looked at the book since college, over 20 years ago. However, as soon as I held it, I knew there was an obvious reason for me to read.

Several hours later, I had been struck many times with small rushes of confirmation, excitement, and growing awareness. This fascinating book is not only a guide for the dead, with detailed instructions on how to move through the changing phenomena of the bardo (the realm between death and rebirth) in a conscious manner, but also for the living. There were many phrasings that echoed Barney's words, such as "the Art of Dying" and I was particularly drawn to one section of the book.

"So, are we going to talk about projections today?" I asked the following morning.

Tell me more specifically what you found and what your question is.

As so often happened when Barney and I convened for our talks, we were already on the same page. Thus, there was no need for an explanation of finding the book, or even what book it was—we both knew. And yet, in asking me to be specific, I felt Barney encouraging me to clarify my intent and focus.

"When I began reading, I found the different stages of conscious dying. One of these stages is called the Seeing of Karmic Illusions. It interested me because it is related to seeing—and going beyond—our personal beliefs, cultural ideas, and emotional holds. So, I'm thinking *karmic illusions* is maybe another phrase for projections?

On a more expansive level, this is so. And, as Zak once alluded to, karma is a belief system. I am not an expert on karma in this sense, but I can tell you that through shapeshifting I have learned about projections in another way.

This is what I mean when I say there is one major road to death, though many sidetracks. When death is studied as a conscious initiation, one begins to get a better feel of the map of death. It is wise to study death for exactly this reason. One becomes more familiar with the map, and thus the territory. Though, as you know, this sort of knowledge can never replace experience itself.

Much of the fear around death has to do with confusion. If you begin to study the paths of those who have gone before, you may begin to develop a degree of confidence. You may become familiar with possible things to expect—pitfalls, side trips worth noting, and so forth. In this respect, it is about being prepared. Knowledge allows you to be more prepared. At this stage, categorization is a good thing, for you begin to make sense of the chaos.

For example, the image you have been dealing with lately is of a circle-loop that recirculates itself, one 'end' becoming another.

Barney was talking about a Chinese notion I had recently been reading about. It was a deeper aspect of the yin/yang symbology: namely, that as Old Yang (a preponderance of older male energy) dies, it redevelops as Young Yin (young female energy). This, in turn, matures into Old Yin (older female energy), which eventually dies and develops into Young Yang (young male energy), which develops into Old Yang, and the cycle starts all over again.

Taken as a whole, each stage of the circle represents an appropriate part of one's path—though we also come to a point where the next step is to go beyond the circle itself. For some, this is an inversion of the loop; for others, a penetration of the circle. There are many ways to describe this metaphorically.

Let us return to projections. I can share my experiences of many lives as a teacher of shapeshifting and how that led to my teachings about death. In some ways, shapeshifting is the study of various projections along the circle as well as how to penetrate that circle of projections.

In very early times on Earth, there were only a few forms through which spirit could enter. So much of early life was about adaptation and new creation. That is, spirit entered form and adapted to that, becoming comfortable with it. Some spirits then used that adaptation mechanism to create new forms. Thus we see an evolution of sorts. More and more forms came into being. They became ever more specialized and, within each specialty, even more specialized. One visual symbol of this might be the roots (below the surface) or branches (above the surface) of a tree. A few major roots or branches emerge from the trunk, which then branch off to others, and others beyond that. This 'family tree' metaphor is also used to denote the evolution of species.

Now, as one mode of specialized evolution reaches a summit, there is often an apathy—a restlessness, a desire for something new. And so a new form of evolution begins (a new branch!). Remember that I am speaking in general terms, so even while one phase of evolution may be coming to an end, there may be some branches that have already died off, while others are still growing. In general, however, the summit stage reveals another path or level of evolution.

Sometimes a planet will go through crossbreeding of species, mixing and matching what is available to achieve a new outcome. Another version is reincarnation/transmigration, where spirit hops around and becomes various species, to learn more about different forms and patterns of consciousness, through a variety of lifetimes. And yet another version of this is shapeshifting, which is more of a conscious 'in life' process of transmigration. This is where my own interest was piqued many, many lifetimes ago.

Once again, I speak of lifetimes as a useful way of expressing this. If we were to look at that segment of the circle that penetrates the mysteries of time and space, we would see this as a multidimensional whole. For the purposes of this linear progression, however, let us use the useful fiction of lifetimes.

My initial experiences with shapeshifting were wondrous, though I had a very good instructor and was 'tethered' by this teacher's abilities. However, the first time I went solo there was the element of fear.

Understand that there are various levels of shapeshifting. On one level, you can join with the consciousness of another being and 'ride along' within its mind or body to learn more about that particular form, with its unique thoughts, perspectives, and so forth.

There is another level of shapeshifting where you physically become a form other than your own. The mechanics of this are complex, but basically you reform your body to the matrix or pattern-template of that species. It is a mini-death of sorts, because in the full shapeshifting process your thoughts—or, more specifically, the mode in which your thoughts are thought—are transformed to that particular species' mode of thought.

To some degree, that is also what is happening when we speak, Dawn. You 'hear' me with your thought patterns, though what I am communicating to you are my thoughts. Our communication is a meeting of two thoughtforms. A certain degree of translation does occur. Just as a certain amount of projection.

"I have been thinking of projection lately as not necessarily a bad thing. As you say, there are places on the circle/cycle where projections of our own repressed material are an obstacle—in that we believe those projections are 'real,' but at another point, we see that even thoughts and perceptions are projections—not so much 'real' or 'unreal' as simply ways of helping us to talk about and understand different aspects of ourselves.

Exactly. And this is crucial in understanding shapeshifting as well as the art of cutting through those karmic illusions. As long as a belief system is held as 'real,' reality is governed by the rules that are mandated by that belief system. True?

"Yes, that makes sense."

It is not enough to say, 'This makes sense,' or even, 'Yes, I believe that.' For, at certain levels, it must truly be felt or experienced to move onward. You have had this experience recently.

I laughed and shuddered at the same time. Barney was referring to a series of dreams I had in which a "devil boy" was watching me. At first I was afraid of his dirty, taunting appearance, but in later dreams I attempted to talk with him. Each time, however, he would run off and hide within the muscles of my back. Only a few days prior, while receiving deep-tissue massage on my back, I suddenly remembered the devil boy from my dream. I saw him in my mind as the bodyworker sank her thumbs along the muscles of my spine and moved upward. He was smiling at me—but the smile he used I recognized as my own. The effect was a spontaneous recognition that the boy had been created by my own beliefs. This wasn't an intellectual realization, but a deep down knowing—through feeling—that the devil boy had been formed by a webbing network of beliefs. A huge shiver snaked through my entire body as the muscles released.

"Right," I said, remembering. "When I realized that 'devil boy' was my own belief system, there was a lightening, as if a whole heavy layer of thoughts and beliefs just lifted up and floated off me."

Yes, that is an appropriate description. For beliefs do form a type of ceiling or sky above and around one. That construct is your 'world,' the way in which you see the world. This has been discussed often by others and there are many fine works on this subject, but unless this is truly experienced in the body as being real, no amount of words can help to fully explain it.

"I think you are right. It wasn't until I felt it that I really knew it."

Let us end there, said Barney as I heard a gentle sigh from below the desk. *The thread we will take up next time is how the evolution of shapeshifting can lead one to dissolution of the conscious form in a more conscious manner.*

I could hardly wait.

A REVIEW

Let us review the art of shapeshifting, began Barney the following morning. *Under the broad category of shifting shapes, there are many variations as well as many levels of moving toward a more conscious awareness of this art.*

From surface to core, this would include learning more about an animal (or other being) from a shared-thought conversation—much as we are doing now—to moving one's consciousness so as to 'ride along' with an animal and see through its eyes. At deeper levels, this includes merging one's consciousness with the animal while retaining consciousness of home base (body consciousness) to a fuller sense of mergence wherein one actually becomes the animal itself.

"What happens to the animal's consciousness at that point?"

First, it should be noted that this is most often done with mutual consent for education purposes and, thus, is beneficial for both participants. After all, that is part of the joy of diversity—that so many creatures see, hear, feel, think, and experience reality in different ways. By holding a more conscious awareness of many 'different' views, you come to appreciate a fuller experience of the whole.

Back to your question. In a consciousness-merging situation, the other being's consciousness may simply be on 'hold' for a time. It is often there, alongside your own, though in a more dormant mode. (In extreme cases, consciousness can become displaced, though this is rare and any mutual consent would provide for a backup agreement wherein as your consciousness leaves, you make sure the consciousness of your host is back in place.)

As one works more with shapeshifting, the desire is often to experience form in ever deeper ways. It is a patterning I have observed: as one expands on a particular level, there follows a desire to deepen. At this point, one may wish to not only consciously but also physically become another form. There are several ways, each with its own subtle variations.

One way is to physically reshape your body into an already known shape. At a cellular matrix level, there are a large variety of known shapes to choose from, and your physical body actually takes on an alternate shape within that matrix. You might think of the werewolf myth here—an ability to physically become a wolf, or other creature. One not only moves in consciousness, but also brings one's transformed body along. Thus reality is experienced not only as consciousness, but emotionally and physically as well. A variation of this is to become an extinct species or even an unknown species. This is a more cumbersome process, though it is useful in certain situations. On Earth at the present time, however, this tends to be thought of more as a 'dark' form of shapeshifting.

"Why is that?"

It is a very old form of shapeshifting and was originally used when working with manipulating the course of evolution or the growth of consciousness in a certain area. It was also used by the darker forces as a method of perpetuating chaos. In general, this type of 'creature transformation' has to do with manipulation—both physical and mental. Though at certain periods of time on Earth this was very useful, and there is nothing inherently 'dark' about it.

Yet another type of shapeshifting is to keep one's body in a dormant *mode (resting or sleeping) while using consciousness to both manifest and animate a second 'body.' That is, one's body retains its usual shape and one's consciousness enters into a temporary creation—like a double—to experience the world. Again, the tendency for control and manipulation is higher at this particular time in Earth's evolution; thus, these latter types of shapeshifting largely remain hidden within the forms of stories, legends, and mythologies.*

'Ascension' is also a type of shapeshifting, though in yet another direction. We might think of it as the inverse of the latter forms, for ascension is activation of the light body at the physical level. That is, it is the spiritualization of the physical—a shifting of the division of physical and spiritual into a type of melding.

Do you see how it fits with shapeshifting?

"I didn't see it in that way until you mentioned it. But, yes, it is a shifting of the old duality into a new form of physical-spiritual consciousness."

Correct. Ascension is a matter of engaging the flow of connectedness while simultaneously expanding one's consciousness and body into a different form. The outer form may look the same, but the inner form will be of a different vibration. It will hold light in a different way, thus allowing experience of the world and reality in a different way. This, too, is a form of shapeshifting.

The same metaphor applies to death—it is shapeshifting into a larger, more expansive perspective of 'time.' The challenge of ascension at this time is to do this in a conscious, physically based way. In a sense, it is to shortcut death—for rather than going from form to nonform and back into form, you will learn to consciously move from form to form. It is more about a change in vibration than in physical shapeshifting, though it is the same core pattern.

At this time, I encourage you to work more deeply with animals, to ask if in the course of your relationship they would allow you to 'come along' and observe life from their perspective. Many may desire to learn about life from your perspective, too, and this would also be valuable.

A period of experiential experimentation is in order. I will be near.
I will help monitor and steer you in the right direction. I have done this
many times before, and I both invite and honor this role in your life.

"Thank you, Barney," I said. "I would certainly be honored to have
your help and guidance in this as well."

THE BIG SCREEN

True to his word, Barney helped me to "ride along" with the consciousness of others, while also attending to his own path. He slept more and
ate less, and it was obvious he was winding down. Although I would
check in with him almost daily, our talks were suspended to give me
time to visit other animals' perspectives.

One morning when I was particularly worried about him, Barney
ambled under my desk and announced that he was in no pain and
expected to stay for a few days longer. *You needn't put me out to pasture*
yet, he said with the hint of a smile.

And then he explained: *I am recalling a life as a horse, a white horse.*
You have had an image of this.

"Yes," I said, recollecting it from yet another dream. "And now I
see you as a white horse with wings." The image came to me superimposed on the memory of the dream.

Ah! That is another form! exclaimed Barney. *Most usually I have*
lived long lives—long in relation to the length of days that is normally
given to a particular species. Now, in this life, I am coming to an end. We
spoke briefly last night about endings. Do you remember?

I recalled our short chat the night before just as I was falling asleep.
"You were saying there are a number of choices of how to leave, how to
exit."

Correct. I tend to favor the older ways: a walk into the wilderness,
finding a spot to lie down and give oneself to the earth, to the animals.
Or to stop eating. Or, another very old way—simply to stop breathing.
That is an elegant exit.

You ask what I have been doing these past few days, appearing to be sleeping and resting so much. And I have told you there are plans to make. I will explain more of this, as a means of helping you to understand how this voyage can be more consciously experienced.

Barney took a long pause, a subtle reminder, perhaps, to deepen my awareness into the pauses of life. And death.

Much of my energy has recently been shifting to other modes of being. I think of it as shifting the spotlight of consciousness—moving the light of my inner being onto other aspects of myself that I wish to focus upon in more detail. Much of what you might call my conscious experience is being shifted to other layers, other modes or aspects of myself, so that the information can be used. It is not 'remembered' as you know remember, but rather synthesized at a pattern level. It is bare-basic feelings, emotions, and understandings which I am speaking of here.

This is difficult to explain without an experiential reference. Let us do this as a journey together, as a story unfolding. Okay?

"Well, of course!" As I closed my eyes, Barney asked me to consciously report on what I was experiencing. The first image I saw was of Barney as the White Rabbit and myself as Alice. *What kind of a harebrained dream is this!* I wondered.

"We are in front of a large black hole," I reported to Barney as I watched the scene unfold. "And you are telling me, *'Remember, remember!'* You push me in and then you jump, too. We are going down the hole, but actually the sense is more of going inside the hole. And now we come to a cozy underground room where there is a huge wood cabinet. You set about preparing to have tea while I look at the cabinet. It is confusing to me, because I can only see one small part of it at a time, not the whole thing. You tell me to step back, that sometimes looking too closely at something actually obscures one's view.

"So, I move back and sit with you at the table and we have tea. When I look at the cabinet again, out pops a huge screen, like a television screen. It is light blue—a really beautiful blue that also emanates light. You give me the remote and tell me to surf around. The first thing I see is a war show, when all of a sudden a cartoon version of White Rabbit pops through, as if superimposed on the show, and you tell me, *'See—that is the realer reality! Watch the rabbit!'* And then I see that you are Barney the dog again, but you are wearing glasses.

"You are telling me to have patience, that there is something here for me to see, but I am not so trusting of this television metaphor. You keep telling me to watch the rabbit, and I see how he darts into the television screen, playing through various scenarios in different shows. And now it is as if they are all aligned one on top of the other on the television screen, and they can be flipped through, like pages of a book. *'Mix the metaphors,'* says the rabbit. *'Mix those metaphors!'*

"And now you show me how if I change the channel, it's still the same. You are saying, *'See, it's all the same—always the same.'* And finally I understand what you mean, because White Rabbit is always himself, no matter what scenario is playing. *'That is the awakened one,'* you are telling me. *'No matter what the scenario, White Rabbit does as he chooses, because he is awakened unto himself. He doesn't buy into the scenario because he knows it is just conjuring, like a television show. That is a good metaphor for you.'*

"Now you tell me it's time to go into the television. You say we have to run, so I run with you and we jump into the blue light. And it becomes the ocean! Ah! And you say, *'The Grand Return! That is what it is like to die. To awaken to the idea that this is all illusion; all a scenario designed to get you to remember. That is the point of this game—not accumulating things or loving or learning. Simply to remember. Because when you remember, you awaken to your true self—or at least a more conscious version of your true self than you have been led to believe was you.'*

"Whew!" I said opening my eyes as we came back. Looking down at Barney, I lightly rubbed my toes against his back paw.

"What about that last bit?" I asked cautiously. "What about love?"

Love, in the way it is understood by many humans, is love of things. Even when you feel it is love of a person, what you more often love is a thing: a stylized or idealized version of a reflection of yourself as projected onto another. The emotional tone of love holds great power, for it can be an inlet to the grand ocean of remembering. But to stay focused on a love of the screen—rather than jumping into the screen—is nonproductive.

Sometimes when you tell me you love me, you cling to relationship of a particular sort. You know, I too have enjoyed my stay with you. But let us take this to a higher understanding, Dawn. Let us not saunter about in old ties of the past. Let us bring this to a more conscious and real relationship, where there is flow and movement and the nowness of becoming.

"How do we do that?"

Begin to let go of the idea of Barney the dog. Begin to see the light that flows within all of us. This is your clue-in to shapeshifting, what I first explained to you as a method for 'becoming' another being. When you enter into relationship on this vibration, we can be together at any time, because we are—and always have been—one within that flow. You will feel my warmth, as I feel yours. We can experience our incredible diversity yet still partake of the same tone of oneness. You are feeling this now?

Barney's words touched something inside of me, as if tapping a memory, urging me to deepen, to feel the flow of merging energy. I was aware of being in two places at once—both within my heart, on a river of warm flowing connectedness, and within my head, amidst a burbling up of images, ideas, and words. Somehow, this seemed right, as if I was settling into knowing something about myself that had been calling to me for a very long time.

As you move with the river of heart, you will open more deeply and warmly to all things. And yet it is important for you to retain your intellect, for it allows you to translate this experience into words. That is what is being asked of you at this time: to experience and translate for others. You are a forger of the new path, one of many. By being open and sharing/translating that to others, you make it easier for the path to be found and followed.

6

———

A Conscious Death

Barney was now sleeping deeply for much longer periods of time. Several times I watched him walk across a room or down a hallway, only to stop abruptly, tilt his head and stare into faraway spaces. His body would sometimes shake then, as if rippling shivers of energy were moving through him.

"Do you have something to share today?" I asked him a few days before he died. "Can you tell me about the shaking? Is there something I can do for you?"

The shaking is a loosening of my spirit from physical form. This is a practice I have retained from another life—another aspect of being. It is a way for the conscious self to begin to separate from the shell of the body. It is not painful. When it began for me (in this life) it was involuntary, though I am now flowing with the process and it is easier to accommodate.

I am indeed preparing to leave, though I cannot tell you exactly where or when. I am working with dying on a conscious level, in a conscious way, and still have some physical, mental, and emotional preparations to make.

Part of the reason I had you look at The Tibetan Book of the Dead *is to familiarize you with the nature of ritualizing death in a more conscious way. There are many ways to do this, though—as I am fond of reminding you—the way you do it yourself, in connection with the deeper levels of who you are, is always best.*

I am calling to teachers and guides, friends and other beings with whom I am close. You are among our circle, Dawn. As such, something may be asked of you to conduct this ceremony at a conscious level. You are our link to human consciousness, just as others in the group hold conscious links to other realms.

In this regard, I would like to remind you of another scenario, one in which I was a teacher and you were a pupil (or perhaps it is happening even now as we speak). There are numerous students and we all work as a group to help each other realize more, re-member more, at ever greater and deeper levels. All of us are working both individually and in our group. Each of us has areas of specialty and expertise. Now we will be using these areas in an ever-deepening focus, both to help others and to deepen the process for ourselves.

That was a group message. Barney paused and looked up at me. *For you, the focus is to seek expansion, learning at deep levels, taking the gist of any bit of information and following it down to the core of connection where you can feel it resounding in your own body and being.*

Periods of quiet and self-reflection are good for you as long as they do not become ego- and/or intellect-indulgent. Your process is now twofold: to quiet, center, and deepen, as well as to listen, take in words, images, thoughts, perceptions, and feelings from a wide variety of other beings.

In essence, what you are working on is connection at a very deep level. Remember the undercurrent of connection that you are able to feel. Always use that as your connecting 'hold.' Become familiar with its 'feel'—its sound, essence, taste, and all other varieties of perception. It is fine at this point to ask questions, though it is best to 'feel' your responses, to integrate them at a physical level.

You are right to apprehend that death is actually much more of a group process than you have been inclined to believe. Humans tend to portray death as a solitary journey, but that is not a truth I know. My experience has revealed that death is much more group oriented than living can be at times, though living, too, is most often a group process.

Death is a journey of becoming and, as such, there are always help-ers along the way. I think at times humans desire to make it a separate experience in order not to open to the shared commonality of our ever-becoming. Perhaps there has been planted a fear about death so that humans would not try to seek out smaller deaths in which they would be given the opportunity to see other perceptions, access other dimensions, and glean the nature of other alternate worlds?

Once you pierce or go beyond the veils that hold these fears, you will see that death is a momentary switch from one mode of reality to another. In order to shapeshift, you must become familiar with death, understand-ing of its nature and ways in the world. Death is the Big Fear that must be worked with in order to approach the deeper layers of shapeshifting, and it is why I call one's relationship with death an art. As one becomes more familiar and adept at this art, one soon becomes an apprentice to death, and death begins to reveal her secrets and her majestic smile.

I felt Barney signing off, but I had to ask—just one more time—if there was any other way in which I could help.

What you are doing now is fine, he said. *Thank you for the water. I don't always remember that and at this point I don't always feel thirsty. But I do need water. The shaking will continue. It is fine—and pleasur-able—for you to be near me, to hold me. Remember to call in the aid of others if you need some support. We are all in this together.*

INTERDIMENSIONAL PATHWAYS

The following morning Barney continued to sleep long after the time for our usual conversation. Still, I had an intuition to tune in that morning, and to be open.

Today's lesson will be a bit different than most, began a voice inside my thoughts. It sounded old and oddly familiar.

I am speaking to you now directly, as your Higher Self. This, too, is a valid means of accessing information. Although the feeling of this voice did indeed seem like a deeper aspect of my self, it was not at all as I might have imagined a "higher self" to sound. And yet, it connected to me within that deeper flow of becoming that Barney often mentioned.

Some of your thoughts are on Barney, continued the voice. *He has been an instrumental guide not only in helping you to access communication with animals, but also as a means into your understanding and further evolution of shapeshifting.*

As you know, Barney is preparing to leave his body. There are some emotional ties that you hold onto him, and we—many of us—would request that you begin to more consciously allow Barney to leave when he chooses. This is his death, not yours. Therefore, it would be best if you allowed him free reign, so to speak, as to the manner in which he chooses to leave.

I felt tears begin to well up as the full journey of our "Death Talks" beginning so many weeks before flowed through my memory. The review slowed as I saw myself finding Barney behind the stone smoker in the backyard, just a few short days ago. I recalled the look Barney gave me, and his words: "Ah, we're going to do this your way, are we?"

A part of you wonders if there is anything you can do to help him. Only to be with him, to reach out to him, to allow him his freedom and movement into a larger sphere. Barney will continue to work with you, albeit from another vantage point in spirit. In some ways, this communication will be easier for him and more profound for you.

Barney has stayed with you longer than originally anticipated, and everyone here agrees that he has far exceeded his aim in terms of a successful link-up and communication with you. To some degree, Zak, the 'energy dog' as you call him, has aided in this process. Barney did not originally choose this, but higher spheres of orbit felt this would be beneficial—as did I, you, and various aspects of our group.

Today is a favorable day to grant access between us, as there are numerous interdimensional pathways open on Earth for clear communication. This particular time in the 'here and now' affords great levels of acceleration. You will begin to access multidimensional worlds and aspects of yourself. Stay focused, stay centered, and you will be greatly rewarded and pleased with what you find.

I vaguely understood that the "favorable day" was in reference to the energies of a lunar and solar eclipse that had recently occurred, and a Grand Cross that was occurring over the next two days. This astrological conjunction was said to be relatively rare and powerful. It was called a Grand Cross because all of the major planets (except Pluto) formed a cross in which they were either square with or opposite each other. Although at the time I didn't know much more than that, I came to learn that the Grand Cross was significant not only for me because it coincided with Barney's death and all he wanted to teach about conscious dying, but also for the destiny of global evolution.[1]

Your eyes are also going through a change, the voice continued. *Your vision is turning inward, to focus on inner planes and more subtle connections of imagery-oriented communication. For example, eclipses are often times of inner brightness—made powerful by the 'dark highlight' of shadows. Think of the solar eclipse—when the sun's light is eclipsed by the moon, owing to its position between the sun and Earth—as metaphor. So also, your inner brightness—your connection with All That Is—is for a moment brightly shadowed, or eclipsed, by a strong focus on earthly matters. Here comes the interplay of the shadow and its immense power!*

All the shadow-work you have been doing is in preparation for this. Allow shadow issues to emerge and work with them. There is an easy method of slipping into alignment, feeling the emotion, and then slipping out so as to realign or transform that emotion into its higher nature. Stay tuned to all aspects of shadow and allow each to have its say. Work on yourself in the sense of seeing, hearing, feeling, tasting, touching, sensing all aspects of yourself that desire to communicate with the conscious you, so as to become better integrated in evolution and advancement of understanding.

This time is for you, for the conscious you to make use of what you have learned and to open to a greater dawn. This is your awakening . . .

WHAT HAPPENED IN THE NIGHT

It was very early the next morning, around 2 a.m., when I woke and had the idea that Barney was thirsty. I was in that half-awake, half-asleep state of consciousness in which I did not question the feeling. I simply knew I had to get up to get the dog some water.

Since Barney was weak, Bob had been picking him up and placing him gently at the end of our bed each evening. As I pushed back the covers, I wondered if I had been dreaming, but Barney raised his head and I saw that he was awake. Maybe he did want water.

There is a pale, blue-gray Alaskan twilight that bridges late evening to early morning hours in the middle of August. It is a beautiful, dreamy light, thin yet veiled, as if made of the palest of shadows. It filled the room and leaked out the door, spilling itself around me as I moved through the bedroom and down the hallway.

At the end of the hall, I turned into the kitchen and noticed that the chairs around the dining table had been pushed outward, as if people were sitting there. The big picture window behind the table had no curtains and I naturally turned my eyes there, as I did each morning to greet the trees and mountains. I realized then that people actually were sitting around the table. I blinked, in that still-sleepy way of just waking up, and saw the "people" more clearly with my inner eye. They may not have been of the physical earth I was familiar with during the day, but they were real people all the same.

I realized they had been talking and had suddenly stopped, for I was aware of the abrupt quiet hush in the room. They turned their heads to look at me, expectant perhaps, or maybe curious. They were clearly not physical people, but they were not what I'd term ghosts either. Spirit people perhaps—people who existed on another level of being, or in a different dimension. At the time this did not occur to me as strange—rather, it was like being awake in a dream in which things that happen do not seem unusual. And so I merely waved to them and asked who they were. They said they were friends of Barney.

This seemed funny because it was obvious—as if I should have known all along. I told them I was getting Barney some water and they nodded in encouragement.

I filled a small bowl with cool water and carried it back to the bedroom. There I stood at the end of the bed, holding the bowl to Barney, watching and listening as he lapped slowly, finally putting his head back on the bed. I set the bowl on the floor, crawled back under the covers, and returned to sleep.

In the morning, I woke just a few moments after my husband. He was sitting up and there were tears in his eyes. "Barney's gone," he said.

I sat up and reached over to feel Barney. Because he was still warm, I was convinced he was still alive. Intuitively, I knew what my husband was telling me was true, but another part of me wanted to believe that Barney was simply sleeping very soundly. I got up and crouched near the end of the bed. There—his chest seemed to be moving. I lay my head against his ribs and listened for the heartbeat.

Such a curious, empty stillness. There was no heart beat, no breath, and yet it must have been just a few moments since he died, his body still so warm, smelling so much like Barney.

COLLECTING ROCKS, LAYING FLOWERS

There is a Zen proverb that goes something like this: "Before enlightenment, chop wood, carry water. After enlightenment, chop wood, carry water." It's one of those big, ripe, wise Buddha-smile truths packaged up neatly in only a few short words. As such, no matter how much you try to analyze it or explain it, you won't come any closer to really knowing it until you are there.

The essence of that Zen adage was how I felt after Barney died. There was a deep, quiet calm throughout the house. I felt it flow through myself and my daughter and husband as well. I sensed a quality of light in the air that I had never noticed before—as if light was not something that simply shined upon you, but was ever present, glowing from every speck and mote of being. We did not have a plan to prepare Barney's body and return it to the earth. Rather, actions tumbled out of us and we moved with them in a kind of graceful, grace-filled dance.

We first went to collect many large rocks, gathering them wordlessly, yet connected and content in this joined movement of activity. Alyeska and I then collected wildflowers, while Bob dug a hole for Barney in the corner of the backyard, just in front of the magnificent fireweed—their brilliant purple blooms nearly at the apex of the stalk. Remembering a baby blanket of hers that Barney had especially liked, Alyeska ran to fetch it.

With the blanket wrapped snugly around his body, we lay Barney in the hole in the ground. We sat on the ground in a circle of three. Zak and Max, our big black Labrador retriever, came and went—making us four, then five, then three again. Sitting there, under the early morning sun, we told stories and memories about our friend and teacher. We were all especially happy that we had just taken him up to Hatcher Pass, a mountain area we all like, and that he had played and run around like a puppy, barking at ground squirrels and paragliders. For every memory one of us told, we would add a flower. Sometimes we laughed; sometimes we cried. When all the flowers were gone, we scooped up handfuls of earth and filled the hole and made a stone circle over the grave.

It felt good to say good-bye in this way, and I was glad we did it all together. It made me wonder if it wouldn't help when anyone dies—beloved human or animal—that we might take a more physical and active role in helping to return their body to the earth, saying good-bye with our hearts, not just pretty words, crying if we feel like it and laughing if we feel like it, and thus opening ever deeper to the experience of death and living.

Hours later, the sun shone brightly while the skies hummed a cool,

Barney's grave

deep, intensely gorgeous blue. Whispery snaps of breeze swept through the trees and across my face. As I stood on the back deck, alternately warmed by the sun and cooled by the sky and wind, I looked out over Barney's stone grave and was reminded of another old saying: "Today is a good day to die."

A most excellent day, indeed, I thought as I smiled at all that had come thus far. *"Good-bye, Barney,"* I said—not just with my head and heart, but with all of my being. *"I will miss you. Hope you have great fun, pal, wherever you are."*

7

What Happens Next

I had read that there may not be communication with those who have died for some time afterward—maybe days or weeks or even months or years. Presumably this is because the soul is adjusting, or resting, or attending to other things. However, I simply wasn't thinking of this the day after Barney's death, and so it did not enter my mind as a possibility. Or a limitation.

As usual, I got up early, made tea, went downstairs to my office, sat at the computer and opened to the flow of the connection portal. It seemed only natural to talk to Barney, and so I asked if he was around, if there was anything about the death experience he wanted to share.

Instantly, I saw a very clear image of Barney's grave. He showed me himself both as Barney and as a light body or spirit form. The two aspects were superimposed and I watched them float above the grave, drifting closer in view until they were hovering over the object that caused our goofy black Lab, Max, to bark whenever we jumped upon it: the trampoline. It was a curious image but I smiled as I felt Barney— his energy, his humor.

Then, in a very precise manner, Barney slipped into the law of gravity and plunged down upon the shiny black circle of the trampoline. Curiously, his light body bounced up, soaring up, up, upward into the sky, while his dog body fell down through the trampoline, down through the grass, down into the earth. I lost sight of the spirit dog but, in a funny shift of vision, watched the dog body falling further: limbs sprawled outward like a toy stuffed animal, swirling down through a dark void and—pop!—into the sudden sunshine of another world, into the outstretched arms of a little girl. It seemed as if we had moved into and through several barriers of energy. And now, again, Barney was two: a stuffed animal dog and a Barney dog at the same time. The little girl was holding him tightly and he was licking her face—both as a real dog and as a little girl might imagine a furry stuffed dog to be licking her face. The young girl was laughing and very happy and, in the image, Barney the dog said to me, *Another life perhaps.*

"Is that really another life, Barney?" I asked. "What does that mean?"

These are dream images—let us call them 'dream ideas' that float across my screen of vision. I was with you at the ceremony yesterday. I heard your words and felt your feelings. And, you are correct about the other ceremony as well—the beings you saw the night before. That, too, was another type of meeting and saying of good-byes.

The experience of death is very personal in that each being has his or her unique transitional experience. I can share mine with you, but be aware that this is not how it is for everyone, though a few of the touch-stones—that is, the basic happenings or modes of transition—do happen to a great many beings.

Death for me was, as you noted, very easy. But I have been working at this for what might be called a long time. I have had many experiences of death and have been learning to become ever more conscious in each transition. In a way, you could say that many of my lives are about the death transition and to some degree that is the focus of my teachings in your world.

As I have already told you, the 'shaking' of the body is a very old technique, one that was first given to me in this life slightly beyond my conscious memory. However, when I was able to connect with that par-ticular vibration, I remembered the value of the shaking muscles as a means of releasing certain autonomic circuits and diverting my energy into a more focused concentration. This is simply a method, one that I am familiar with and have used before as a means to allow me to detach part of myself from my body before fully leaving it. You noticed how I stared off into space more than usual, and you were right that I was often in other places or realms or realities during that time frame as you saw it.

It is somewhat difficult to describe the process of death in the terms of the living, as time is greatly changed. That is part of what I was working with in preparing for a more conscious death. I wonder if one of the things humans become so disoriented with is the time change phenomenon. It is not really as if time changes. More, it is as if your constructs of time simply evaporate. Time is seen more as a fluid ever-presence once one leaves the confines of the body. For domesticated animals this is also something of an adjustment, though not nearly as problematic as for humans, or let us say humans who live in a society that has a very highly structured sense of time.

For me, death was an experience beginning several days before the actual leaving of spirit from body. There were periods of reacquainting myself with the out-of-body mode. This is also done at times by animals in their bodies, but these last few days for me were very focused on moving seamlessly between the worlds—again, hard to describe, but the gist is that I kept my conscious awareness of all worlds in simultaneity. If I had been more adept, you would not have seen me 'staring into space,' for I could have maintained this awareness as I moved around or jumped or performed any action. There are masters on the planet who do this, and their death is truly a magnificent spectacle to witness, for they simply whisper through the door and sometimes you aren't even sure they were present to begin with!

For me, this process of holding various worlds in consciousness was my primary purpose in preparing for death. The moment of leaving the body was thus simply one of focus. I moved all conscious awareness from the body to another realm—another body, so to speak. The heat you felt from me was a gathering of my energies, a concentration of life force as it was redirected to other aspects of my greater being.

Now, the consciousness of Barney the dog was nearly all absorbed or redirected to this other being, but some bit remained. If you liken it to a computer, you could move all the software files onto another computer or zip disk, but some of that first computer would still retain shadows of old data, trace files of what it once held. So it was with the Barney body—and this ties in with the image you just saw: the Barney dog who is loved being redirected down to a very easy, open level—that of a young girl who loves her dog. That, in fact, was the base blueprint for Barney the dog.

This is a very deep and multilayered subject, Dawn. Let us continue tomorrow with more. We will talk about the movement of consciousness into spirit and some of the varied experiences one might encounter as that transition occurs.

Thank you for the ceremony and your heart-thought words. I am pleased that you are sharing with others in such an open way. And I will be available to others who choose to talk with me, though for now my focus is on our group and helping each one of you to deepen and benefit from this shared experience.

RIDING THE BANDWIDTH

Isn't it wonderful how little details of life often bring us confirmations of the most unexpected sort? Although I wrote a short personal account about Barney's death and shared it with many others via e-mail, I did not tell anyone of the vision of Barney with the little girl. The following morning, while reading through some loving e-mails from those who had known Barney, I found a note from my mom:

> Hi Dawn: Thanks for sending your Good-bye to Barney piece. It did help and I thank you. Still miss him terribly, though I do have thoughts/ visions/dreams of him happily trotting in the sunshine next to a little girl. So who knows—maybe his new life? Lots of Love, Mom

Still smiling over the e-mail, I tuned in to Barney and asked, "Are we continuing this morning?"

As I closed my eyes, I was reminded to more consciously open the connection portal. Instead of the usual river-of-energy metaphor, this time I saw a long split down the middle of my body, from low belly to throat and forehead, with golden magma pulsing inside and moving, just like the river of energy! With a small *aha*, I understood the importance wasn't so much about the image, but on physically *feeling* that connection and flow. And, more than that, perhaps it is actually *feeling* that holds the physical, emotional, and mental bodies in matching attunement for, say, talk at deeper levels to occur.

Your theory is fairly on the mark, Barney chimed in. *You are correct in picking up on the 'holding' of one vibrational band by a variety of bodies—as you note, physical, emotional, mental, and some layers of spiritual as well. In truth, there are many emotional bodies, not just one—and it is just the same with physical and mental bodies, and more.*

The key image, however, is that for communication to occur, a certain bandwidth is chosen. This allows communication between species, as well as communication between various 'bodies' within your physical body-being. This ties in well with our subject today, which is the ways in which consciousness joins with spirit. In truth, conscious does not so much join with spirit as it is held by spirit, or becomes the vehicle through which spirit may either know itself in one mode or express itself in another mode.

First, it must be noted that there are numerous layers or dimensions of consciousness. In this discussion, I will use 'consciousness' to signify the more enlightened aspects of your everyday living consciousness.

Let us begin with what occurs in the after-death experience. When consciousness leaves the physical body—and I am talking here specifically of conscious deaths, in which some degree of awareness has been cultivated through living one's life—a 'lightening' occurs. This is a falling away of various constructs, such as the time mentality. (With deaths that are not consciously motivated, this would not necessarily occur—the consciousness of the dead being would strive to hold on to these old constructs.)

So, in this sense, death is a reawakening to a deeper essence of conscious-ness—what we might call somewhat ironically a more 'conscious' connec-tion with spirit. At this point, consciousness is still experienced as separate from spirit because it has not fully identified with spirit itself. Spirit sim-ply is—*consciousness is still involved in being (thinking, acting, doing, and so on). Thus, some level of 'personality,' if you will, is involved.*

To distinguish spirit itself from conscious expressions of spirit, I use the term spirit-beings—*meaning these are conscious parts or movements of spirit. Of course, you can follow the flow of spirit all the way to Source—it is always there, part of the flow. But in order to move in the spirit world, separate out and manifest in body again, there is necessarily a driving force of consciousness.*

Do you understand?

"What I hear you say is that there are different levels of conscious-ness beyond our physicality, though these are not necessarily fully real-ized states of awareness."

Correct, though we have already covered that. I am speaking more of the divisions of spirit wherein the mobility to separate and use conscious-ness as a vehicle of expression is possible.

Barney paused and I sensed the equivalent of a sigh.

You are having some trouble maintaining connection this morning, he pointed out. *Let us hold off on the talks about this for the time being. Spend a few mornings with other animals and see where that takes you. Does that sound agreeable?*

There was nothing to do but agree, for what Barney said was true. "But there is a part of me that wants to keep in constant contact with you," I said.

Yes. That is not necessary, really. You need to trust the flow more deeply. I think it will serve us well to have you involved on some 'field trips' for several days. Enjoy yourself. Learn new things. This will ele-vate your energy levels and allow some enthusiasm to bubble up and help make you lighter. This is what is needed.

I am still here. I am working with our group, some of whom are doing quite well, while others need more help. We are all in this together. So, let us all do our part to the best of our ability and intention. We will soon begin to have more conscious group meetings, and the sharing of information will be a boon to all.

A TALK WITH ZAK

Soon after Barney died, Zak and Max began changing in their relationship. When Barney was around, both dogs deferred to him. Max, a stout black Lab, was by far the largest of the three, but he had a placid nature and rarely challenged the other two. Now, with Barney gone, Max and Zak seemed on edge.

After several days of intermittent growling, I had a talk with Zak. I wondered not only about his experience of Barney's death, but also whether he was willing to work things out with Max.

Zak began: *Barney's death was known to the two of us at different times. On 'the dog channel' we knew this was happening in elemental ways: by smell, vision, taste. We sensed something was 'wrong' or ill with Barney. On more cosmic levels, yes, I did know this was happening. I thanked Barney for sharing his home with me, and we engaged in some mutual exchange of information before he left this body. He was a fine dog to live with. He was also a gentle ruler.*

You observed how he was the king of us dogs, even though he was the smallest. It was important for Barney to have that position for a number of reasons. In this life it was particularly important, and we all agreed to that.

Now that Barney's body is gone, however, the rules change. There is again the issue of dominance, or order in the canine world.

Zak paused, as if sensing how to best phrase his thoughts.

There are many threads here, he said after a moment. *I do not want to make it seem that my 'spiritual' self doesn't care about my positioning within this family, for that too is part of who I am—my dog self. Zak the dog needs to assert his dominance over Max. I am the older dog and to be respected. Size is not everything. Because of his size, however, Max seeks to challenge me.*

At this point, I see it more as an empty threat, but still I must make my positioning known. I estimate this will go on for several weeks. You are right to 'call' us on it and claim your position of authority as well.

That is all I have to say on this matter at this time, though perhaps we can refer to it again when discussing other situations. Why don't you speak with Max about this too? A good exercise for you . . . Zak, signing off.

A TALK WITH MAX

I took Zak's advice. And so, after a short time playing with Max, we settled in for a conversation. "Max," I began, "Do you want to talk to me about Barney's death and what's going on with you and Zak?"

I am sad for the loss of Barney in our family. I will miss him. I liked him. He was a good and fair dog, and he was always kind to me.

I don't want to make trouble in this family. I am happy here. I will be good.

"Of course, you are good, Max," I said, a bit disheartened by his words. I felt a little wave of sadness that I didn't talk more often to Max, for I sensed that maybe he felt I cared more about Zak and Barney. But Max did not often express interest in conversation. Rather, he carried himself as a big, goofy, kindhearted dog and our relationship was based more on throwing balls, massaging his jaw and ears, and feeding him good food and treats.

"We do love you, very much," I said softly. "But I'd like you to not be so jealous of Zak. I love you both. Sometimes I would like to pat Zak and be with him, just like sometimes I spend time with you. Do you think we could work on that a little?"

I will try. Sometimes I get nervous.

I felt another tug of sadness for Max and his early life. Although I had asked him many times what had happened before he showed up on

Max

our back deck during a winter windstorm, he would sidestep the question. As our feelings touched, however, I sensed that he had not been cared for well by humans and was perhaps overly sensitive in wanting to please.[1]

I like you very much. I love you and this house and home. I will work to protect you from anything, even other dogs.

"I know, Max; thank you," I said, "But I need you to know that just because I pat Zak doesn't mean I love you less." I remembered, then, the first story Max had told me. It was a dream-sharing of sorts in which he showed himself to me as a mother bear, with two cubs sleeping in a den. "Think about that bear life you told me about, with the two cubs," I said. "You didn't love one less just because you were playing with the other, did you?"

No. I loved them both. So, we are your cubs?

I laughed. "Well, I'd like to think you are both your own dogs and that you live with us, and that I love you both, just as I love the others in our family. I would just prefer that you and Zak wouldn't growl with each other. I feel Zak is now top dog because he is the oldest. And I want you to know that when I pat either one of you, I will be happy to pat the other, but please wait your turn."

Good manners . . .

"Right! I'd like you to have good manners. And, while we're at it, maybe not to bark so much when you see other dogs or people or cars outside. One bark will do!"

It is hard to stop once I start.

"Like when we are jumping on the trampoline, Max. No need to bark at us."

You are flying into the air! Doesn't look safe!

I had to smile as I realized from Max's perspective it probably did look like we were flying up into the air.

I would like to jump with you, said Max after a moment.

"Your nails would ruin the trampoline. Maybe we could walk with you more. Would that help?"

And throwing balls and things for me to fetch. That would be very good.

And so it was that the big black Lab and I came to an agreement on this and many other things, and the dog wars between Zak and Max abated.

A RESURGENCE OF ENERGY

Barney was right: I needed to take a break and enjoy my 'field trips.' I was glad to continue meeting and talking with animals—as well as trees and plants, clouds and glaciers and mountains. I took notes, recorded conversations, and read whatever called to me. And all the while, I felt something simmering just beneath the surface of consciousness.

One morning, the simmering bubbled over and offered up an idea: write a book with Barney, looking at death, through his story, along with experiences in shapeshifting.

An excellent topic, said Barney when I approached him about it, *and I am pleased and honored and committed to working with you in this regard. To some degree, then, this is our book—and I mean that not from a possessive perspective, but from the view which holds us in a certain level of teaching and understanding. This is not a review of death, dying, and shapeshifting. It is simply experience from our perspective. In this manner, the whole group is involved, with some additional material from others. Sound interesting?*

"Yes," I nodded, "that would be very interesting."

Let us begin with the topic of caring for one's dead. This is more for the living than the dead, of course. For example, I felt the way you handled my body as I was leaving from it was very respectful and I was pleased you chose to take such an active role in sending my body to the earth. On the one hand, it is only a body—a residence of the soul or spirit. On the other hand, it is a marvelous temple that holds its own memories and functions and amazing abilities. Returning the body (any body) to the earth—whether by fire or burial or at sea, or by dispensation through other creatures partaking of it—is always a recycling. That is how the planet Earth operates. It is quite elegant in its simplicity.

For another round on what happens when the soul leaves the body, let us focus again on conscious dying. There are various forms of conscious dying. For myself, I knew when I would die. It was to be a choice. I do not mean to say I knew the exact minute or day, but I knew it was to be determined by a congruence of timing and inner development. I was 'feeling' for the right time to die.

I chose to die at dawn, both for your namesake and to be near you, on your bed, because we are linked and this life of mine was partly to help you bring forth memories and understandings and experiences to your conscious self and to others. Do you remember bringing me water? About being the Water Bearer?

"Yes," I said, feeling the weight of that curious title: *Water Bearer.* It felt old and worn and hefty in my head, yet cherished as well.

It has to do with memories. Water holds memory. I was pleased you were able to awake and remember the value of water. Did you know this was a touchstone to your role as a Water Bearer in past lives, or other scenarios of life? You brought me water as a sign of one of our existences; and, by doing so, you brought yourself the remembering of this. Do you wish to explore this further?

"If it's part of where we are going to go."

It may bring up more than you realize. I want you to choose. Look inside and tell me if you are ready.

I pondered deeper. "Well, my first vision is of a treasure chest at the bottom of the ocean. The water is dark, but there is definitely promise in that treasure chest. I guess the question is: Do I have the courage to go down and get it, to open it up and see what's inside?"

Always a good question!

I laughed. "I'm ready." For what could be so scary?

Then let us deepen and focus upon a life which links us via water, via the Water Bearer. This is an early Aquarian-age life, as the horoscope emblem/sign reveals, and is of a much older time in Earth's history. It also ties in with creation stories—and, as such, with destruction stories. We are actually going to a more mythic life. So, let us hold this in mythic terms. This is very deep—as you saw, the treasure chest is at the bottom of the ocean floor, and you can be assured that the pressure at that level is very different from your normal breathing levels. Therefore, you need a protective suit. It is in this sense that we will use the mythic format—as a protective suit—to go 'down' in the self and retrieve the treasure chest of memories.

Breathing deeply, slowly, I focused on a swirling black hole of water that began to pull me down. But after a moment I panicked and bounced back up to the surface. Sun sparkles glinted on the waves and the water stretched to the horizon's edge of a temperate blue sky. As I looked further, I saw an island and, over there, a raft—with Barney disguised as an English sheepdog!

Let us begin again, said Barney, patient as ever. *Remember, the purpose is to go down and face the treasure. The raft and island are diversions. It is not safety you are looking for—it is the treasure. It is the memory at the bottom of the ocean.*

So, once again, I focused deep. As I felt the swirling of the water, I let it pull me down. And, once more, I felt panic and the awful sensation of drowning. It was as if my body's memory held the fear as a barrier, and it took some time for my breath to carry me past this, down, down, to the floor of the ocean, where the water was murky and dark. I heard a voice tell me that I could not have the treasure to take back unless I answered the question. And the question was: *Who Are You?*

I was surprised to hear my bold underwater self reply without hesitation, "I am Dawn. I am the owner and caretaker of this treasure box. It holds my treasure. Let me take this back up to the surface."

And so the treasure box was released. But not, of course, without a hitch. For at just that moment, a shadowy Captain Hook character appeared. He told me I must first open the locked box, for if the treasure was really mine it would open.

And then, in that way of mythic journeys, I was aware of a key hanging on a cord around my neck. Taking the key, I approached the box and inserted it. Lo and behold, it opened wide. And—to my incredulous surprise—out of the box sprang a small, startled, alien being.

"Oh brother," I said to Barney. "Do you want to tell me that we are from outer space, from other planets? Is that it? Is that the secret?" I could already feel my thoughts going judgmental and wiggy with the idea.

And that we came to help begin a new understanding among the people here. There was a core group. You and I and many others are part of this group. It is all of us really, since there is no difference between you and I and everyone else, but in this level of the play, from where I stand, yes, this is the remembering scenario we are working with. You came here to be a dawn, a morning, an awakening to others. This is part of who we are.

I shook my head, annoyed with the direction this little adventure was taking. "Calm down," I told myself in irritation. "He told you to hold it in mythic terms."

And your mythic work of the scenario shows that you do hold the keys, that you are ready, and that you do hold the voice that is willing to claim her birthright. Barney paused, as if deciding what path to follow here. *In some ways, this was more of a testing procedure, to see your holds, your blocks. What do you think those might be?*

"I don't know about that," I said, still in frustration.

It is because you don't want to see. It is about the 'end of the world' becoming reanimated and active with life—it is about manifestation, creation, new life, and new awakenings. We use these words and images in metaphoric reference. This is about new birth. This is about awakening fully to who you are.

And, this is about resistance to the new—preferring to drown in the old. You have had several lives of drowning and of giving up and of feeling you have failed. You tend to be too hard on yourself. You hold resistance to death because you hold resistance to life. You would benefit from loving your experiences—all of them—and so you would begin to have and hold greater love for yourself.

I shook my head again, trying to shake away the tsunami of chaos and hot tears rising from within.

This will be our segue into the deeper mysteries of shapeshifting and discovering who we really are, said Barney, leaving me in a blur of uncertainties.

As the tears finally popped from my eyes, I had the uneasy feeling that part of me was zipping open. As if that key really had opened something. As if some pocket door inside my mind was sliding open, revealing a room I never knew existed. A quiet, spacious, empty room, clean and clear and still. And I was standing there, my foot poised to step beyond the doorway, wondering: What happens next?

PART 2

*Adventures
in Shapeshifting*

8

——·——

We Are All
Shapeshifters

Not long after Barney died, I had a dream:

> I am walking up a small path to a house that has an open front
> door. As I approach the door, I see Barney inside the house.
> "Barney! You're alive!" I exclaim. I am very excited by this,
> though an older man—a doctor—appears and tells me that,
> obviously, the dog was just asleep and hadn't really died. I be-
> gin to argue with the man, but it is no use; he insists that a dog
> cannot die and come back to life. I see, then, that he is stuck
> in a belief and no amount of arguing will change it. I surprise
> myself by slapping him across the face, saying firmly, "You saw
> it. He was dead. And now he is alive!"

On waking, my fingers actually tingled from the slap, and the visual
"open door" of death seemed deliberately funny, despite the parts of me
(as evidenced by the doctor) that still wanted to deny that truth.

*This is a beginning, an indication from your inner world that the
division between life and death is not as you once believed, nor as others may want you to believe,* Barney commented later that day. *You are*

already guessing that the doctor in the dream represents an older, male-centered, authoritative way of seeing the world that you once held as true. That you slapped the doctor indicates your moving away from these views, though notice that it still entails an argument. A part of you continues to want 'the doctor' to believe you; thus, you are not necessarily fully centered. This is fine; this is where you are. It seems a human pattern that leaving a paradigm often involves some type of struggle.

Once you get past this division of life and death, you see that it is simply another choice of form. This is where shapeshifting can play an important role for you and other humans. Essence does not die. Most religions understand this to some degree, though the cloaks or myths through which they deem this is possible (such as, heaven and hell, bardo, reincarnation) vary widely.

Let us go into reincarnation for a moment. Some humans believe reincarnation includes a continuance of personality or ego. I have seen this occur in some instances, but have found these are, for the most part, rare. This continuance is often done as a type of conscious dying—that is, bringing the personality program of one physical being through the death process and into the body of another physical being. The idea here is to link the consciousness of one physical body to another through the death transition process. The Tibetans are keen on this as a means of continuing teachings from one teacher to another.

As I pondered that, inwardly questioning whether it really worked, Barney sent me the mental equivalent of a shrug. *As I said, it is a special type of life-to-death-to-life process, and requires some degree of inner training. Actually, it is a very unique means of shapeshifting, so perhaps we will discuss this at a later date.*

For now, however, I would like to focus on some misconceptions about reincarnation. Most often incarnation of spirit does not include personality traits from the former life. Although many spirits who begin to awaken in their physical bodies may 'remember' past lives or alternate lives, they will find that many personality traits are not similar. They may identify with a personal theme or keynote because, of course, the same essence is involved—so in that sense there is similarity—though it would not be correct to assume that this similarity is personality or ego based. Do you understand?

"You are saying it is not as simplistic as the idea of a small personal 'you' continuing into another life."

Correct. That is a good way to get into this. Upon death, there is a falling away of personality, less identification with the ego and character subroutines that are dominant in the physical. It is as if the soul or spirit form of 'you' may now observe the software program or container you were using while on Earth. Your focus widens to a larger part of yourself, rather than a narrowly focused view, which is most often the perspective from the physical body.

Shapeshifting can be used while in the physical body, however, to effect a change in perspective so that you see not only from your personality-based paradigm, but also from other personality-based paradigms, and beyond. It is interesting that animals often have less identification with 'personality' than humans do. Perhaps this is why to some extent many humans believe animals do not have souls—because they do not see the personality of an ant or a tiger, or whatever animal you happen to project upon. So, do you see how this identification with personality and soul becomes coded at a level beneath your consciousness, of which many humans are not even aware?

"You're saying that we sometimes relate personality and soul when in fact the two are very different?"

Different and yet at the same time related. On the one hand, personality is a program, a unique development that each soul chooses while in a particular body. As such, it is also related to the soul, since the soul has created it. But it is not the soul itself. Rather, it would be like a piece of art or music or story that you create. Understand?

"Yes, that's a clear way of putting it."

Thank you. Let us once again look at shapeshifting as a means to 'wake up' while in the body. By riding along with or becoming other beings, you are able to realize at an experiential level that your manner of seeing the world is simply your manner of seeing the world. It is your perception, based on who you are. Just as a dog's perception is based on who and what he is, or a dolphin's based on her unique view. As Zak mentioned, the amount of soul or spirit you are aware of in your body is dependent on how open you are to allowing that essence to infuse your consciousness. We could liken this to how 'realized' a novel is, or a piece of artwork, or a song.

As you continue to open, you realize that you have many talents, that you are capable of many perspectives, that you can wear 'many hats'— which, by the way, is an interesting phrase that many of us link to shape-shifting abilities.

For example: you open to this voice of 'me' speaking in your head. To some degree, you are creating it in the sense that you are providing the words and expressions. It is your fingers typing, translating the inner words into phrases on a keypad into written sentences for others to read, and your thoughts helping to carry my ideas outward. Can you describe this experience to others?

"Well, it is as you say. I quiet my thoughts and feel for a particular tone of energy and then I listen." For a moment I did just that. The effect of consciously listening to myself listen, however, had a curious effect, rather like being hyperaware of yourself looking at yourself in a mirror.

"I don't know where you're going with some of this, Barney," I said after a moment. "And when I think that thought, I get a little fearful. I know that's silly because all I really have to do is be and listen. It's almost as if when I'm not thinking and just being calm that it all flows the best."

And don't you see how this is great advice for yourself, for your life? When you allow and are 'open,' then your soul can open within you. Then there is the space for more of the greater you to filter into and infuse the physical you. You are enlarged; you become more aware of your total-ity, light, and brilliance. And if you continue with this opening, you will begin to see the brilliance not only in yourself, but also in all other shapes and forms, all other beings. And that is when shapeshifting simply is. It's not even called shapeshifting at that point, because it is obvious—you are all: the ant, the elephant, the kangaroo, the parrot, the dog, the human, the living nowness of All. At that point—which is not really a point at all but a be-ing—there is no longer a need for words.

And, for a moment, Barney and I sat happily in silence.

However, to return to words—to put some of this on paper so as to spark the experience in others—we always begin with who we are, at this moment. That is centering. And, in deepening into that, we become aware of a much greater way of being. You can spread this deepened, centered knowing in many directions.

Think of it as a rock dropping and forming a group of ripples on water, circular ripples moving outward. Now, you may focus on any circle of the ripples or any point along a circle of the ripple. You might follow death into the release of your personality so as to meet your essence. You might follow that into another life and then another, so as to experience the various masks—the various hats—you decide to try on. Or you might experience this all in one life—moving from form to form, asking animals or humans or plants or forces of nature to be your teacher, moving along with them so as to see yet another perspective, another view, another frame of the film. Or, you might focus on just one aspect of yourself, following that ever deeper, ever higher, ever closer to essence. That is a means of shapeshifting also. It is an evolution of sorts—taking one form and stretching with it as far as it can go, until at last you pop through and are once again aware of the larger you—the fullness of your greater being.

We may call all of these means a form of shapeshifting. Life itself is a shapeshifting. I know I use this word differently than some in the human world, but this is the way in which I can relate our understanding of shapeshifting, making it applicable to everyone.

Shapeshifting is a movement, and all life is movement. As any form of life, you are constantly in movement and, as such, you are constantly shifting in your shape: growing as a human, plant, or animal; being weathered; taking in other forms and essences and releasing them, via food or air or water or sunshine or nourishment. This, too, is a form of shapeshifting: the taking in of others and the letting go of that which has become you. Do you see how this is all interwoven, interrelated?

Life and death is this: the taking of one form and the letting go of another form; it is the taking in of the 'other' (such as eating food or join-ing in union with another) and the release of that which becomes, for a time, a part of you. Do you understand this at a deeper level? Can you experience this continual interaction of all life? It is at this level that physical shapeshifting is understood for what it truly is: a continual move-ment. And once you become aware of this, then you have opened to the understanding that shapeshifting offers.

"Whew!"

This is all for now, said Barney with a small laugh. *This is another way of seeing shapeshifting. Let us continue to describe this in a way that helps our readers to feel this in their beings. It will be a good project for your mind.*

STREAMS OF ENERGY

Although Barney was poking some good-natured fun at me, he also was planting a seed. Sure enough, my mind readily took on the project, playfully exploring the nature of describing shapeshifting for several days. Then, one lazy autumn afternoon, I had an experience. It came in the form of a key teacher who had been hopping about my life ever more frequently: Rabbit!

We are the energy of the Rabbit Links, meaning the energetic presence of that which connects the rabbit form to spirit or soul, said this unex-pected aspect of Rabbit, stylishly springing up alongside my conscious thoughts as if he or she had been listening patiently all along. *We work to link the quicker, finer vibrations of spirit to the denser, physical mani-festation of rabbits on this planet.*

Sometimes situations like this call for introductions and polite

questions. Other times they do not. This was one of those times. As I
settled in to listen, the voice continued:

*Rabbits are capable shapeshifters, and are often guides into the deeper
nature of this art. Recall White Rabbit in* Alice in Wonderland. *It was
the rabbit who led Alice into the hole—or entrance to another vision/ver-
sion of the whole.*

*Rabbits also have a connection to the heavens, which ties in to your
rabbit experience [of the rabbit leaping into the night sky]. In this sense,
rabbits link dimensional levels of consciousness. That is, we work to
forge deeper ties of awareness between various levels or grids or planes
of emotional consciousness. For this reason, rabbits are often pictured
as leaping or jumping. We are indeed capable 'hoppers' when bridging
dimensions.*

*Many animals chase rabbits, not only for food. As prey animals, rab-
bits appear to some humans as being 'scared.' You may have seen rabbits
being chased, eyes wide, their focus seemingly intent on escape. However,
rabbits do not hold fear in the manner that humans often project upon us.
Rabbits have a secret life. Many times rabbits serve to guide other animals
to another space inside themselves. Rabbits work with the energy of . . .*

And here Rabbit paused, suggesting that I feel this energy rather
than categorize it.

Well, what else can you do but gamely accept when Teacher Rabbit
offers an experience such as this? Settling in, I soon came to feel
the energy Rabbit was directing me toward. It came upon me like a
whoosh—a surprisingly smooth, fast, deep-leveled sense that all is well,
all is as it should be, all is in order, even with a fox chasing a rabbit.
Ah! It was then I saw the image of a rabbit and a fox in pursuit. It
was not as we humans usually understand a one-guy-chasing-another
pursuit, but an intrinsic flow of a much deeper, much bigger, much
more vibrant version of reality. I was particularly aware of a shimmering stream of energy, like a heat wave, both trailing and preceding the
chase, as if it were simultaneously occurring in the past and in the
future and in the now. The rush of this discovery—the feel of fox and

rabbit moving as one, as part of a larger stream—was magical to me and I excitedly wanted to follow it further.

Rabbit Teacher, however, had other plans. I felt a patient request to slow down and focus on becoming each animal—fox and rabbit—in turn.

Taking a few deep breaths, I began with fox. Without a plan, I opened, feeling myself expand and diffuse like a warm current of air—a cloud of consciousness flowing into the moving form of a red fox with sharp, quick eyes:

> We are moving fast, chasing a rabbit, a brownish rabbit, along the outskirts of a wood. I can smell the rabbit—a musky scent that holds a link of connection—not just a smell as humans know smells, but an actual energy line that trails the rabbit. Like the stream of energy, though this is finer, more precise. Part of this is fun, like a chasing game, though I know my prize will be to eat the rabbit. Of course the rabbit could also get away. It is smart. I know this from experience. Ah! Suddenly the rabbit disappears—down into the ground again. They have many holes around here, where they pop into the ground; even if I try very hard, I will probably not get him. He is gone, though I can still sense him. He is quiet and his heart is beating. I will sniff a while longer, but the game is finished. He has won.

And then, with a simple shift of intent, I was rabbit: a swift brown rabbit running from the red beastie:

> I was being bold, letting him smell me. I was in a clearing—not a good place to be—but I was being still, focused on a little bit of tasty something on the ground, not wanting to leave it but knowing the predator was near. That began the chase. I know the amount of distance that I can outrun a fox. Other animals have different distances—so many leaps. Foxes are not as smart as they

seem. They are distracted easily, like dogs. The ones we have to watch for are the owls and birds from the sky. Hard to watch for the swoopers! The fox explained it well. We were in a chase, a game. I was not in fear of my life in this one. It can always happen, of course, but I didn't feel it would this time. I knew where the hole was, part of my family's hole. We have a system of "safe places" all over these woods. We are well prepared in that way.

I laughed as the experience ended. "Whoa!"

What we wish to impart to you at this time is that this chase, this game, is part of an overall educational system, designed to illuminate one small strand of the web of greater life. Just as humans learn history or any particular study, so do various animal species have a focus of study.

On one level, rabbits learn about being well prepared—working with family or community to know of and to share the 'safe places' as our small brown friend termed it—and helping to create them for others. On another level, rabbits help to move animals from one area (such as a forest) to another. You see this with desert rabbits as well. They are part of a movement system designed to encourage the interaction of species. The chase is one segment of this learning.

Sometimes species are forced to work together. As with humans, this often occurs as a result of natural disasters. With a fire, for example, almost all animals are in exodus. There is rarely any hunting in this pursuit; all are moving in a common flow, side by side.

Rabbit paused for quite some time then, as if waiting for me to comment.

"I'm not sure why you are telling me all of this," I said at last. "Sometimes rabbits prepare safe places, and other times they work with animals to escape danger. Maybe there is a deeper point here, but I'm not getting it."

Sit with this for a moment. This is part of the rabbit's shapeshifting nature. There is much power rabbits hide from first view. Rabbits are about silence, about deeper meanings, about holding the secrets of cre-

ation. Part of you is a rabbit, didn't you know? Haven't you guessed by now? You have had a rabbit teacher in more than one 'lifetime.'

And, as so often happens when an unexpected awareness suddenly looms large, I felt wavelets of fear rising within.

As for fear, responded Rabbit straight away, *I will tell you this: Rabbits work with the deeper layers of fear. We work very deep—at the level where fears both come into existence and are nearly ripe to be released. That is our 'birthing' ability. We are able to help those who are ready to release fears do so in an instant. The 'cover' for this is our innocence, our gentle nature. On the surface, no one believes a rabbit is capable of such things, and yet this is our shadow nature—our seeming innocence. The cover of innocence is, in fact, where many fears are hidden away and, thus, begin to grow. There is much about hiding fears under so-called innocent pretexts that many humans hold, and it is here that rabbits serve as excellent teachers.*

EXPRESSIONS OF SPIRIT

It would take some time for me to integrate Rabbit's message, for there was so much there, in such a small package. Just like a rabbit! I also felt Rabbit had delivered several time-released teachings, tiny tendrils designed to blossom in my consciousness (or yours) when the moment is right.

In addition, the notion of shapeshifting was ever shifting its shape. I had come to see that in a larger context, shapeshifting is not simply about shifting the shape of the body but about shifting the shape of our thoughts, our consciousness, our being—the very experience of who we are, and who we are becoming.

We are all shapeshifters, a birch tree said calmly one autumn evening as I sat on the back porch, watching the rays of an almost-setting sun glow golden pink upon the mountains. I nodded, appreciating the tree's shared imagery of its graceful movement through the seasons: bare branches to buds to leaves and back to naked branches once again. It caused me to ponder the deeper implications of shapeshifting as movement. For, as Barney noted, "Shapeshifting is a movement, and all life is movement." How then do we distinguish shapeshifting as anything other than the movement of life becoming? Well, maybe we don't. Maybe this deeper, subtle shift is so obvious and pervasive that—oh! And then it came to me.

Perhaps the key to shapeshifting has not so much to do with the forms—the shapes of becoming—but the transition, the shift, the movement itself. In becoming the place in between forms—which is to say the deeper movement of life, that energetic "glue" which holds things together—we not only access a deeper knowing, but a keen awareness of the mechanics of shapeshifting. Perhaps shapeshifting shakes us up so much because by doing it often enough we finally wake up to the knowing that we really are *that*—the essence within the form and the essence that is beyond form.

It would be so much better to see us all as expressions of spirit—incredible, diverse, varied expressions of spirit, said Barney, calm as the tall, handsome birch. *Spirit speaks through all of us, in ever changing ways. That is a very real truth on this planet. That, too, is an awakening: the awareness of spirit moving through us as part of the larger unfolding. That is a grand remembering.*

"'*Tat tvam asi*'*—'Thou art that,'" I noted. "We are one."

Yes, said Barney. *And this is, coincidentally, exactly what most animals mean by 'we are one'—one not in the sense of we are all the same, but we are of one essence expressing itself.*

At this stage of your learning you have chosen to 'see' through the variety of form. There are other ways of doing this, though my feeling is that the art of shapeshifting is an elegant way of opening. For it honors the creative diversity—which is to say, beauty—of this world. It has the added benefit of helping you open to other worlds and other modes of being.

---

*A Sanskrit phrase, originally from the Chandogya Upanishad, which reveals the essential oneness between soul/spirit *(Atman)* and ultimate reality *(Brahman)*.

If you are to journey much further, however, you must learn to trust at deeper levels, as well as pay close attention to the circumstances that unfold around you. Much information is given to you in dreams and about dreams because your life is indeed a dream, and you are the only one who can awaken from it. Do you understand?

I nodded, touched by Master Barney's gentle manner of support and persuasion.

We can speak whenever you like, about anything you like, he added. *You do not always need an agenda. For, many times, the best thoughts or ideas occur simply when two friends are sharing.*

9

—·—

This Mosaic Called Earth

One early morning as I was making coffee for myself and breakfast for the dogs, I noticed something very surprising: Zak wasn't Zak.

There was the familiar body of Zak, of course, but he moved differently. He held his head and body differently. He even ate differently. Yet these differences seemed familiar. With a start, I realized: it was Barney! Barney was inside Zak's body!

"Are you really in there?" I asked. "And are you still there too, Zak?" I wondered if this body-sharing was a form of shapeshifting. It was more than just 'riding along' in consciousness, for Barney seemed to animate the body. "Why are you doing this? *How* are you doing this? What's going on?"

You have numerous questions! Let us start with a basic overview. This is Zak speaking, as if you could not tell. Er—you are able to tell?

Actually, I could. I was reminded of hearing dogs barking when I'd had a fever and learning how to identify energetic signatures of being.*
As soon as Zak spoke, I sensed him back in his body, whereas just a few seconds before Barney's "signature" had been present.

"So, following the energetic signature is a way to identify who's in what body?" I asked Zak.

---

*See beginning of chapter 3.

Barney and Zak

Exactly. It is the spiritual being, the soul or spirit-being, who inhabits a body. The body is the shape. You have also had a shift and so now, when you speak about shapeshifting, you are talking from the perspective of the spiritual being, are you not? That is an important perspective to consider. From this point of view, it is not so much about your shape changing, but about your being shifting into another shape. A small distinction, but enormous ramifications.

Consider the experience of resting your physical body (keeping it on 'hold') and allowing your consciousness to enter another body. In this way, you use your being—not your body—to shift shapes. Your body is still present as it was; it is your being which has shifted views or perspectives. For basic understanding, this is a good way to approach shapeshifting.

There is, of course, the ability to cellularly shift the shape of one's physical body. This requires larger amounts of energy and, at this point in your development and the development of most of humanity, it is not particularly wise to focus upon.

"Because we first need to build a base of spiritual grounding?"

Yes, that is rather at the base of my thoughts for you and other humans at the present time. It is easy to get caught up in the power and amusement of shifting shapes, but unless one has a deeper reason or plan for playing such a game, then it is a diversion and may not really serve one's larger purpose. Best to first understand the importance of shapeshifting, why it might be exercised more by humanity, and why it is an essential aspect of your evolution.

"Why is that?"

What do you think?

"I suppose it serves as a quickening process. As we open our consciousness to animals and other beings, we begin to really know, and appreciate, one another so much more intimately. It can't help but change us—how we see the world, and each other, and ourselves. And I imagine if we begin to truly feel and know and live from that connection which unites us all, we might move into a whole new shapeshift of evolution unfolding."

This is certainly a good beginning on the mental level. That can be your 'game plan' for now. What is still needed is more experiential knowledge. You have an ability to understand and see things on the mental level rather quickly; though as you have learned, knowing something with your head and feeling it in your body and heart is another matter. Isn't this so?

I nodded. "Sometimes I'm in the flow and other times I'm stuck in the streambed."

Part of you is frustrated because you feel things are not happening quickly enough. Another part of you is afraid. You hide fear quite well from yourself. You have an ability to see with your mind, but your body is often reluctant to follow. Our advice here is to trust, to continue to ask for help and to focus a bit more when asking a particular teacher to work with you. Barney and I are willing to help. Part of the purpose of our interchange and sharing of bodies is for you to notice and learn from this.

"Yes, I'm interested in knowing more about that! What's going on?"

Barney is doing some fine-tuning adjustments in comparing spirit vibrations to physical vibrations. I have agreed to help by loaning him the use of my body for short periods of time. He will be 'in' and 'out' for several days. Think of it as a scientific experiment. He is revisiting the physical as a form of remembering so that he can complete what might be called lost data.

It is easy for me. I am familiar and comfortable with the ability to leave my body and I have a trust built with Barney so there are no fearful overtones. Some animals allow this type of sharing to occur over long periods of time. Humans sometimes involve themselves in this practice—what is known as a 'walk-in.' There are times when this is not entirely helpful, though other times it is accomplished in a well-planned and useful manner. It can be diversionary, however, especially for those who choose to believe they are walk-ins only as a subconscious design to escape their current version of reality. This can be quite destructive.

Let us return to a more helpful vibration: what you are learning now—this shifting of perspective. As mentioned previously, it is often best to begin by asking a teacher if you may ride along with his or her consciousness. This is a nice introduction to another's internal home, and you will gain confidence as you observe more from 'inside' an animal. After you have had more of these experiences, we will delve into deeper topics. It is a pleasure to help you in this regard.

I thanked Zak, and then asked Barney if he had anything to add.

Only that I am nearly finished and do not plan to visit much longer. As Zak informed, I am doing some personal work with fine-tuning energetic frequencies. Remember the shaking that occurred near my death? I am working on aspects of that, along with the ability to disappear at will. . . . Though I may have to incarnate next as a cat to fine-tune it to the degree that I would like.

We both laughed, appreciating the noteworthy abilities of Cat.

Although you have done shapeshifting many times already, the focus is now to become more conscious. I will be happy to help you 'see' from my perspective and I can show you some wonderful places out of body. One initial suggestion is to let go of the idea that you see through your eyes. You see internally, with your mind's eye. Let go also of expectations and ideas about what you might see. Even if what you see is not physically possible (according to you), allow it to come into being. Suspect and suspend judgment and interpretations. There is more time for that when you return and record your experience.

Oftentimes there are very good reasons for journeys beginning in a mythological or even nonsensical fashion. Rely on your dreamwork abilities. Allow us in by breathing deep and opening to what is. Remember: we are all working together.

SHARING WITH PLANTS

As Barney noted, the more I opened to the 'what is' of life unfolding, the easier, more engaging, and more fun the flow became. Living in such a way brings us unexpected delights, teachings around every corner, the shine of brilliance and deep-down knowing in everyday events.

One morning, while watering a philodendron, I felt the quiet nudge of an invitation. Well, this is often how it begins! Just the faintest little feeling, a wisp of a sense, a wink, the shadow of a smile. The gesture is extended; it is then up to us whether to accept or not.

Putting down the watering can, I sat in a chair, easing the potted philodendron onto my lap. Closing my eyes, tuning into the hum of energy that connects us all, I felt the deeper presence of the plant. I sensed her guiding me, helping me to feel the fluid growth of her leaves and vines. She shared a stream of images that were supple and sinuous, flowing in a way that was akin to the budding and growth of her leaves. I came to know how plants are connected and how this particular plant moved by 'leaving,' or putting out leaves in the direction she wanted to travel. Words evaporated in a shared stream of brightly glowing, green liquid consciousness—a deeply filled inner light of growth and movement and plantness being.

Another morning, it was a Christmas cactus who extended the call. Improbably, she introduced herself as "Jen." In moving with her energy, I felt a solid, self-sustained, inner strength—very different from the connected energy the philodendron had shown of its relation to others of its kind. As I wondered then how cacti were connected, or if they were aware of their connection to other cactuses, Jen flashed the image of a map revealing a sprawling overlay of Christmas cactus arms. I saw them in long extensions, like an uneven fence, with blossoms in red and pink, yellow and orange, sometimes even shades of purple.

In sharing energy with an animal or plant (or any other being), we are also sharing ourselves. I would forget this at times, falling into the role of an observer or reporter. And so I was surprised when the little cactus commented that I was similar to her, for I liked to keep my secrets inside. I liked to hold things close to myself, she noted, like certain cacti who didn't care to "spread out in an ungainly manner." As I took this in, Jen offered to teach me more about cacti, connecting with plants, and sharing secrets.

CACTUS STORY:
A TALE OF BEGINNINGS

The following day, Jen's lesson involved me holding her and feeling into her root system. Although I tried various ways, I wasn't getting anywhere. She then related that cacti hold their nourishment inside their stems and lower leaves (trunk) and that is what I do, why often I do not feel a sense of having roots in any one particular place.

You carry your roots like a cactus, Jen remarked. And before I had a chance to respond to this, she went on with her lesson by offering to dictate a cactus story:

In the beginning of time, cacti were not yet formed. It may surprise you to know that we trace our origins to lava, the hot fire of the earth. These are the tales of our beginnings, from the time before we had form . . .

Accompanying Jen's tale was vivid imagery of a vast brown land with massive volcanic craters in the distance. Sparks of red-orange fire seeds spouted high into a darkened sky. I watched as their dazzling points of light arced downward, landing with flickers and sizzles in a slow-moving, glowing blob of molten lava. There was no sense of time or place; this was simply where Jen's tale began.

As lava flowed farther and farther, it came into contact with the rushing water of a river. There was the need, or perhaps the desire, for new plants—plants who would hold the consciousness of fire and water together, and this is the spark of idea from which we formed.

Along the banks of the river, there was the idea to cover the lava that had met the water with green plantness. When we pull back to ancient times, we remember the flow of lava meeting water, traveling along the cool river and being covered with the idea of green leaves. We all have that flowing within our being, our body of cactus. We all have an inner river, from which we trace our origins back to the first river of life.

In the beginning, many plants could move from place to place. You are thinking of walking, though it was not exactly like this. Rather, the ground was more fluid than it is now and we had a way of shifting ourselves, moving from place to place to find the best circumstance of weather, ground conditions, sun, and shade to accommodate our needs. Many plants were able to do this, not just cacti. This was before there were many animals. Though we were acquainted with a few insects.

Cacti would have liked to travel farther, but owing to our encapsulation of fire and water, we had a need to stay in warmer climates. Some of us went to the mountains; many congregated in desert areas. Some of us grew near and among stones. Others went to less temperate climates where we developed a 'leaving' manner that we learned from other plants.

Jen distinguished here between prickly cacti and 'leaving' cacti (those with growing leaves—though humans might call these 'stem segments') such as herself.

There are other differentiations as well, she added. *We have differing consciousness, and you might enjoy talking to a prickly cactus to get that point of view. Now, do you have any questions?*

"Is this a science-myth of how you came into being?" I asked, wondering how Jen related to the tale.

It is a story, a way of seeing things. We do not distinguish between myth (as 'made-up' story) and science (as 'real' story) in the manner of some humans. There are many ways of seeing truth, many stories to relate. This is just one small view of how we evolved. The prickly cactus may have another view. This is the story that our kind relates to, the way we see our beginning. Just as humans have differing ways of seeing their beginnings, from originating in a garden to the growth of other beings [primates] into humans.

"Yes, that's true," I agreed. "And other cultures offer different views of our beginning as well."

Our feeling is that the more stories there are to view, the more we might appreciate the glory of our beginning, and of how we have become what we are today.

I nodded. "Each aspect contributes to the whole—and by holding all, we are able to sense something bigger, something greater than just one view."

This is our be-leaf as well. Our focus is on being.

MORE ON MOVEMENT

The following day I had more questions for Jen. I was curious about the positioning of plants relative to energy grids on the planet. Groups of animals had related to me their notion of protecting, nurturing, and working in alliance with the energies of certain areas on Earth. Were plants conscious of their role in holding energy in similar ways?

In her distinctive way of answering, Jen asked me to first connect as deeply as possible and feel for my own answer. As I did so, she began hers:

Just as all living beings do, plants have a force field of energy emanating from their tissues and inner being. Different plants (and likewise, different animals) hold what you call different 'signatures' of energy. In general, different kinds of plants work with different aspects of the earth, interrelating with her to bring about certain conditions that are deemed necessary or desired.

Plants do indeed move. We shift and grow—both upward and outward, above ground and below. Some plants move more quickly than others do, but we are all aware of our 'movements' both within and upon the face of the earth.

Plants have a unique connection to Earth in that we are physically rooted to her—we are a part of her, and cannot exist without her. Even houseplants have a sense of this, as soil removed from the earth still holds a field of consciousness that remains in constant remembrance of Mother Earth.

The plant kingdom is different from the animal kingdom. We work with both land and sky in a way that is often difficult for humans to understand. We often think of ourselves as growths or extensions of Earth herself. We are her taste buds, her nerve receptors, her senses—vision, hearing, taste, touch, smell, and many senses of which humans are not aware. We work with the core energies of Earth as well as with her more surface-conscious aspects. Many plants are connected at very deep levels and we are able to transmit . . . we hesitate to call them 'messages,' since they are not what you understand as messages, but similar . . . plant messages to and fro. Disease, for example, is often a communicated parcel of information. Some species of plants choose to leave the face of the earth. Humans and animals destroy others. Sometimes they come back; sometimes they do not.

Many plants hold valuable information for humans, and many animals are already aware of the plants that keep them in balance or help restore them to balance. Though some animals (like humans) do not listen to us and some die from eating or touching us, others gain health by respecting us and asking us for our wisdom—which we most always share. We do not mind being eaten, by the way, for we have a larger view of life cycles than you do. By being eaten we become a part of the being that consumes us, and we often retain a sense of existence even after being pulled away from our roots and traveling through digestive processes. Some of us begin life that way, as digested seeds, which are later expelled back onto earth, to become a new life as a plant in another locale.

Our relationship with humans is designed to help you refocus your connection with the land, with the forces of this planet, and to see on a larger scale how all aspects of Earth are evolving to a common goal.

Most of us enjoy sharing our wisdom and enjoy the company of animals and humans. As a whole, we perform many incredibly useful functions for animals and humans. You would not be here without us. Many of us would not be here without animals. Humans are unique in that most all other forms of life could survive without you. And yet humans are in some ways the common evolution of all of us—you are our future in many senses since it is your species that has chosen to break away so as to discover another mode of being—a uniquely conscious way of connecting what we all hold. In this manner, you are helping all of us to see and appreciate life in a new way.

THE HUMAN ROLE IN EVOLUTION

As quickly as Jen's lessons came to me, so too did they end. Although I sensed I might contact Jen later, she made it clear that her instruction was finished for the time being and it was up to me to determine how clearly or deeply her message might unfold. She certainly left me with plenty to ponder!

The topic of movement was still keen in my mind, and over several days I began thinking of how humans move vertically while most animals move horizontally, with their bellies facing the earth. What does this tell us? Is our upright posture about a decision made at some point in our evolution to move in another way? Does it have to do with free will (being that our third chakra—our will center—is not directly in contact with the earth)? And how does this relate to Jen's statement that humans broke away from knowing as animals so as to discover another mode of being? What is our role in the evolution of all beings on Earth?

Big questions! said Barney, who was no longer using Zak's body, but nonetheless acutely present.

Each species has its own way of moving through space and connecting with the land and planet. Some are more specialized than others. You could move your consciousness to an earthworm and learn about mixing up soil and enriching the power-energy of a certain spot. Eels can show you about creating new gridlines and repairing old ones, about altering circuits. They are in some regards the 'computer technicians' of the under-water world. Sharks hold knowledge of different 'histories' of Earth and how she has moved through each learning phase. (And let us remember that Earth herself is sentient and evolving along with all of us.) Birds approach the matter differently—and fish have yet another perspective. Many creatures have fine-tuned their connection to a certain area, whereas other animals (such as migrating birds or caribou) spread their connection over a vaster space.

It is helpful to discern the way different animals move. You are correct that many animals move with their bellies facing the earth—a homing device of sorts, a reminder of our connection to the land and to distinct pathways of energy. It is as though the land holds maps for various animals to follow specific trails. That is the 'magic' behind cats and dogs finding their way home, even from hundreds of miles away. Barring accident and hunger, they can find their way home.

I recalled when Barney was still alive and shared with me how he experienced moving. Lying on the floor next to him, I could not only see through his eyes as he dream-ran, but could also feel-see a flow of energy that helped to guide him as he ran. Like a living map, I now understood. This further clicked into place as I recalled the experience

THIS MOSAIC CALLED EARTH   111

of how rabbit and fox ran, which compared in an altogether different yet complementary fashion with the way the plants moved. Such rich diversity!

Humans are another story and did indeed evolve along different lines, moving more 'vertically' in order to appreciate their connection to the earth in a unique way. In a sense this is about evolving instinct and intuition, which is to say evolving an innate connection with the earth to a form of conscious intuition. It is to say humans chose to lose, hide, or forget certain connections in order to refind—and, in the process, refine— them. It is a choice human species made long ago—severing part of their innate connection with the land, animals, plants, and natural world, in order to rediscover it in another way and come to know themselves through yet another perspective.

Each species holds a distinctive connection to the earth. We are all part of this mosaic called Earth. We all hold knowledge that others may share and learn from. Humans, too, hold distinctive, detailed information about many things, and some animals would appreciate a chance to learn from humans as well.

This is a secondary phase of animal communication,* in which humans share knowledge with animals—and many other beings—in a more conscious and giving way. We have access to some human knowing, but not all, mostly because our receivers (brains and senses) are adapted in different ways.

Much depends upon humans and animals coming together and working together. As you open to animals, you open to deeper levels of awareness within yourself. Your connections to the sky and land and sea and subterranean places within your own being become more accessible. As humans gain a greater awareness of the abilities of animals—as you as a species come to know that we all have souls and depth and families and consciousness—you will be more open to sharing yourselves, so that we can all work together in a new way.

---

*The first phase is awareness of our inherent connection with all life, and opening in telepathic communication with animals (and other beings).

10

Limitless Possibilities

The first time it happened was on a brilliant summer day. I was wandering through a mountainous area, no real destination in mind. Occasionally, I'd look up to watch the clouds bump around the bright blue sky. As a bald eagle glided overhead, my eyes naturally followed its path, and I wondered what it would be like to see from the eagle's eyes. And suddenly—for just a moment—I saw from the eagle's point of view. It was such an abrupt shift in perspective that I gasped and blinked in amazement, thus losing the vision nearly as quickly as it had come. However, there was no mistaking it: for a few precious seconds I had glimpsed the world through the eyes of an eagle!

Clearly, my consciousness was not yet so flexible or expansive as to fully accommodate this immersion into Eagle—or that part which was still 'I' wouldn't have been so shocked by seeing through the eagle's eyes. So also was this experience rather impulsively called into being—not so much intended as simply a wandering thought of wonder.

It wasn't until I began working consciously with Barney on shape-shifting that I used more focused intention when requesting to see through the eyes of another. As experiences followed—raven, goldfish, jaguar—I was less shaken and better equipped to spend longer periods of time sharing consciousness with others.

Each of the experiences had a different quality. Raven shared the unfolding of wings and uplifting of feathers, the feel of air beneath our body not only as a support but as a living presence. Jaguar revealed the vision of golden outlines around plant leaves and branches as we leaped across a fallen tree and moved through a shadowy path of jungle-earth brightened with rich, yellow patches of filtered sunlight. And through Goldfish I came to know a deeper sense of liquid flowing through me, around me, as part of me—our gills fluttering open, our fins oaring, our long, filmy tail rippling in a dance of supple undulations that moved in living relationship with the larger presence that is Water.

There were small amusements, as well, such as the strange heaviness I felt pushing upon my eyes with Goldfish—only to realize it was the pressure of water. So, too, did Goldfish cause me to laugh as, coming out of the experience, I shared my sense of self, lying on my back in bed. A flurry of concern came my way: *No, not on your back. That is death. Flip over, flip over!*

Sometimes I was able to simultaneously see through my normal way of perceiving and through the animal's manner of perceiving—as if I had an eye in each of the two worlds. Other times, I was more fully immersed in the animal's perspective. These moments were truly a world unto themselves. It was transporting the experience back into our human world of categories and words that was the tricky part.

With each experience, I was more keenly aware of a subtle yet profound change. This was difficult to articulate at times because the jump from "being" the animal (or, at least, sharing in consciousness) to regaining my own sense of consciousness often seemed too great a distance. Much got lost in the translation. This is why to describe in words what I saw from the eagle's perspective is already to lose sense of what it was. Concepts such as "mountains," "land," and "water" (ways in which I might have described the scene) were not part of the eagle's consciousness, not part of his way of seeing.

What I eventually came to know—not just mentally but through experience—is that in shifting to another's eyes it isn't necessarily *what* we see that changes; rather, it is the way *in which* we see. (And, because the way *in which* we see changes, *what* we see changes as well!) Thus I realized a deeper aspect of what Barney had been telling me all along: the value of shapeshifting isn't simply seeing through another's eyes; it's deepening that experience within ourselves—knowing that as part of the greater "us."

THROUGH BARNEY'S EYES

One morning while connecting with Barney, I sensed a deep, blue calm. It was as if an expansive cloud filled with rich blue light was settling inside of me. It was opening me, refreshing me, focusing me in a way that was both grounded and centered yet spacious and airy. As I filled with that soothing blue light, I had the idea that I was looking through Barney's eyes. And with that idea came the awareness that he was settling—shifting *his* shape of being—into me. I was surprised by the feeling of immensity, not only as if his spirit-being had matured, but as if it had taken on a lighter, airy quality that was also remarkably vast.

Barney directed me to lie on the floor, just as he used to lie, on his side, beside my desk, several yards from the bookshelves, legs and paws outstretched. It seemed funny to do such a thing, but I knew there was something for me to see, and so I did as Barney requested, stretching my body on the carpet as if it were his when he had been alive. A second wave of settling came over me, along with the feeling that I was Barney in another event-field in the flow of time: sleeping and resting as he used to do, several years prior.

When I opened my eyes, I was seeing the books as Barney had once seen them: vertical strips of color of different heights and thickness, lined up one after another. Of course, the categories of "height" and "thickness" and even "color" were not present in the seeing; this is a translation. And the colors were not as humans know color, but different shades—similar to what we know, yet qualitatively different.* The textures of the books were also not as I, as a human, knew them, but slightly fuzzy, as if I could see the movement of slight vibrations rather than the appearance of solid objects.

What was more amazing to me, however, was the feeling I got while looking at the books. *This is how humans store their thoughts!* I saw, from the dog perspective, how these slim "strips" could be pulled from the walls as neat rectangles, and then opened further and unfolded to reveal markings that held stories and thoughts. What an amazing way of storing ideas! Not only was I seeing the way in which Barney-dog grasped this concept, but also comprehending the idea of books in a completely new and different way for myself.

"So, this is another perspective of shapeshifting?" I asked with some excitement as I sat up on the floor.

We are on the wide track now, said Barney. *We are choosing not to teach you a specific system precisely so that you can break open some of these limitations of definitions and spectacled ways of seeing the world and the flow of life. It is healthy to be flexible, to be able to jump from one view to another, and to hold many in simultaneity.*

I recalled a line from Walt Whitman's *Leaves of Grass:* "Do I contradict myself? Very well then, I contradict myself. I am large. I contain multitudes."[1]

Yes, this vibration is full of potential and limitless possibilities, Barney agreed. *Another way to work with shapeshifting is to* allow. *Just as you allowed me into you and were enabled to see how I see through*

---

*Some humans believe that dogs do not see in color. However, as many animals have noted, what humans believe is not always how it is. While we must keep in mind that we do translate and interpret our experiences with animals in the sensory ways available to us through our body software, the experience of color was something that Barney (and other dogs) showed me time and again. It thus became my experience that dogs do indeed see with color—though some colors were not as bright as others and the overall color spectrum was perceived differently than humans see it. Years later, I ran across newer scientific research confirming much of this.

your world (which is, indeed, a kind of shapeshift), you can allow others into your eyes. Many animals very much want to learn through your eyes, just as you learn through theirs.

That is all for now. Digest. Deepen. Be aware. Events will occur when you are ready for them to occur. It is very true that you create your own reality, as does every other being. This cannot be stressed strongly enough. Many humans seem to take this in a philosophical, mental, New Age sort of way, but it is quite literally true. If you knew this with all your being . . . well, reality would be a very different thing indeed!

TELEPORTATION

Still trailing along the vibration of potential, I was to meet another example of what is possible a few weeks later. While relaxing at my desk in between projects, I closed my eyes and moved into a contemplative state. I was feeling very tranquil until an abrupt shudder wobbled up my spine. The movement jostled me into the awareness of being in two places at the same time. I was seated both inside my body as usual and outside my body by a distance of about three inches.

Perhaps I was getting used to strange events, for although the double "me" felt odd, it was also intriguing. As I maintained the state—curious what would happen next—I felt a guiding presence suggest I look and "project outward."

Slowly opening my eyes, the first thing I saw was a small toy rhinoceros that sat on top of my computer. Gazing very gently upon the rhinoceros' horn, I felt the outer me "blow" outward and coalesce in the center of the tip of the horn. The guiding presence then suggested I turn around within my second body and open my vision from there. And with that thought—in the quickest of flickers—I was in my second body, now in the tip of the horn of the toy rhinoceros, gazing back upon my own face.

"Whoa!"

Clearly, this was the limit of my relationship with limitless possibilities for the moment; for with a quick tremble, I found myself instantly back—as one—within my body. I looked around the room, astounded. Even more strangely, when I looked back, I realized the toy had rotated a good twenty degrees.

This is a small example of teleportation, said Barney, before I could even begin to verbalize my usual barrage of questions. *It is part and parcel of shapeshifting in the greater sense. By releasing some old thoughts and ideas and beliefs, you opened to something new. And by shuddering—in this case, an outward manifestation of release—you were able to move your consciousness outward.*

As you practice with focus and intention, you may do this with greater range. In truth, it doesn't matter if it is two inches or two feet or two hundred million miles. Although within your particular space framework it would seem to make a great difference, we are working with consciousness—and consciousness is not limited by space. As you experience this in different and deeper ways, you will find this is so.

You are playing with constructs of space. So much of outer space projection is about inner space. You can visualize this in many diverse ways. Another form of shapeshifting, for example, is to see the universe inside yourself—inside your body, or inside your essence.

The important thing to realize is that it doesn't matter which metaphoric image or projection you use. The point is not the projection, but what lies beneath the projection—the connection. The projection is merely a tool, a way of getting you to feel the deeper flow of connectedness. Understand?

"Yes."

Next question?

I laughed. "Okay, so part of me wants to know if I really did turn the toy rhinoceros."

That was a little joke for you—and a foreshadowing of things to come. Remember what you learned about teaching and learning? The two work together. So it is with shapeshifting with other beings. It is not a singular process. It is all about relationship. When you are in relation with something, you affect it, just as it affects you. The toy has a different sort of 'consciousness,' though most humans would not speak about it in that way. But, yes, by interacting with the toy you did 'shift' it to some degree, just as it allowed (or enabled) you to shift.

As I considered this, Zak chimed in from his place on my office floor. I startled yet again, for I hadn't known he was there, or listening.

As you become more consciously tuned, you begin to appreciate the humor of such incidents, he observed. *There is a grace, a natural beauty, a sense of irony and comic appreciation of these unfoldings. This is truly a living game. A game that takes place on many levels at once—mentally, emotionally, in your dreams, in your waking life, symbolically, with animals, with plants, in any way that you can imagine and probably more than that as well! It is all your show. It is how you design it. The manner of learning is as creative as you can be.*

BECOMING LIKE WATER

I sometimes felt that working with Barney was like walking down an immense spiral staircase, each turn taking us ever deeper into the nature of boundless potential as we revisited material we had already seen, though from a different layer of perspective. That is why one morning when Barney suggested we look again at the role of Water Bearer and its connection to "re-solving the mystery of death," I knew we were embarking on yet another spiral.

Water is for you both a beautiful thing and a dangerous thing, he observed quietly. *You are pulled by it but there is a part of you that fears it. The two work together. Water is a part of you, as it is a part of all humans, animals, and Earth herself. Water also holds the seeds of remembering for this planet.*

Water does not direct itself. Water allows itself to be directed. This is a key, a secret that many masters have spoken of, one that is often hard for humans to hear. Why? Because you are so focused on free will and creating—a marvelous gift to be sure, though it often obstructs you from the deeper teaching of simply being. *That is when you are most who you really are, and when you are closest to remembering: when you are simply being. It is not a matter of becoming—it is only to* be. *You need not do anything. More, it is a matter of lessening your hold.*

This is why during early stages of learning to shapeshift, you might imagine yourself to become like water—feeling its flow, its rush, its song. I am speaking primarily of flowing water, though there are many variations of water. Sometimes water is involved with wind, their relationship evident in waves or typhoons. Or, you might see the combination of fire and water in steam, or earth and water in mud, and so on. However, for the initial stage of becoming like water, I mean water as in a river—the flowing of water simply being.

As you dive into this connection, you may feel yourself as a point within water, moving along the river and riverbank. As you continue to deepen, you may become the whole river, from beginning to end, rushing down from the mountain source, all along the earth, meandering, flowing, flowering, and becoming one again with the ocean.

At even deeper levels, you are larger versions of water: the rain, the river, the lake, the ocean, and even water that is absorbed into living beings, into the earth, then pulled up into the sky and washed down again as rain. Thus you might move from a larger cycle only to return in a smaller cycle, in another form. Or, you could become even more. You could become the essence of water and follow an expansive cycle that spans from farther reaches of space to deeper places within the earth and deeper senses of being.

Now, you understand how shapeshifting occurs at many levels, even as one flowing into another, hmm? And do you see how there is no real beginning or ending, except from the perspective of smaller cycles? It is all about shifting and flowing. More than any element, water holds the memory of this for the planet, for you, and for others. It is a large responsibility—and an accolade—to be a Water Bearer.

See water within you, becoming a part of you, flowing from you out to the world—which is just another aspect of you becoming the world. Play with this metaphoric shifting and soon you will begin to feel it at a deeper level.

THE SOUND OF THE EARTH

Several weeks later, my experiences of becoming like water had pro-
duced some interesting results. For one thing, I no longer felt so caught
up in having to make hard-edged sense of things. I came to see that
knowing was like flowing. "Things are shifting," I remarked to Barney
one morning.

*Indeed they are! As you continue to deepen, you tap into a vast, deep
reservoir of energy. It is like an underground river—old, ancient. It
flows beneath the surface of things, which is to say, at a deeper layer than
appearances. It moves to a deeper rhythm, pulses closer to the heartbeat of
this very earth. To our way of seeing things, that is where the real core of
nature resides—in the deep.*

"Our way" of seeing things? I suddenly sensed a presence besides
Barney. "Who else is there?" I asked.

*We are guardians of the earth or, more specifically, guardians of the
deeper nature of things. We could tell you a title, but it would only be that,
a label, a way for you to order things. We offer assistance to beings who
work with recovering (or uncovering) the deeper nature of Earth herself,
discovering how evolution, especially of animal forms (including humans)
began from a single river of thought, of life-giving form and energy. You
might think of us as Underground People who spring to the surface of the
earth when someone is attuned to hear our words, our thoughts, the gifts
we have to share.*

"Well, this is going to be interesting!" I thought as I settled in to
listen.

*All molecules of living things connect to the Earth herself, to the soil,
and even below that—to deeper waters and matter of the earth. We are
not apart from the earth; we are a part of the earth. When you tune into
this way of seeing things, this deeply connected perspective, you cannot help
but know that hurting the earth is harming yourself.*

*We would suggest that your studies would be well served by looking to
the core of the Earth herself. For here you will find a richness in interspe-*

cies communication and the becoming of shared forms. As you look to the origin of human beginnings, to the ways in which your particular form evolved—individually and as a group, species-wise and as a planet—you will see that all of these events are interrelated. There is not one line of evolution without all others. That is essential to understand.

It is in this sense that you can 'move' into the form of other species. It is this type of evolutionary planning that allows you to share consciousness with another species' being. There are other realities that do not allow for this . . . let us call it 'ability.' Earth is interesting in this respect, unique in the sense that she has evolved in a very creative and specialized way. There are not many other planets that have evolved in this particular way.

"Hmm," I said, knowing this was a big thought I would have to ponder some more. "Is there something else you'd like to share?"

First, we wish for individuals who are working with the energy of the earth—and this includes far-reaching aspects, from gardening and farming to conservation, water treatment, pollution treatment, as well as working with animals, shapeshifting, even many forms of ritual energy making—to focus first on deepening, and making contact with the earth beings.

There are many, many varieties of earth beings who work at different layers. For example, some devas and fairies work close to the surface of the land. Another layer includes energy beings or guardians of the land, each specific to a certain place. So, too, are there energy beings of the soil, the plants and trees, of the mountains, lakes, rivers, marshes, ponds, deserts, rainforests, and so on. And yet other energetic beings link the earth's surface with deeper layers—of molten energy and deep-water energy (and within these layers there are many more specialized energies unique to fire and the waters). A bit deeper you find us, the guardians of underground rivers and currents of energies (some even of air), and of stone. And there are deeper beings yet, some who reside at the core of the earth. Those beings are very powerful, very compact, very bright; their emanations can be felt right out to the surface of the planet and beyond. In fact, many of those beings are responsible for bringing in communications from other planets and galaxies, including other dimensions.

Second, we wish for all beings in this work to attune in common pur-pose. This is difficult for some humans who are focused on agendas and schedules and rules of order. We do not mean it in this way. What we are speaking of is more the notion of a tuning fork: our wish is for all beings to feel within, to attune to the inner vibrations that serve to link and unite this planet so that we may all work better together.

The earth has certain discordances at this point in space/time, in this event-field reality. There are other dimensional beings on the earth who work to fine-tune these vibrations. Some have already established a tone for the planet and are working to help others to 'hear' this sound of the earth.

"I think I've heard this!" I said, recalling a low, cavernous hum-ming tone.

Indeed you have. You hear other tones as well.

And the earth guardians then pointed out a series of different tones I had heard throughout my life. I smiled in wonder, in a blessed feeling of having these moments arise again in memory.

To return to the larger context, there are many sounds that humans may tune into, if they choose. The very act of 'tuning in' helps to change them, to attune them to another mode of being.

And in this sense, you see, everything in this world is about shape-shifting—about shifting the shapes of your being! You are surprised with this?

"No, I know what you mean," I said. "When Barney first spoke about shapeshifting, I thought it was very specialized. But the more I experience, the more I realize we are constantly experimenting with different ways of being, constantly shifting the shapes of our conscious awareness. And the more we do, the more we realize we are all of this, and more! I don't mean that in a vague, amorphous sort of way, but— more like the way you speak of the tone of the earth. That tone—that way of being—is always present, underlying everything, though it is not until we consciously attune to it that we enter into a more aware rela-tionship with it. We move into being with it."

Yes, agreed the earth guardians. *There you go . . . and here you are! Here is the deeper sense of shapeshifting, the deeper essence of what we speak about. When you think in this way, it is as if you are drinking from our river, for it is this type of fluid connection that is at the essence of all creation, all evolution.*

We encourage all humans to continue deepening, connecting and experiencing the vibration of 'being' at more essential levels. Remember to listen to the tones; listen for the sound of the earth. That too, is you, all of you—all of us.

11

———

Deepening Dream Awareness

One early morning, I awoke from an experience so energetic and tangibly real that at first I wasn't sure if it was a dream or some astral-travel version of shapeshifting.

Only moments before waking, I was within the body of a professional ballerina. She—we—were on stage performing. I was utterly aware of the woman as a separate individual with her own life, and was not in any way connected with sharing her thoughts. And yet I was so fully immersed within her, keenly responsive to the way our body moved—the gliding, outstretched reach of an arm; the sharp, tight turns on the tips of our toes; neck tilted, curving upward just so from spine. Never had I been so fully aware of muscles and movement! As we ran-leaped-sailed across the floor, I knew exhilaration as never before. Our skin flushed in the bright heat of the stage lights; our nostrils drawing in the sweaty, musty smell of the stage. Fine particles of talc swirled in the air as we twirled in elegant precision, held within the dance. The colorful, flashing movements of fellow performers created a vivid tableau, and our body sensed, with an exact, finely tuned inner knowing, every nuance of connection within the shifting configuration of players that danced upon that stage.

This was different from other dreams, for not only was I lucid, but also aware that this was a *real* woman performing on a real stage somewhere—perhaps in a different city, perhaps in a different time— but nonetheless having an identity other than a dream creation. Or so it seemed. Was it a dream? An alternate self? Or, perhaps a larger way of dreaming? Whatever it was, I knew it to be a tremendous gift. I just wasn't sure what to do with it.

Later that morning, I sat down to tap into the energy of the dream—to ask the dream creators how I might bring the teachings of such dreams to consciousness.

Your questions are improving, as are your abilities to stay conscious in your dreams for longer periods of time, remarked a voice that sounded faintly amused yet approving. *I am a liaison between the dreamworld and the conscious, waking world. I help to both translate and awaken deeper senses from your dream experiences.*

Let us recall that some dreams are designed to reveal problems or issues from the unconscious to the conscious mind. Other dreams, such as the lucid dreams you have been experiencing, are designed to bridge the dreamworld with your conscious waking world. And shapeshifting dreams are designed to give you additional experience with shape- shifting. These are a type of 'student designed' dream, in which you set up exercises for yourself as a type of template. It is often easier to shift in dreams than in waking life, and so these dream experiences are designed to help show you—to help 'feel' you—into the experience. They are no less valid than experiences in your waking life. In fact, they offer a measure of safety and security because they occur in the dreamworld. It would be wise to use the dream sensations as a tem- plate, a physical reminder of how to feel into a shapeshift, how to feel into the body of an animal or person with whom you are experiencing a shapeshift.

One of the prime directives *for shapeshifting, to borrow that term, is to experience the shift—not merely to talk about it or study it, but to feel it within yourself. That is the crux, after all, of shapeshifting itself.*

INTEGRATING DREAMWORK

I took the dreamworld liaison's advice to heart and began using both waking and dream experiences as templates for other states of awareness. Many animals—spider, skunk, hippo—offered to share consciousness as well as insights on how to use vibrantly charged experiences (in any spectrum of life—dreaming, waking, or other states in-between) as a kind of multilayered stepping stone, a way of linking waking experiences to the dreamworld and dream experiences to the waking world. It led me to wonder: what else could we do in dreams?

Let us discuss dreamwork and how it relates to shapeshifting, said Barney one morning as events, and questions, continued to unfurl.

To begin, let us observe that many humans have a way of separating dreamworlds from waking life. In addition, you have a wide variety of states of consciousness within the day during which you perceive, receive, and experience life information in different ways. Let us observe that you are capable of many types and levels of consciousness. It is to some degree your 'wiring' and 'software' which makes some states conscious, others subconscious, and others superconscious. It is also some degree of cultural conditioning and habit that separates these various states of consciousness.

For some cultures, there is not the distinct separation between dream state and waking state. For yours, however, there is. In addition, your private daydreams and meditative exercises (including shapeshifting exercises, for example) are often done internally and in that way deemed separate from your waking life.

In reality—or let us say in another version of reality—all of these states of consciousness are fluidly connected. And also available are a great many more that you do not perceive.

As with your abilities to communicate with animals and other beings, these skills must be learned and relearned to some degree. The deeper you allow your connection to flow at an emotional level, the easier it will be for you to communicate consciously in dreams. In the dreamworld, remembering is not a mental activity. It is an emotional/feeling activity.

Back to the connection between shapeshifting and the dream experi-
ence: In order to program your dream, which is part of what you are ask-
ing, you first need to be in familiar territory and in good relations with
your dreamworld. Dreams are messages from your unconscious state—
from another part of you. They are the primary (and a very powerful)
way in which you may speak to this part of yourself. Therefore, to go in at
a conscious level and decide you know better can often lead to disaster.

So, the best way to approach this is to ask your subconscious if it will
allow you some time to practice with shapeshifting abilities. In effect, you
begin by asking to forge a link with it. Perhaps you will be given time
every night, or one night a week, or perhaps it will work out differently.
This is between you and your subconscious.

As you have observed in the past, the manner in which your conscious
self responds to messages from the dreamworld often has direct influence
on the continuity, volume, and quality of messages. Do you treat your
dream messages with respect? Do you work with them? Or do you merely
forget them or tell them to others as if they are a joke? This is a very clear
reflection of your relationship with your subconscious. And thus you will
know when and if you are able to work with your subconscious in a way
in which dream shapeshifting can occur.

There are many who have forged this relationship. In some cultures,
it is part of a practice—cultures in which magic and a connection with
the natural world are not separate from 'ordinary' waking life. In these
instances, certain individuals are called to work with shapeshifting, and
they will honor the signs and images from the dreamworld as well as from
their waking life. Teachings from the dreamworld and waking world
often work in tandem, and the individual may experience an overlay, one
upon the other.

It is a curious state, this overlay, for it is one in which you are walking
in both worlds as well as between the worlds. In advanced states, it is simply
to be aware of your multidimensional self. In these states, there is no longer
the 'weird' effect (as you might call it) of being aware of two or more differ-
ent states of consciousness or of participation with more than one world.

Questions?

I was following so intently, I had no room for questions. "Not right now."

Let us continue. In the dreamworld, it is much easier to shift one's form or covering. You have already had this experience.

I remembered just then a dream about being in an office building. Dressed in my usual jeans, sweater, and clogs, I realized that I needed to be in a suit to attend a meeting. As I walked down the hallway, I closed my eyes and imagined a dark blue business jacket and skirt and high heels, and my clothes instantly changed. Although this was not remarkable in the dream ("simply think it and it occurs"), on waking I noted how seamless the shift had been.

But wait—did I really dream that? Suddenly, I had the strange feeling that another part of myself had just now dreamed this dream, but remembered it as occurring "back then."

Yes, said Barney with a small snort of humor, *and there you have a quick perception into how time works in this way as well. You remembered the dream and had an inkling that the dream was put there from 'now'—which in a way is true. It is like writing fiction—as you write a story, you tie details or characters from one point of the story into other points, so as to weave a more interesting web. In truth, that is how your life works. There is a part of you forever weaving strands of connections in space and time, both from one self to another and in this particular life of Dawn. Other selves are also connected with you—since they are you—and there are similar interconnections for them as well.*

To return to shapeshifting: in the dream state you are able to partially access that part of yourself which creates reality; as you 'think' what you want to wear—or what shape you want to be—you flow into it. There are no obstacles of 'I can't do that' or 'That isn't possible.' When this type of magic is alive, you are able to accept it, to use that energy and make the shift you choose. It is really quite simple. It is only your construction of thought that deems it is not simple, or not possible, in other limited versions of 'reality.'

EXPANDING HORIZONS

Barney's point was well taken, of course, for it's an ancient truth that as we focus our thoughts and intentions, the universe reflects agreement. It was true for me as well, and the more I played with the interconnections of dreams, waking awareness, and shapeshifting, the more opportunities arose to learn.

One night I dreamed of being in an old, empty red-brick building. It seemed to be an abandoned warehouse, massively long and narrow. Although I was on the top floor, there was no roof, and an intense, blue-black evening sky, pulsing with tiny brilliant stars, loomed above. Even so, I felt safely enclosed, for there were tall red-bricked walls on either side of me. The walls were punctuated by high, narrow windows, through which I could easily see as they were placed closely together. Still, owing to the size of the walls, I felt small within the open room.

In that strangely urgent way of dreams, I was trying to get from one end of the building to the other—but what a far way to go! As I ran, I thought of leaping; and as I leaped, I thought of flying; and with that small step-stone of thought, I woke up inside the dream. As I sometimes did in lucid dreams, I moved my hands together in front of me, arms outstretched, as if launching myself upward. Very easily, I jumped up and into another level of space. Thus I was flying, completely horizontal and comfortable. A smile came over my entire being, though I cautioned myself to keep the flow of consciousness light—lucid, yet not too hard-edged or rational—so that I could maintain this state within the dream. It was great fun, and I loved the feeling of flying through the building, under the cool, dark, wide-open sky.

Upon waking, I recorded the dream in a journal, noting the links between dreaming and shapeshifting. *Dreaming is often a form of shapeshifting,* said a voice that eased into my thoughts; *that much is obvious from the start.* As I closed my eyes, to better hone in on this unexpected visitor, I saw the image of a large gray rock, which at that moment "held" the shape of a human. As time unfolded in the vision,

I saw the human figure dissolve through the rock to reveal a brilliant nightscape of stars against a dark blue sky.

This image reveals another facet of the nature of shifting forms—a visual example of how so much is interrelated beyond what is apparent, continued the voice. *When you think about dreaming and shapeshifting, yes, of course there is a link. This is a broad and general observation. But rather than compartmentalize, we feel it is best to experience each moment as an aspect of connecting to other realities. That is our view on shapeshifting.*

"Who are you?" I asked.

We are the beings who regulate the interconnections between stone and sky—one aspect of the many links between earth and heaven. The picture [of the human in the rock who becomes the stars] is ours. We show it as an illustration of melding realities—that is, not simply a shift from one view to another, but an example of being in which you are aware of both realities (and, as you become more adept, of many realities) in simultaneity. The highest 'enlightenment' teaching we carry is a stance wherein all interconnections are held at a conscious level (though this does not correspond exactly to your notion of consciousness). In other words, one is fully aware of all aspects of one's being.

"And there is even more awareness beyond that?" I asked, sensing their implication.

There is always more, they agreed. *Always.*

When you tune in to your dream, you see the aspects of stone (brick walls) and sky (through the window). Between the two, you fly—though note how you fly: still within the confines of the building.

It became obvious to me then, though I hadn't noticed it before: even though the sky was wide open above me in the dream, I flew only within the boundaries of the walls.

As you become more aware, you open to greater possibility and may choose to fly beyond your walls, above your walls, into the open air. And, after many such adventures, perhaps you will be willing to work on holding both stone and sky, keeping a perspective of each. Your dream would change then, of course.

I had the distinct impression the beings were smiling.

We seek to educate those who are interested in and open to knowing more about the interface between open space and closed space. By that we mean the seemingly open space of air and the seemingly closed space of solid objects, such as rocks, stones, walls.

There is a phrase you have: 'running into a brick wall.' It means you are held by apparent limitations. These limitations are of your own making, of course. Some choose to go beyond their limitations while others turn in defeat. We work with the ones who choose to go beyond the wall, to learn how to move beyond the limits of held belief.

Our nature is not only of stone and sky, but also about outer and inner, visible and invisible, and other dichotomies. We work primarily with merging these through shifting realities.

In pure forms of nature, we are about mountains and air. When you see mountains shrouded by mist or clouds, we are at work. Our being is a misty sort of presence, one that blurs boundaries, encourages climbers and wall pushers to go beyond. In fact, we work often with climbers and explorers. In a sense, we are the underlying spirit of adventure when it comes to doing what has not been attempted before.

That is our part for now. Look for us in your dreams. Perhaps next time you will attempt to fly out of your building. We will be happy to assist you!

GUEST LECTURER: THE DREAM GUIDES

You are truly having some unique adventures! exclaimed Barney later that day. *Occasional morning talks will help to tie up loose ends, but you might explore more on your own and share your findings with our group. As you engage other realities, so do we all. That is it for now. If you want to see me, just 'think' me and I will appear. But, for now, see where your experiences take you.*

Thus Barney began tapering off our morning talks. I felt his subtle, spirited encouragement as events unfolded, and I was also pleased when he made introductions, connecting me to other animals, plants, and beings whose interests or areas of expertise related to my growing adventures.

One morning, a group of beings introduced themselves before I even tuned in. *You might call us a guest lecturer,* they began, *for we have worked with your group many times, and Barney is a friend of ours, as are you.*

We are an energetic—beings not in the sense that you normally understand the word, but a mode of energy—that works to aid other beings to become more aware of the subtle processes of their own conscious, subconscious, and unconscious minds, and the links between them.

To answer your unspoken question, you might call us Dream Guides. We work with connections, with linking the conscious mind to the unconscious mode of creating. And, in a specialized way, we work with manifestation. For many, it is much easier not to be conscious when dreaming. If there is a seeming measure of uncontrol, then one can plead that one is 'not responsible' for one's dreams. At one level of reality, this is quite true.

The area that we focus on, however, is helping individuals such as yourself to become more conscious of the process of dreaming and your role of responsibility for manifesting your dreams. We mean that not just in the sense of how your dreams are portrayed in the inner theater of your mind, but what you do with your dreams, how you 'hold' them as you wake up and throughout your days, and the manner in which you approach the sacred act of dreaming and dream interpretation.

To review some of the points that you already know: there are several types of dreaming. We may relate this to the way in which there are several types of shapeshifting.

Did you know that when you watch a shapeshifting occur (let us say you witness a 'magical' event in which a person becomes something else—a woman to a wolf, a being to a field of stars, even someone shifting in space very quickly or seeming to disappear), you too are part of the shapeshifting? This is analogous to early stages of dream awareness in which you might recall your dreams in the morning and repeat them to others. Both occurrences carry a note of incredulity at times—a sense of strangeness or the bizarre. Often this is an introductory invitation to deeper awareness. Some might say that if you have enough 'personal power' to lead you to a shapeshifting situation, then you may witness the event. The event has its own reality, and what you see may or may not correspond with the shapeshifter's perception of the event, but believe us when we tell you that you are brought to the event for a reason.

Now, a more intermediate step is that you are involved in the shapeshifting in some way. Let us say part of the shift involves you: your arm or hand begins to look different; you notice the colors of your immediate environment changing, or something shifts in your landscape. This is a 'close encounter' with shapeshifting. In the same way, this might be likened to waking up in your dream. For a brief moment, you are aware that you are dreaming. You are aware that something unusual is happening. You become a part of the dream and, in doing so, have forged a conscious link to your deeper subconscious and unconscious modes of creative thought.

Another step occurs in dreaming when you take control for longer periods of time, or when you actually shift the dream itself. As in a recent dream, you chose to fly and so you flew. In its correspondence to shapeshifting, we see this when one consciously desires to become an animal and does so. There are many, many degrees of this, as noted by your friend Barney. You deepen in your control of the shapeshifting as well as the dreaming. In a dream, for example, you might desire to have a different set of clothes or a different body, or desire to meet someone you know, or change the environment. There are many different forms of this and many times you are not aware of how conscious you actually are or can become in your dreams.

Beyond this step is the conscious creation of the dreamworld. There are many references to this in your moth book[1] and other books as well. From our way of seeing, this is connected with entering alternate realities and engaging more expansive energy fields. It is to bring the dreaming to a more conscious plane by making it manifest—or entering its manifestation—on the physical level.

As you are becoming aware, there are many versions of reality, many layers of reality that often exist side by side, so to speak. It is not a different geographical space that you must enter, but a different vibration.

In essence, what all of this leads to is the ability to become more conscious of your multidimensional nature in any given moment. What might be termed bleed-throughs *begin to occur; perhaps you remember different times or different lives and are 'in touch' with those aspects of yourself in those lives; perhaps you begin to see other worlds, where the layers between the realities are thin. This can also occur both with shapeshifting and with dreaming, both unconscious dreaming and lucid dreaming.*

To return to our original distinction: the difference between unconscious dreaming and lucid dreaming is a matter of degree and orientation. In a sense, it is a difference of perspective, though the two modes are sufficiently different to warrant an explanation.

Often unconscious dreaming is meant as a lesson for the conscious mind to discern or learn from. It is a reflection of other dimensions— sometimes a reworking or re-imaging of problems with which the deep psyche is wrestling. In many ways, you might think of it as an anagram for some aspect of your life.

There are also prophetic dreams wherein there is a bleed-through from past to present or from future to present, or even from alternate lives to present life. These are of a slightly different order and are more oriented toward providing guidance or resolution of a problem.

Lucid dreaming is in some senses a more advanced form of dreaming, but only from the perspective that you are situated in now. In other situations, cultures, and times when lucid dreaming was widely practiced, unconscious dreaming was considered more advanced since it was seen as a gift from the gods, from the deep nature of one's being.

So, our opinion is not to judge one better than the other; rather, they are different forms of the same process, and one is wise to use the gifts of all.

12

—·—

Moving Through Fear

My dreams were overflowing. So much so that it seemed an intensive dream workshop was occurring. Some nights I'd live through epic dreams, filled with intricate plots and an abundance of detail. Other times, dream messages were short and symbolically concise. Some mornings, I would recall three or more dream-tales. I later found some of these to be interconnected with subsequent dreams, forming a larger picture, like an ongoing television series. I met people and animals from other worlds and dimensions; some offered advice and ideas, others stood silent and inscrutable. Most times, my dreams were a lot of fun and offered many new understandings. I marveled at how true it is that all we need to do is give awareness to something and we are richly rewarded.

Every so often, a dream would show me something about myself that I didn't really want to see. These dream stories often seemed harmless on the surface, but I was *feeling* my dreams now—a whole different ballgame.

Just before my birthday, I dreamed of being in an enclosed trailer with three huge elephants. Although the trailer was fairly spacious, with room for the elephants to stand and sleep, along with a living area for humans, only a few thin wires separated me from the elephants. As I stood watching them, one lowered her face and looked me directly in

the eyes. Her deep, brown-eyed gaze was extremely gentle and percep-
tive. And yet, even though she was calm and loving, I began to feel
fearful. I thought how easily she could trample me, she being so very
big and me being so very small.

On waking, I recorded the dream and noted that some of the
totemic qualities of Elephant include strength, power, and ancient
wisdom. For me, this corresponded with the look in the female elephant's eyes. I was disheartened that I had been so afraid. Surely in
waking life I would have been joyful to connect with the elephant's
gaze. As I felt into my sadness, I sensed the stirrings of emptiness,
an aching soul-sadness peeking up through another part of me. How
amazing that a simple image can touch us so deeply! And so the
dream cracks us open . . .

Later that day, Barney challenged me to look into the core of this
fear. It felt old and associated with childhood, though perhaps a childhood of many lives long gone by.

Where does the fear come from? Barney inquired. *Can you feel it in
your body?*

"In my heart. It feels like betrayal."

Yes, he agreed. *That is a clue for you. We could examine that scenario
if you wish.*

But that was the last thing I wanted to do. "Is there another way,"
I delayed, "or do you really feel this is best?"

Well, it is the more interesting way. Let us try. If you are willing.

I knew the drill: best to breathe deep, open to experience, and
report back with whatever I saw.

*Begin by remembering a time when you lived among elephants, or
perhaps first met elephants.*

It took a moment, but there—beyond the fogbanks of forgotten
lives—I saw an elephant. She lay unmoving, near a watering hole, on
her side. "The elephant is very sick," I said, "maybe dead already. I feel
terrible. I am with a group of people—my people. We did not kill the
elephant directly, but we are responsible for the watering hole turning

bad. We didn't think it out properly, and now no one can drink there. We can't even eat these animals or we will get sick.

"I feel such a sickness about it, but I can't say or do anything. I am too young, too small. It is wrong, what we did. Everyone is pretending we didn't do it or it wasn't our fault. I am very sad for the elephants, and for us, for our tribe. We have a soul sickness."

Let's shift that, suggested Barney. *What if you become powerful—someone with a strong voice in the tribe? What do you say?*

"I tell the people that we have done wrong. That it is our fault and we must make amends to the elephants. They might not forgive us, but we need to show we are sorry and try to help. Most of the people see this is right, but there are some who don't want to do this. Their energy is closed—a sick, green color, like poison. It is the heart turned bad. I call to the older members of the tribe and many of the women agree with me. I say how important this is, to walk out of our denial and to make amends. Many want to do this.

"But I am challenged to a fight from the man who holds the most sickness in his heart. We use spears and he kills me. I was just a child! I feel betrayed, just as I betrayed the animals and didn't have a chance to fix it. I feel betrayed by my people."

What do you do now? Barney asked.

I take another deep breath and let the story unfold. "In spirit, I go to the dead elephant and apologize for my actions and the actions of my tribe. The elephant stands up, in spirit. I see now that she is a great teacher. She says she has come to help some of us 're-evolve' through our depression, our sleeping sickness of the soul. I feel such a love for this elephant! It reminds me of a time when I was a young boy and was with her—Oh! That is another life! I remember now how much we loved each other. And as I crawl on her back—just as I used to in that other life—she begins to fly. In spirit, we fly up into a golden sky. We have a great deal of love and I know this soul from many, many lives! I know her very deeply.

"She is here now and fills me with a golden light. She says, *'We love you. We are here. You are always home with us. See past these dreams, these plays. Let us work with you. We can change this world as easily as you have changed the dream in your mind. Have trust and love. We say this to you over and over again, in many ways, because it is the truth. Follow the lead of your heart. We will shine with you and through you. We love you."'*

How does the fear feel now? asked Barney.

"Like it has shifted," I said, laughing and crying at the same time. "There is an opening inside of me, and I feel such love. It's very real right now; I feel I could stand with elephants in the wilds of any dream or reality and not be fearful."

Continue with this work and you will clear other fears as well, advised my wise friend and guide. *When an animal comes to you, you have asked it to come. Use the opportunity. It may not happen again for awhile.*

And then Barney and I were quiet for a time, his presence warm and close to me, just as he had been when he lived within his body.

All is for a reason, he said softly. *You know that. Trust what comes to you and what appears, even—especially—if you do not like it. There is a reason for all that happens. Like the elephant teacher showed you, it was all a charade designed to open the heart of the tribe. Know that the tribe called the elephant and the elephant agreed to play this role. Trust, trust, and trust . . . key words for your inner evolution.*

RELEASING THE
CONTAINERS OF FEAR

The Elephant Spirit stayed with me for many days. I felt boundless love from the Elephant People—not only for me, but also for Earth and all her diverse animal, plant, nature, and spirit peoples.

I began wondering if some spirits prefer teaching in animal form precisely because the human form is so often caught up in having to prove something, either to oneself or others. Does working with an animal teacher make it easier for humans to learn? But what of humans who don't believe animals have souls?

"I don't know that any of this can be made into a general rule," I said to Barney as the thoughts whirled around. "What do you think?"

Let us begin again with the fact that spirit is. *Spirit can choose to experience itself in any way you can imagine: humans, animals, plants, trees, angels, dirt, stones, rivers, wind, mountains, land, planets, other dimensional beings, events, circumstances, and so on. All is infused with spirit-knowing.*

It is wise to be cautious about applying labels and making general rules. Once you shift to a view that sees life as an unfolding, a weaving in and out of itself, a flexible happening, the need for rules lessens. Rules and order help to fix ideas and concepts in time-mind and, for that period of time, may be very useful. But experience is, by its very nature, a move-ment, an unfolding, a feeling of life. Rules seek to hold and contain. Life simply flows.

When humans make up rules about spirit—such as 'soul can be in a human form but not in an animal form'—they are playing with contain-ers. So, in that reality-container, all they can see are souls within human forms. These humans might then distinguish between 'us' (with souls) and 'them' (without souls). This distinction creates a fear: 'They' who are different; 'they' who are invading; 'they' who are evil. And, in that framework, 'they' serve to hold all that these particular humans cannot allow themselves to see within their own present being.

If you move from that perception to one in which souls do reside within animals or plants or stones—or if you simply perceive the infusion of spirit within all of nature—your reality shifts. Now, spirit is every-where; there is nothing that is not spirit. So, you have engaged another version of reality.

"And neither reality is 'better'?"

We could say that for those who hold themselves in the 'soul in human form only' rule, the situation is perfectly situated so that they will learn what they need to learn, so that they will experience themselves in the way they most need and want. It is choice. For those who see spirit everywhere, that is the situation they choose and need and want to learn. This is also perfect.

"And when these two realities come into contact?"

Each will see the other in terms that are appropriate for the individual. Some will see one face, others will see another. The trick is to know when you are seeing the face of the other and when you are seeing the face of yourself. And the paradox is that one is the other.

"So if I met someone who believed that talking to animals was the work of the devil, then I would be seeing a face of myself?"

Do you believe that it is the work of a devil?

I laughed. "No."

Though you've previously referred to others, or even yourself, thinking it is crazy. Isn't that a type of devil fear? Couldn't the devil be in secret charge of that—making you think something is real when it is not?

"So the reason I'm even asking the question is because there is still a little fear inside of me?"

There you go. Why don't we work with this one? Up for another experience?

I rolled my eyes. What a set up!

Look into that part of you that still believes talking to animals is a little loopy. Feel into the part that worries what others think. What part of you still searches for yourself in others? Why do you put your authority outside of yourself? When did you first give it away? Tune in to this at a deep level, the first time you became aware of this in a life . . .

With closed eyes and a few deep breaths, I see the generational history of a life in which people had just begun to move away from communion with nature, toward viewing ourselves as different from animals and nature. As I wonder how this happens, I see a big disaster: the sky becoming black and many dead.

"There are fires and floods," I tell Barney, "a time of chaos and confusion when food becomes scarce. We were driven by fear that manifested into greed—the need for more, especially food. But as food became more available, we extended that need into wanting land, and we defended against other groups of humans. And somewhere in there we got caught up in the fear. Still, a part of me remembered what it was like to be without that fear.

"And now as I follow that thread of 'me,' I see a child who was close to a grandmother, a caring, loving woman. And when I'm with her, I remember what it's like to be one with nature. It is like we all forgot, but every once in a while I can remember.

"I have lessons with this gentle grandmother—not talking lessons, but inner lessons, while she is cooking or walking. And also in our dreams. We know how to shift our shapes and become one with the creatures—it's a type of remembering, so we can re-know ourselves with nature. Sometimes we go on walks and move into the trees—becoming one with the trees and watching the forest life from there.

"But I know not to speak this out loud. There is too much craziness in our group; maybe this is where the fear comes from—fear that if I say anything they may become angry. And maybe in later lives I did try to share, but was hurt or silenced."

I opened my eyes. "So that is where the fear is still stuck? In another life?"

It is a deep knot, well placed, because you hid it there yourself. If you work with that fear, you can lessen the hold—and lessen the need for it to hold you.

"How do I do that?"

By realizing that it is merely the way another part of yourself saw the world. It chose to see 'They will not understand me.' You still hold that in your present world. You still hold the fear of telling others that you talk to animals, and of sharing what you experience. There are many who will be very interested in this. There are many who need to hear or read your words so they can be sparked inside to their own adventures. You truly are a dawn, and part of your job is to awaken to that fact and begin what it is you came here to do. You are already doing it, of course, but there is more. And we would encourage you to lessen this particular fear. It will make it easier for our word to go out, and for you to blossom into the full-ness of who you are.

So, our talk today has been a roundabout way of seeing that you are holding yourself within your own container of fear. And by stepping out of that, by expanding your container, you come to experience another percep-tion of reality. You will, in fact, create a new world as you come to see and participate in a new world.

All this talk of new worlds is true, you know. If you feel this deeply and open to it, you will know it by experience. You change, and so the world changes. Don't think about the words—feel the shift. That is the key into deeper experience.

As you open and release more of these self-imposed limits, you—and everyone else—will have more success across the board. It is fine to doubt information that does not feel true, or comes to you from sources that seem disjointed or out of place. Go within that information and see it through a larger lens. Always ask to see through a larger, more expansive, clearer lens.

And have fun. Laugh! As you know, this helps to jog loose old infor-mation and make room for new. Experience the unfolding. This, too, is who we are.

FEAR AS GUARDIAN

All this talk of fear got me thinking about how we sometimes fear our fears so much that we don't allow ourselves to see them, thus uncon-sciously projecting outward onto others and the world. I wondered how, then, we can come to see the fears that we cannot see. As I was pondering this, Zak looked up from his place on the floor.

This topic could be called Fear as Guardian, Fear as Gatekeeper, Fear as Foe, Fear as Friend. Though all these attributes have less to do with fear itself than with your personal relationship with fear.

The energy of fear is an interesting one. It begins very early in the evolution of most species. It derives from an essential misperception—

and it thus stands as a central truth that misperception is at the core of fear.

You want to know how to work with a fear you cannot see, sometimes cannot even feel. Correct?

"Yes, that is the question."

To begin you must find a means of meeting fear—a common space wherein you gain a deeper understanding of the working of fear in relationship to you. One way of doing this is by inviting fear into your life. Some people do this by courting danger—speeding, stunt work, high-risk missions. This is not your way.

Another path is to approach an area that feels uncomfortable to you so as to explore the outskirts of fear. For it doesn't help to delve into the core of fear if one's nature is to be paralyzed by fear, does it? However, one can become a detective and begin to gather clues about one's relationship with fear.

Keep in mind the core of misperception as you gather your clues. Your logical mind will enjoy this work, for it is analytical and can be pattern based. But as you delve further in, you will be asked to work with this emotionally as well. This is what stops you from going deeper into shapeshifting. One of the ways in which you deal with fear is by shutting down.

"You mean by diverting energy or thinking other thoughts so as to not 'see' what's going on?"

Yes, by shutting down invitations to explore the deeper work. You choose to analyze, which is fine, though you mistakenly accept this as the ending or answer, when in fact it is only the beginning. To work with the deeper roots of fear is to do the long walk, to resurvey every aspect of yourself and trek deeper into shadow terrain. It is also to be ruthlessly honest with yourself. If you are not prepared to do that, then I would not advise working with fear. It will eat you alive.

"Gulp! Any more advice for me, Zak?"

This is your *dream. Make it magnificent.*

KARMA IN A NUTSHELL

Make your dream magnificent—I smiled more than once in appreciation over Zak's wise words to live by. And, in a funny twist of canine
advice pawing through the multidimensional spectrum, my dreams *did*
begin taking on a peculiarly magnificent shine.

For several weeks thereafter, I had a series of vivid dreams in which
I met Fear in various guises. The magnificent part was my dream-self,
who seemed magically transformed into a superhero. On waking, I
was often surprised by her boldness. Each time I met Fear, my dream-
self acted swiftly and confidently, with a self-assured, inner knowing I
couldn't help but admire.

In one dream I met an angry old woman who raised a large knife
to stab me. I ran to her, abruptly embracing her with such energy that
she dropped the knife and hugged me in return. In another dream, I
was surprised by a man hiding inside a cabinet. As he jumped out at
me, also with a knife, I drew back my fist and socked him so hard that
he flew back into the cabinet, disappearing in its shadows. When he
reappeared, I socked him again and—pow!—he disappeared. We did
this several times until he emerged with a grin, offering to shake hands
and part on friendly terms. On waking from these dreams, I felt as if
layers of heavy, dense energy had slipped off my head and shoulders,
heart and body, revealing a cleaner, lighter inner clarity.

"I was thinking of how this ties into karmic illusions," I said to
Barney one morning. "It feels as if my psyche is clearing up some old
irritants of fear. And when I look at all the ways these fears were re-
solved—with an embrace, a punch, shaking hands—I see it's not necessarily what we do, but how we do it; though even that isn't exactly the
formula. Rather, it's determined in the moment of relationship. Is that
it? Is that how you'd say it?"

Barney took his time in responding, and I felt a warm wave deepening between us.

We are reaching a point of communication where we are beginning to merge our thoughts, he said at last. *Yes—it is 'determined in the moment of relationship.' That is exactly how I would say it because I did say it— with you—as a larger thought.*

I mention this to remind you of what is possible in the shapeshifting journey. Think of it as moving from one cycle to another. On this level, you begin to merge with other energies to create a new reality. In order to do this you must be fairly secure with what is your energy; you must be fearless enough to be open to a merging of this sort; and you must be spiritually developed enough to allow this to occur.

As you hop about on multidimensional levels, it may first appear as if you have gaps of knowledge on the 'Dawn-level' you are most familiar with. And so I remind you of the notion we spoke of once—that multi- dimensional selves, events, knowings, and experiences may simply come to you when needed—not necessarily in what you might think is logical order. It may help to remember the 'now' that is present in each moment as a very good means of accessing these deeper layers of connection, and by tuning in to what is happening throughout your being—throughout the larger multifaceted continuum of you who is experiencing.

Back to the dreams: yes, they have had a powerful effect on cleaning up certain fears you were holding. Be advised that it was not only you who participated in creating or clearing these fears, however. Other selves have been working on this and so, by virtue of your link with them, you also benefit. It is interesting that this is another variation of karmic illusion, though we might understand this in the sense of karma not as a 'bad' thing but as a 'good' thing in helping one to move through fear.

Let us readdress karmic illusions since you mention them. Karmic illusions are those emotional charges that hold an experience or event in time and place and 'stick' to you as an evolving being. Think of them as knots. As you progress and move faster, you recognize that the knots create drag, and so you realize it is to your advantage to untie the knots.

As you work to untie a knot—especially if consciously aware while doing so—you come to see that the emotion that made the knot was an illusion: Perhaps it was something you drew to yourself as a note to help you remember; or a misperception that you held, also designed to help you remember; or a created event that your higher self manipulated—again, designed to help you remember. All karmic illusions are in this sense 'good' in that they are designed to help you remember various aspects of your being that at some point you wanted to release early or throw away or dwell upon in a way that was not particularly helpful to the fuller version of you.

Pay attention to events that bring up themes of pain and fear, and you may unwind more than you think possible. Great things can open when you move with the flow of these events. This is what is sometimes called a window of time. Note that you do not consciously create these windows—as in forcing or willing them to appear—and yet at another level you do indeed create them, for parts of you 'set it up' so as to facilitate your own development. This is karma in a nutshell.

How much more alive you become when you simply open to the moment of now! As you move into a more awakened relationship with All That Is, you will find the conversation deepening, and more sharing occurring. Shapeshifting is an intimate sharing of experience, as you will soon discover.

13

—·—

Other Voices . . .

From time to time, Barney's spiral manner of teaching was more notice-
able as he would review and examine in greater detail concepts we had
already visited. Although initially it would seem he was merely providing a quick summary, I was inevitably amazed how retracing these
threads would bring to light richer, deeper perspectives. It was as if the
threads themselves shapeshifted, suddenly revealing an entirely unfore-
seen fabric of reality.

Barney was also becoming increasingly fond of surprise visits—popping in from a different angle or position—as for example, through the
body of Zak. One morning, he noted that he was coming from an energetic level that was capable of viewing—and engaging with—several of
his multidimensional aspects.

*The level at which we are speaking is 'behind,' if you will, the forms
of Dawn and Barney,* he explained. *We are communicating at a level
behind the form, beneath the form, beyond the form. This is one manner
in which to tune in to the shapeshifting paradox.*

*As we know, some may use shapeshifting in a very elemental manner—
that is, merely to shift the shape of their appearance. We might link this to
an illusion of sorts, though it is quite true that one can literally shift one's
shape. I use the term* illusion *in the sense that it takes place on the appearance level, and appearance, all so often, is an illusion to start with.*

As one further explores the nature of shapeshifting, one realizes that the shifting of shapes is a tool to access something deeper. For it provides not only a teaching, but a vehicle. You are thinking correctly here of South American shamans who become an animal or travel with an animal guide to other worlds to obtain information for healing or wisdom. There are many variations here—one may use an animal guide, the energy of a totem, or one may literally become an animal and travel with the animal spirits to better understand or fetch a healing remedy for body-mind or soul. At other times, shamans journey via entering the consciousness of an animal and traveling with that animal to discover secrets that other animals hold or possess. One might also travel out of body and enter the consciousness of various star guides or otherworldly beings who serve as guides. Or one may travel in light-body form—another subtle form of shapeshifting.

For the purposes of our discussions, and for the majority of this book, the type of shapeshifting we are dealing with is the type in which one shifts one's consciousness to a different form. By virtue of entering another form, one has also shifted one's shape. How we perceive the world and how the world perceives us are actually linked at a deeper level than most humans believe.

"Hmm. Can we explore that a little bit?" I wondered.

Are you ready for another experience?

Do you see how it is? Ask a question and you get an experience in return! Can life be any more accommodating?

Let us imagine that you have no prior knowledge of me, Barney pressed on, as if my query were all part of his seamless plan. *Let us imagine that one day you simply close your eyes and hear a voice inside. I am the voice that is now speaking to you. How would you proceed?*

I laughed. "I would ask questions: Who are you? Do you have something to tell me? That sort of thing."

And let us imagine that I told you I was an entity speaking to you from a different dimension.

"I would probably ask you questions about that dimension."

And if I said to you, 'Why don't you try this on yourself? Why don't you come into my consciousness—I will help you—and explore from my perspective for yourself?' What would you do then?

"I suppose, with no prior knowledge of you, I would be very cautious. What if it was some kind of trick? An interdimensional scam?"

Barney did not respond to my feeble attempt at humor, and I felt him waiting for me to discover my own answer.

"Okay, on the one hand, if you are something other than me from another dimension, how can I trust you? I would have some fear and mistrust. On the other hand, maybe I have just made you up—so what harm is there in exploring this voice? Except that maybe I am having a delusion—and, would I make myself psychologically ill by talking with these voices?

"So, perhaps you are telling me that this is why we are doing shape-shifting a little bit at a time? That it takes time to unfold and that I needed a gradual unfolding, especially in the matter of trust, so I wouldn't freak myself out."

Anything else?

"Well, perhaps these two different projections—that either the voice is an untrustworthy one from outside myself or a sick one from inside myself—are really two faces of the same thing?"

You have done well with this. Don't you agree that it is much more rewarding when you see this for yourself? When you unfold the wiggles of the paradigm inside yourself? Can you not trust your own words and ideas?

"So, what are you really saying here?"

I sensed Barney laughing. *Dawn, you are being shaken awake! You are still sleepy, still liking your dreamtime. Some of us—or perhaps some parts of you—are shaking you awake. In your drowsy state of consciousness you prefer to stay where you are, to rest, to enjoy your dreams, and to not look at the list of what you have to do today. But imagine yourself in an hour from now—an awakened hour from now—well on your way into an awakened day. Isn't it much more rewarding to be awake and playing in the world than still sleeping, merely imagining you are playing in the world?*

There are many kernels here for you to chew on, Barney added after a pause. *Others have forged this way as well. Keep the link open. You will not be disappointed.*

MEETING THE GROUP

Keeping the link open seemed simple enough, but how easy it is to fall into the trench of habit and routine, a million times daily! We often don't notice this, for routine and habit have become so much of who we believe we are.

Take the group, for example. Ever more frequently Barney made mention of a group of us involved in studying shapeshifting. In the beginning, this felt distant and safe—I figured I was just one among many. Or perhaps the representation of a study group was metaphoric, not altogether real.

Slowly, however, I became more aware of a distinct group energy, as well as idiosyncrasies of particular members. Barney advised one morning, *I would suggest that you begin to listen more carefully to the adventures of your comrades. As you engage other realities, so do they. It is intention that allows you to 'hear' or 'see' their adventures and share in them. That is the agreement for our group.*

So, just who were the members of this group? One who introduced herself early on went by the name of Nexus. It felt to me as if Nexus was female, though I sensed her form was not human. Her short introduction sat in my journal notebook for quite some time: *I work in between matter and manifestation. My vibratory rate is one of sound, of creation of form through sound waves and balances of complementary tones. When you tune in to the angels singing, you tune in to a group I also work with. It is from this family that I bring the gift of voice, of tone, of harmonic vibrations to our group here.*

Another member was a being named Tau. Although he initially

portrayed himself as a free-drifting animal spirit, my impression of Tau was as an adventurer. I later came to know him as a counterpart with an unusual expertise. Intriguingly, it was Tau, Barney suggested, who was most similar to me and "together, you might accomplish much more than you think."

Our group was small (about eight members), and Barney described it as follows: *We come together to learn of shapeshifting. We are not a special group in the sense of being exclusive, for we are open for all to learn. And yet, we have joined in special study, at a common level of progression, working together to share our experiences, knowledge, insights, and desires. Our main focus is creation, specifically through the ancient art of shapeshifting.*

There are many, many ways to learn about shapeshifting and countless experiences available. One of the reasons you joined our group is because you are more comfortable learning by yourself, which is to say by direct experience, not by following a leader or one particular method or teaching. Our group is designed for just this type of desire to learn. Part of our focus is to learn more by direct experience about the mechanics of incarnation, of death, and of shapeshifting within a three-dimensional vehicle or form.

As with so many ideas that were slightly outside the range of my comfort zone, I let thoughts about the group simmer on the back burners of consciousness. Barney was gently persistent, however, encouraging me to speak with Tau in particular. As he also was fond of reminding me, *Experiences come to you for a reason, when you are ready for the opportunity.*

THE VOICE OF MANY:
A FISH, A PLANT, A FELLOW STUDENT

Even with Barney's kind nudges to focus attention, tender prods to feel into this or that, or humorous Post-it notes to welcome the unexpected, I was not always the best of students. I often procrastinated, was entranced by diversions, slipped and skidded into the more mundane routines of being. And yet, Barney and the others persisted. When I didn't follow up on contacting Tau, they brought Tau to me.

We are trying something new today, announced a bright, sparkly voice one morning. *You have been opening to a variety of voices. Today there are several who join together so you can feel the variety of our voices in one 'compacted' message.*

"I am here, now in eel form, though formerly a tropical fish you once spoke with."

"And it is I, Jen, the cactus who lives in your home."

"And I am here, Tau. I come as an observer and to help you with discerning voices of an individual pattern within messages such as this."

We wish to talk about the larger concept of shapeshifting as it relates to the fullness of vibrational realities. By way of example, this message comes to you as a joined effort, though all three of us could separate—as we just did—in our own individual voices.

This is our group voice speaking. How is that possible, you wonder? Certainly one is in charge of the group voice? Sometimes this is so, as when a herd or group of animals is speaking. Often one animal in particular will take the lead, and it will be with that individual's voice, focus, and personality that you receive the gist of the message from the group.

We give you the image of a sled dog team. All dogs are pulling the sled, but only one dog leads. One dog is in charge, yet that single dog cannot pull the sled alone. That is a partial metaphor of how some animal groups work.

Our voice comes to you in a different sense, however. We all speak our piece and then fashion it to form one message, so that the words you receive work as one chord. Our individual voices are as strands that make up a rope—each a part of the vocal cord that you 'hear' speaking.

The correlation of this is that there are numerous aspects of you who are receiving this message. Within your body, various bodies work to allow your conscious mind to hear this and allow you to translate through numerous impulses these impressions-feelings-understandings into words.

And, let us be aware: there are numerous translations along the way—a fish, a plant, and a visiting spirit, all working toward sending a human a message! There is an art to the cohesive way in which we speak, and you hear and record. It can happen very quickly at this time, though that was not always the case.

Let us return to shapeshifting and again assert that time quickens as your abilities open; or, time becomes more fluidly understood as you vibrate in a clearer relationship with time. In truth, time can speed up or slow down according to the state of consciousness you hold. Why? Because time is a form of consciousness—a software program, so to speak. When you open up the program and play with the variables, you will find that you can speed up or slow down time and interact with it in many amusing and interesting ways.

"Plants have a different understanding of time. The shift is now coming to me, Jen, and I will relate to you that for many plants, myself included, time is more experiential than you understand it. We do not have so many divisions of time—rather, we are focused on a movement of time. Plants are very much about movement, as I alluded to in our prior talk about plants moving through the earth. And time is in many respects the same for us. We can reach back into ancient times or pull ourselves into future times. We have an open access to many timelines in simultaneity. In general, we see time in a much larger framework than many humans and animals."

"I will speak of time also. I am Tau, from your group, though perhaps you may think of me as an animal spirit. I have lived in other dimensions and have experienced many features of time. I also experience alternate dimensions of time while in the 'now.' I work with what you might call outer space energies and have particular fondness for certain dimensions that Earth does not generally recognize. I also have interest in Earth as it is one of the planets that is 'time encoded' and so time is worked with on this planet in a very specific way . . ."

At this point, there was a loud crash upstairs and I needed to quickly leave my office to attend to two feisty dogs who had knocked over a plant on a table. When I returned, a few minutes later, I settled back in and picked up where we had left off.

"I find the ways in which you move and interact with other beings remarkable," said Tau. *"It interests me how you manage to hold separate your encounters via consciousness. My experience of time and relationships is very different. Perhaps we might talk later and share events in order to better understand each other's mode of perception and experience."*

As I agreed—cautiously, but encouraged too—another voice took over.

"And now I speak, currently as an eel, though formerly a tropical schooling fish. I chose to move from a group consciousness with other fish (though we did have our individual lives and focuses) to a more solitary sea creature. I am amused by this body—it is so long!—though I still have a good deal of fish-mentality within myself. My incarnation was very quick as I chose not to spend much time in the spirit world. You could say I am on a fast track in incarnations as I chose several lifetimes ago to incarnate as a variety of creatures. (I am speaking to you from a higher dimension right now; my eel self is only dimly aware of this grander plan.) I wanted to experience many different aspects of relating under the water—I have been a whale, dolphin, porpoise, seal; I have been many varieties of fish and will be a shark for several incarnations as well. My transition was from sea mammal to fish, and I chose that for a specific reason. I am something of a scholar—a historian—and wished to experience many different varieties of seeing and feeling and knowing the underwater world of Earth."

We now return to the group voice for we wish to reveal how several small individual voices can create the tone of a larger voice. Each voice is important to the whole, and if one of our members were not present in speaking, then the group voice would have a different quality and flavor. This idea has a parallel in shapeshifting as well. Barney and others will comment on that in future talks. Thank you for opening. Please keep your channels open for more.

VIEW TO VIEW, YOU TO YOU

While the idea of keeping my "channels open for more" was surely good advice, I often felt such messages were tinged with sly humor. As if the messengers already had an idea of what was in store for me.

During the next several days, for example, I began seeing ravens: ravens perched on telephone poles, ravens hopping in parking lots, ravens soaring in the sky. While this initially brought the trickster energy of Raven to mind, I felt there was something more. Just as Tau, Jen, and the eel had formed a group voice fashioned from individual tones, I sensed another "voice" with the appearance of Raven in my life.

Looking for pattern, I realized that seeing ravens coincided with my thoughts of a disagreement several of us were having with one of our neighbors. The problem was a minor issue that had blown entirely out of proportion. Although I had arranged for a neighborhood meeting to talk through the issue, it ended badly, with the neighbor storming out.

How or why was this connected with Raven? I wasn't sure. A few days later, while driving and wondering how the situation might resolve, I saw the logo of a raven on a passing car. Although I smiled in recognition, another part of me felt insecure, desperately scrambling to decipher: what did it *mean?* And then—with perfect timing—a raven flew straight at me. It was if Raven were staging a direct course of collision—swooping very low, lifting up over my car only at the last possible moment. This was very unusual behavior for a raven, of course, and a clear message to pay attention.

But to what? Again, meaning eluded me. It seemed a new kind of puzzle—not only involving the teaching or medicine of Raven, but also something personal, entwined within myself.

We would remind you to always remember that the web of life is alive with interconnected strands of being, commented Raven the following morning.

Humans have a tendency to relate everything back to them. Not all species do this in this particular way, you know. Many of us are more comfortable in circular thought rather than the direct, straight line you are so comfortable with.

"Do you mean by my wanting there to be a meaning to this?" I asked. "By saying 'this means that' or thinking in terms of cause and effect?"

To some degree, yes. Likening this to mathematical formulas, we could say you like 'this plus this equals that.' Whereas we are more likely to think in terms of 'this plus that plus this plus that,' one thing linked to another, with less emphasis on what it 'means' or a final answer. Though I wouldn't want to get too rigid on this metaphor.

We offer in the way of feedback a simple rule: Arguments and misunderstandings are about inner conflicts, arising when desires of the inner world do not 'fit' with the outer reality. Inside and outside are the same; when this is not seen or felt for each individual, a disturbance in the psyche occurs. This becomes translated to an argument, disagreement, fight, problem, trouble, or war with the outside world. What you see is what you are: a basic precept.

The raven-haired woman is a reflection of you. You are now being given the opportunity to treat her as you would a part of yourself—for this is who she is. This is the deeper nature of communication—not simply to make good points or speak eloquently, but to move people, to move one's self. This is communication of the soul. It is the beginning of poetry between hearts. It is the deeper nature of shapeshifting. For as you see her as a part of you, you shift your form which pronounced 'Dawn' as the central player in your drama. Dawn is all these neighbors—and many more.

What is different and what is the same? These are two aspects of the one central question as we strive to understand the deeper purpose of our meaning, our lives on Earth.

Much of our communication to you is about extending communication and understanding not only between species, but also between members of your own species, as well as between the seemingly different aspects of your own self. As you open and embrace more as yet unrevealed aspects of yourself, you come to realize the deep inherent oneness that pervades everything.

That afternoon, while contemplating Raven's message, I sat on my back deck watching a trio of ravens soaring and swooping under the rich blue canopy of sky. Jagged lines of snow blazed white on mountaintops in the distance, and the dark angular shapes of the ravens formed a brilliant counterpoint.

As I closed my eyes, I saw a close-up of Raven's face, black eyes glinting. He moved his head slowly, side to side, or, as he put it, "view to view, you to you."

We speak about the poetry of the soul and the movement between hearts because this is the way we perceive the world, he remarked in a calm and thoughtful manner. *This is our way, a flow of information, a patchwork of sorts that centers not so much on meaning as on overall cohesion and deeper knowing on a symbolic level.*

One of our qualities is as messenger birds; we carry information from one aspect of One to another. We work between species and within species to help enhance communication at a deeper level of intimacy in shared, mutual understanding.

Many humans feel you have reached the pinnacle of linguistic development, but countless animals will tell you time and again that this is not the case. There is even now, as we speak, a throbbing pulse that reverberates within the world of which so many humans are not the slightest bit aware. You have heard it described as the Sound of the Earth, and this is an apt description. Many animals are able to tune into this sound, this song, at any moment. We are never alone, for we have the ability to 'hear' from any other species who participates in the orchestration of sound and feeling and shared knowledge.

We would like to tie up some loose ends about communication and shapeshifting. To use words to reach another being is to move outward and touch that being. And, in turn, that being reaches out and touches you. When a deep and meaningful interchange occurs, a communication channel is established and brought to life.

Even now, you are reluctant to share personal information, but we encourage you to do so. To reveal more of yourself so that more will be revealed to you. We maintain you cannot engage in shapeshifting if you are always guarded. You must open—not only to those around you, but to the deeper nature of your own being. As you delve deeper into this arena, you will find infinite amazement at what you hold within yourself.

We feel shapeshifting is about opening to this essence. Once you hold this key, you are free to ride along with any form, marry any aspect of being, in order to marvel at the myriad forms and manners of perception and ways of being that oneness chooses to manifest. This becoming is joy.

When I opened my eyes, the ravens were gone. Sunlight sparkled all around me and the immense blue sky stretched open, wide and clear. A cool breeze swept down the mountains. Touching my face, it entered my body, whispering through the depths of my very grateful being.

14

. . . Other Selves

The more I listened to the diverse range of voices available to us as humans on planet Earth, the more sensitive I became to issues of hearing and sound. This is no big surprise, of course, for the more we focus our attention on any aspect of life, the more fully we open ourselves to its treasures.

I felt that my inner ears were changing, attuning to subtleties in vibrations. I sometimes heard multiple soundtracks, similar to listening to the director's commentary as spoken over a filmed scene in the "special features" segment of a DVD. Other times, I was simply very aware of the many hums, purrs, whines, whistles, and other assorted tones in daily life. While many of these sounds were easily traced to humans, animals, or the multitude of electronic equipment that surrounds us, some were not.

One morning a specialized group of whales introduced themselves: *We come from a variety of dimensions, both on Earth and from other positions in space. We work largely with sound and the power that sound brings, most notably in allowing us to travel to other dimensional realities. The sounds are pathways that we voice and, by voicing, are able to follow into further reaches of space.*

The whales showed me this by sounding a tone, which then became an actual pathway leading (they said) to other dimensional worlds.

They added that just as creating and then listening to certain sounds allowed this type of movement to occur, tuning in to the voices (or energetic frequencies) of one's "other selves" offered one the ability to move into those alternate worlds.

As I shook my head with wonder, the whales suggested that as they had much more information to share, perhaps I would be open to a download. As they put it, *the information is vast; to load it into you piece by piece, through consciousness, could be a lengthy and overwhelming process for you. The information we send is tonal and will find the appropriate 'file folder' within your being to place itself. This will help you at future 'times' as you open in understanding. In addition, this will allow your operating system to work faster and smoother, more efficiently. We offer you an upgrade!*

Although the whales' upgrade was relaxing, I did not notice any immediate changes. A few days later, however, I awoke with a piercing ache deep in my ear. As I lay in bed, trying to make it go away, I recalled Zak's advice about moving through fear by looking it straight in the eye. Well, why not move through pain by listening to it deep in the ear?

Focusing into the pain, I detected a swirling, high-pitched sound coiling through my ear canal. It sounded tight, as if tautly stretched— thus revealing the sound also as an image and feeling. The more I listened, the more I heard and saw and felt.

As I followed the flowing sensation of the pain, it deepened, blossoming into a low, bass throb. It seemed I had journeyed to another place, far removed from ordinary reality, for as the throb pulsed it formed a cave-like quality in both sound and imagery. I recalled the whales then, and understood more clearly what they meant by a sound having the ability to form a shape, a feeling, an actual place of being.

From within the cave, I sensed a different path that moved-pulsed beyond the throb to another tone. Following that, I encountered a tweaky, high-pitched range—another kind of pain, in another kind of place. Once again, I followed that tone, matching myself with its vibration, feeling into it, flowing deeper.

There were many such twists and turns, uplifting crescendos and peaceful diminuendos. When I came out the other end, the pain was barely existent, and it was then I realized: I had been shapeshifting with pain!

Later, on recording the experience in my dream journal, I considered it from alternate perspectives. "Maybe it is about the fear of meeting my other selves," I wrote in that loose, speculative manner of journaling in which thoughts bubble up from the quiet, less recognized parts of our being. "Maybe it is about not wanting to hear about that."

As I wrote these words I heard-felt the tone in my ear once again—though softer, dimmer, more as an echo. With the tip of my finger, I tapped my ear. I don't know why I did this, but as I did, the tone translated into words:

I am the direct line to your other selves. It is true: you are now at a place where you are called to be more conscious of your other selves, other aspects of who you—as a soul entity—are. This is one manner in which you may receive this information—through inner hearing.

Communication with animals is a way of opening humans to this mode of connection. That is part of what animals do for the planet. They introduce a link, a way of opening, so that you can begin to hear others— and yourself.

Do not be afraid. Fear is what shuts you down and causes pain. Trust this process. Our advice is to not rely so heavily on past expectations or what others think. Rather, be open to the new, to what you are receiving and the unique manner in which you receive. As you incorporate this into your daily life, you will also have the opportunity to meet with other aspects of yourself and grow in this regard. It is indeed a great opening into multidimensional awareness, and your spiritual nature may breathe deeply and expand at this juncture in temporal reference. As you open, others open. As others open, you open. This is the nature of the deal.

ANOTHER FACE OF YOU

There was no need to convince, for the "nature of the deal" made perfect sense to me. I was increasingly aware of how our collective stories not only correspond, reflect, and illuminate, one to another, but also how the experiences of others may directly touch and open us, just as if that experience were our own.

In a similar fashion, certain events revealed how parts of me that struggled stubbornly with awareness were influenced by other parts of self that opened more readily. For even a small awakening to one part of our being has an effect on the whole.

One day I met my raven-haired neighbor, the one I'd had the argument with, in an empty hallway of our children's school. It happened in such an odd, dreamlike way, however, that neither of us was conscious of the other until the very last moment.

Gently swinging two baskets of flowers that had been an unexpected gift, I was walking down the hallway as a woman I vaguely recognized approached. "Look at you!" she said with a huge smile, and I smiled in return. It was only after she passed that I realized it was my neighbor. In that split second of recognition, I also understood that she had taken me for someone else. In disbelief, we each did a double take—turning around at exactly the same moment, as if mirror images of one another. The event seemed so deliberately orchestrated that I could not help laughing, and I heard her do the same. Although we abruptly snapped back to our separate paths, in that moment I knew: something had been healed, whether we chose to be conscious of it or not.

The question of just who our neighbors really are took on greater significance as the metaphor snuck into other aspects of my life. One night, for example, I dreamed of myself as a young girl skipping down the road outside my childhood home:

Although it is late at night, the street is lit with a silvery glow.
I am looking for neighbor kids to play with. Finding no one, I

skip and dance down the road, twirling a long red scarf in big circles beside me. And as I skip, I sing:

I am awake and you are all sleeping.
I am awake and you are all sleeping.
I am awake and you are all sleeping.

But I soon feel a shiver of fear. There ahead, I see someone coming at me. I turn and run, though the figure chases, following me all the way back home. As I try to get inside—through a sliding glass door—I see him up close: a young boy with a gun. Looking into his eyes, I know we are connected in thought; just as he knows what I am thinking, I know he means to shoot open the door.

The following morning, working with Barney, I introduced myself to the boy and asked why he was following me.

I am a part of you that you left behind, from another era, he began. *I learned how to grow up on the streets. I don't like how you are singing your song. You sing that 'you are all sleeping,' but we are not all asleep. Some of us are awake. I have come to tell you that you don't know everything and it's not nice to do a singsong against your neighbors.*

"You are right. I'm sorry for that," I said, feeling a sense of sad heaviness. "But why do you have a gun?"

To shoot through your misperceptions. Once you open all the doors and windows of that old house, then the fears of your childhood will be freed. I would not hurt you. There is really nothing to be scared of. But you believe that there is, so here I am. In a way, you created me so that you could see what you are scared of. But what are you scared of? This is your house and it is for you to open the windows and doors as you please. You are your own leader but you don't want to see this. Once you open up your windows and doors, so will your neighbors. Then you can all dance on the street.

As I considered this, I felt a double rush of warmth: a profound gratitude for finally hearing this part of myself speaking so openly, and a matching gratitude from this part of myself for being heard.

You are being asked to open up, to share your wealth—which is your insights, your unique manner of perceiving reality and the world, the boy continued in a voice that was now more mature. *Your dreamworld has brought you back to the core of your fear so that you can work with me and release this fear. Our job is to open up the shades and windows and sliding glass doors and let the light and wisdom and love shine through.*

I will come to see you again. Remember to hold my hand, to meet me in a kind way. That way we can work together. We can do things that your outer mind might think impossible. But I am with you, and have always been. Together we can do amazing things. I am the Boy Child, another face of you.

"Wow," I said to Barney as the inner boy retreated.

Perhaps it is best if you simply allow this dream and talk to continue to unfold within your being, said Barney. *Remember that when working on the multidimensional level, some experiences may not seem logical or chronological. But it is all a part of the opening process, one aspect touching another . . .*

"Like synapses!" I exclaimed, laughing as the image of multicolored synaptic flashes forming a fireworks display of awakening suddenly came to mind.

Yes, this is a good metaphor, agreed Barney, *for it expresses the deeper truth of how the organs and systems of your body operate in concert, in combination, in holographic unity. And from here it is only a slight shuffle to understand this is also how spirit works in relation to the body. There are continual inspirations—synaptic bursts of opportunity—simultaneous happenings, and multileveled experiences which flow from spirit to body and back again.*

It would help to open your understanding of time, to really feel-know that all is happening all the time. The linear model of time was very useful at one stage in human development, though your species has hung onto it a bit too tightly.

As you open in understanding to the multidimensional nature of your being—as you lessen the fear of living more truly as you are—you also open to alternate facets of reality, time, dimensions, and so forth. The holographic process gradually seeps through your being, and you awaken as a part of it. This, too, is the multiple meaning of 'neighbors' in your dream: bridging awareness with those who are still sleeping—inner neighbors, outer neighbors—and awakening yourself in the process. In truth, all is one, but this is how the illusion of the game proceeds.

OTHER NEIGHBORHOODS
OF THE SPECTRUM

The neighbors are your challenge, Barney reminded me a few days later. I had been thinking of this not only in terms of bringing together inner and outer worlds, but also conscious ego with the expanded self. Yet, how to do this? How to *be* this? And how does this tie in with incarnation—as one moves from an expanded self into a body, no matter the form? What is the relationship between the sleeping self and the awakened self—in living, in incarnating, and also in dying?

These are seemingly difficult, involved questions, though the answer is quite simple, said Barney. *It is a matter of where you focus your attention—to which bandwidth you attune yourself within the full spectrum of being. For analogy, let us imagine the totality of You (which is Us) as the all of everything. Now . . . how to experience that? This was the first question: the first desire of All That Is to experience itself—at least in terms of this universe and what we are doing now.*

In order to experience, there were divisions—not so much divisions as they are known in your world at present, more like gradients or bandwidths of being. Remember: reality is attention-dependent. Where you place your awareness is how you experience reality. Now, here is how shapeshifting comes in, for it is about becoming more conscious of the ability to travel along the many bandwidths of being—from personal being to any form of being—throughout the larger spectrum of All That Is.

Do you see why you chose to study shapeshifting? It is to facilitate the manner in which you experience reality. That is why it is such an old science and art, for it is a means of gathering information from aspects of the spectrum that are normally unavailable to the conscious self.

By shapeshifting, you allow yourself to become more fluid and dance within the consciousness of another being. You awaken to another perception—another neighborhood of the spectrum. The more you do this, the more you come to appreciate the unique ways in which All That Is has come to experience itself. And, the more you do this, the more you see the underlying layers of interconnection between you and All That Is.

To return to your question: incarnation and de-incarnation, or dying, are flip sides of the same event. You might think of it as a valve on consciousness, a magic gateway of sorts. Death involves leaving behind a portal of perception and opening to a larger remembering of all of who you are. Similarly, incarnation involves forging open a new portal in order to experience another aspect of who you are.

One image you could use is a balloon: via incarnation, you blow yourself through the portal into the shape of your body self. And in death, you release your awareness back through the portal into the breath of you. Perhaps not the most elegant metaphor, but a simple way of describing it.

Now, shapeshifting is one means by which you strive to be consciously aware of the fluid connection between your many selves. It may not seem like this at first, but for many—myself included—this is the true gem of shapeshifting. As you become more consciously aware of yourself in incarnation, you develop access to your other selves, as well as connections to other beings (who, in a very real sense, are also other selves). At a certain point this becomes very fluid, very open, and you can glide anywhere you wish on the spectrum, as well as become open on many different bandwidths on the spectrum simultaneously. At this point the metaphor of spectrum has to dissolve, however, because it is more than that. It is an Allness that is beyond the confines of words. It simply Is.

So, does this answer your questions?

"Yes, good job!" I laughed. "Though here's something I've been curious about. How often were you aware of yourself as a shapeshifter in your life as Barney, and how often did you know of yourself as you are now, as a spirit-being?"

This is a personal question, but I will share my experiences as much as I am able, and as much as you are able to translate these feelings and thoughts. Let us remember that reality is dependent on one's consciousness, one's focus of consciousness, and one's software—in this case, the software of a dog living with a family. My perceptions were very different as Barney the dog. Many times dogs seem to be on 'autopilot'—because they are. Humans sometimes project we are bored or lazy as we lay down and nap, but often we are turning on other bandwidths, gathering information. A good many domesticated animals live in more than one reality simultaneously—in nonphysical space as well as in other lives.

As for me, part of my early life before I met you involved cleaning up some matters I had with another family. I was finished, but not finished with my body, and so I came to you. Do you remember the woman who wanted me, to replace her dead dog?

"Yes," I said, recalling how just before I signed the adoption papers at the shelter, a woman asked if I would reconsider, since Barney reminded her of her old dog who had recently died. "I said no, even though I felt it would have been very easy to say yes."

That was an important choice for you. Things would have unfolded differently if you had 'given' me to her. It is one of those points in your life where a seemingly small decision has enormous consequences. It was a fork in the road for you and you chose the path that led you to where you are now. Another part of you chose the other path.

I sensed Barney wanted me to look into this other path, this other life of me, though I was not certain I was ready. However, as he cajoled me—*Let's do it as an experiment!*—I relented, allowing myself to glimpse another aspect of me diverging from that point so long ago: two different Dawns, living two very different lives.

It's just another dimension of shapeshifting, commented Barney matter-of-factly. *We spoke about this in the beginning of our talks—*

about how some, on incarnation, allow their selves to go off on dif-
ferent paths, to explore many different options. I know this is hard
for you to hold at present, but I mention it because some animals use
their 'downtime' to tune into their other selves and compare notes, so
to speak.

Cats often do this. I was a cat more than once and know the cat
form is fond of this—which also ties in with the human observation
that cats have nine lives. They do indeed have many other awarenesses
(or 'lives') that they hold within conscious connection. Think of it as
having an invisible friend whom you tune in to every so often, shar-
ing information, telling each other how the day is going, that sort of
thing. As this takes on deeper meaning and focus, the selves begin to
work together, to merge consciousness and become aware of each other in
a much fuller sense.

Let these ideas play inside of you for awhile. It is not about taking
over bodies or selves—you do watch a lot of horror movies!—but about
joining talents and energies to expand awareness. Think of it as expand-
ing the conscious boundaries of all involved.

I felt Barney smiling, pondering how much more I might be able
to digest.

You have to remember that you are filtering reality through a human-
brain-being that has certain limitations, he said most kindly. *While it*
is possible for you to expand yourself in conscious awareness, when you
express or share this reality-experience with others, it will be filtered
through your unique paradigm. So, there is only so much you can talk
about in this manner. Still, this is quite a lot!

I smiled in return, and Barney and I sat silent. Colorful thoughts
swirled and danced like an unruly passing parade, though even the
most outrageous of these eventually settled down softly beside us. I felt
like a tired pilgrim, having trekked through untold mountain passes
and secluded valleys. Tired, but satisfied, too.

I knew we had not arrived at any final destination. No monastery
or temple or cathedral in site. And yet, none of that mattered. I felt a

contented glow at having found a path that suited me, and a deep peace simply being quiet with Barney.

Let us put it this way, Barney remarked at last. *Shapeshifting is about forging new avenues of creativity, about moving beyond limiting boundaries of consciousness, about meeting other aspects of who you are and what you have created. This is a new way of looking at shapeshifting, one we haven't discussed in any great detail.*

It is a step into the deeper nature of the multidimensional. For it is to walk with greater awareness of who you are, with greater appreciation of the fullness of All. Together with many selves, you may touch off in one another extensions of awareness, gathering power among yourselves so as to become ever more responsive to who you are and all that you create.

"And shapeshifting comes in?"

As a means. As a training ground. Do you remember that is what we first spoke of: that shapeshifting is a particular course of study designed to help you get past the illusion of separation—to help you to discover, or uncover, the innate beauty of all forms in the All-That-Is scenario. By experiencing a great variety of forms, you become more aware not only of others but also of yourself. And as you become more aware of yourself, you become more aware of your other selves. So, in a sense, becoming aware of the other and becoming aware of the self yields the same thing. The joke is that essential oneness permeates all, though each goes about discovering this, experiencing this, in his or her unique way.

And this is our bridge to the following section, the remainder of our path: the Art of Greater Living. It is to share the essence of experience with others, to spark in one another new modes of being, to awaken conscious relationships between all the 'you's' who operate in a multitude of varied realities, and so to evolve more consciously together.

As I opened my eyes, I felt the nudge of a wet nose under my forearm. The gesture was unmistakably Barney—playfully executed, perfectly timed. No matter that no dog was present in the room, for thoughts on what was and wasn't possible, what was and wasn't real, had long ago begun to lose their hold. Shining through, a feeling of inner knowing pressed on. There was more adventure to come.

Be open and aware, suggested Barney in closing. *I might meet you anywhere.*

PART 3

The Art of
Greater Living

15

——

Embracing the Yeti

The yeti: a large, shaggy, solitary creature said to wander the remote upper ranges of the snowy Himalayas—an area sometimes referred to as the rooftop of the world. Bordering countries of India, Nepal, Tibet, China, and Bhutan offer an array of intriguing stories about this seldom seen, elusive being. Some report the yeti as being helpful and shy—for example, nursing sick, lost explorers back to health—while others portray a more intimidating version, and still others claim the hairy beast is actually a Tibetan bear. Expeditions to find the yeti have yielded no definitive evidence, save for a few footprints, blurry photos, and dubious artifacts, including scraps of reddish brown hairs, hand bones, and part of a scalp. Most of our knowledge of the yeti thus remains couched in legend, speculation, and the remote rooftop of our imagination.

In my early twenties, a yeti made a series of noteworthy appearances in my dreams. Unlike the traditional dark-haired yeti, mine had long, silky, white hair. He was most often silent and calm—more kindly observer than threatening presence. In early dreams, I spied the yeti from a distance in the wild. Though as the dreams progressed, I came to sit beside him, often near a campfire under the twinkling black sky of a secluded region. It was there that he began sharing a story about yeti origins. There were no words exchanged between us. Rather, side by side, gazing into the small fire, I saw from the yeti's point of view. Not as if seeing through his eyes, but as if remembering—recalling a series of images from another time. It was like watching an old film, for these movies within the dreams had the feel of early black and white travel documentaries, complete with jerky movements and muffled sound.

The story the yeti shared was related to the monks who lived in the far, mountainous regions of Tibet. Tall snowy peaks and shaded valleys were the landscape of these dream-memories, with gatherings of squat, sturdy buildings set within the folds of the craggy mountains. The yeti's tale revealed that when the monks needed to leave on pilgrimage or other long journeys, they used their minds to create guardians. With the tremendous powers available to them through meditation and thought control, they harnessed their inner vision to imagine immense, imposing creatures to protect the temples. As if to emphasize this, the yeti replayed scenes of one or more monks fashioning a kind of holographic image that suddenly materialized as thought became form. The next step, the yeti showed, was for the monks to add weight or substance to the image—a third dimensional component that activated the thoughtform and made it tangibly real. This "reality" could be turned on or off as the monks desired.

The guardian—the newly fashioned yeti—was placed at the entrance to the temple in its invisible form: as a contained, undetectable force field. But if someone came too close, the thoughtform would be activated and the yeti would appear. Once invoked by someone stepping past the invisible wall and activating the need for the guardian, the thoughtform—the yeti—became alive and acquired a life of its own.

The trouble, the yeti showed me, came many decades—or perhaps centuries—later, after the first yeti was created. For there was strife, confusion, war—a chaotic disorder in which the peace and balance of the monastery was disrupted. It was at this point in the dream documentary that the story inevitably broke down. Sometimes I would ask impatiently, "What happened to the yetis?" and the dream would abruptly end. Other times, the yeti reluctantly revealed a series of disconnected scenes. On waking, it was a frustrating yet compelling process to make sense of what had happened next. Eventually, however, I pieced together my understanding of the rest of the dream-story as follows:

In one way or another, as the monks left (or were forced to leave) their monasteries, some essential link with the yetis was broken. Perhaps this was because the monks kept the yetis alive via their life force and use of extended meditative techniques. Perhaps with the monks unexpectedly gone, the yetis lost their sense of purpose. Whatever the reason, the abandoned yetis eventually wandered away from their respective birthplaces, roaming the mountains, sometimes visibly activated and other times not; sometimes helpful and sometimes not.

Although I did not know whether this tale was "true" in the conventional sense, the story was shared so many times within my dreams that it—just as the thought-created yeti—eventually acquired a life of its own. At times, I wondered whether I had read about this, forgotten it, and then refashioned it in my dreams. Research on the yeti, however, did not yield much in the way of a connection with the monks of Tibet. (Much later, while reading the books of adventurer and author Alexandra David-Neel, who lived in Tibet and studied with various monks, I read of the creation of *tulpas*—animal or human companions or helpers created by thought.[1]) And so the yeti dream-story remained an intriguing personal mythology for me—neither true nor untrue—until it, like the mysterious yeti, simply faded away.

For a long time, then, I forgot about such things. Other events were happening in my life and the yeti and his story no longer frequented my dreams or thoughts. He was gone entirely—off wandering in distant places, perhaps . . .

Until one day, decades later, when I was facedown on a bodywork table, receiving massage. There was a hold in my back causing infrequent but painful spasms. I felt the knot coiled tightly just above the base of my spine, in the lumbar region. As the bodyworker focused on the spot, melting her fingertips deep into the tissue, I suddenly saw the yeti. He sprang into my consciousness fully formed and present, just as if he had never left. The only giveaway was his pensive, slightly perplexed expression, like a long lost friend who is surprised by meeting once again.

The image triggered a flood of memories that washed over me like a freak tsunami. For one shining moment, I saw myself—felt myself—in several realities simultaneously. It was just a taste, but in that moment I *knew* myself in other forms, as alternate selves; I felt myself as individual and also as an interconnected collection of beings. As quickly as that experience came, however, it was gone. My brain scrambled to hold on to fragments of memory. I was amazed and confused and overwhelmed all at once. It felt as if so much had come so quickly—and then suddenly was gone. Only the gentle-eyed yeti remained; a faint, questioning smile barely visible beneath all that hair.

NOT ME, YET I

Although I was happy to see the yeti once again, I was taken aback by having so easily forgotten him and his story. I felt the peculiar astonishment at how our memory faculties can simply let things slide away—*So long, synaptic links!* And, I was equally surprised by how little it takes—a glimpse, a word, a touch—the massage therapist's fingertips sinking into the muscles of my back—to trigger the fullness of a particular memory back to consciousness. *Who's in charge of such comings and goings, anyway?*

When something as unusual as a yeti shows up in our life, it's probably a good idea to pay attention. We might begin, for example, by asking: *Who is this yeti? What does the yeti represent? What does my yeti show me about myself?* In the larger collective view, it is easy to dismiss the yeti as merely a myth or legend, for we are often more comfortable distancing that with which we are unfamiliar as something out there, different from ourselves. However, creatures summoned from the depths of our psyches *(Why a yeti, after all?)* are valuable clues, calls from shadow selves as invitations to greater awareness. In this light, to recognize the yeti in relationship with ourselves—or perhaps to realize the yeti as a part of ourselves—means moving beyond the superficial façades of "just a coincidence" or "Isn't that weird?" Rather, it is to accept the challenge of the gift: to open ourselves to experience, to welcome the mystery of the yeti who is not me, and yet I.

For the next few months I had many dreams and adventures with the yeti. The more I opened to these explorations, the more I recalled details of those alternate I's with the different lives that had been ushered in by the sudden wave of memory. Some came in dream form, others as concurrent memories, and some as simultaneously evolving "past lives." Barney reminded me of the "continual inspirations—synaptic bursts of opportunity—simultaneous happenings, and multileveled experiences which flow from spirit to body and back again." And I found, through direct experience, that this was so.

In fact, many shapeshifting ideas and concepts were becoming clearer—not just to my mind, but to the whole of my being. I recalled the Dream Guides' observation that "what all of this leads to is the ability to become more conscious of your multidimensional nature in any given moment." The Dream Guides spoke of coexisting realities in which selves of different times and places may meet, merge, or otherwise blend together. Sometimes in very amusing ways.

In one encounter, for example, I was surprised to see that the yeti's hair was no longer white and silky, but yellow-brown, like straw. "What happened?" I asked, holding out my hand with a desire to touch the hair. But the yeti backed away. Then, with an outstretched pinky finger, he raised his great furry hand in a deliberate manner, as if drinking an imaginary cup of tea. Perplexed, I shook my head, but the yeti only repeated the gesture. A flash of associations brought to mind the medicinal tea my acupuncturist had recently prescribed for my back. The Chinese herbs were dark and bitter, yet I steeped and sipped the pungent mixture every day. Was Yeti absorbing the tea as well? Was the nature of interconnected realities really so porous? That his lovely white hair would turn yellow struck me as visually funny, yet the act of connecting to me in such an intimate, personal way was so endearing that I felt even more affection for the good-natured yeti.

True to his tale, the yeti also proved to be an attentive guardian. For several years I continued to work with the alternate selves who presented themselves in the tsunami of consciousness. These memory fragments were like small, hard seeds, and I sensed the need to take gentle care for them to blossom fully into conscious recall. I often felt the yeti's presence while doing this, as if he were silently, carefully observing.

One of the memory seeds was particularly disturbing and significant to my back pain. I remembered it as a past life scenario, as a baby who had been abandoned by her young mother in a forest cabin. Wrapped in blankets, the baby was placed alone in that cabin, on a hardwood board. Crying, screaming, wet and hungry, she was left to die. There were many details and layers to the story, and many impacted emotions that connected to the tight, impacted pain in my back. (As deep body-work may reveal, pain in the back is often related to pain from our past—from what is "back there" in time. Further, as Barney noted, a hold in the back can also indicate a "holding back": a fear of opening to a truth that we continue to hide from ourselves.) Using shape-shifting techniques, I came to know and eventually share consciousness with not only the baby, but her mother and father. Intense emotions of betrayal, hurt, rejection, and more were played out within each personality as we moved through healing in this linked energetic relationship. By engaging in a kind of temporal shapeshifting, we also experienced a variety of different "endings" to this life.

As we reached a sense of completion with the past life scenario, feeling a healthy balance between mother, father, and baby (and, not surprisingly, significantly less pain in my back), the yeti appeared in a dream. He was different now, both his coloring and demeanor much lighter. Although he had the same general yeti shape, he floated like a puffy cloud in the bright blue sky of the mountainous area where we had once met. Sailing low, just over my head, he dropped down a group of small, furry, white yeti-dogs. And as he passed by, I heard the words, *If you take care of them, they will be good to you.*

A TALK WITH SPIRIT OF YETI

For the most part, my communication with the yeti had been through shared images and feelings. This occurred in the dreaming world, the waking world, and many worlds in between. Even though this worked just fine, I still attempted to engage the yeti in verbal conversation. Most often he ignored my requests. One day, however, a voice "behind" the yeti offered to speak, to answer and clarify various questions I had pondered over the years. In keen anticipation, I began to organize my thoughts. Was the dream-story the yeti shared with me historically true for all yetis? Or was the yeti's tale something my dream-mind fashioned to suit me alone? Indeed, what was the "reality" of yetis? Before I could let loose my racing avalanche of questions, the voice began:

This is Spirit of Yeti. We are more alive in certain mountainous parts of the world, in certain peoples who hold a consciousness that is open to our type—which is, for the most part, of a mythological origin. That is not to say we are not 'real.' When we are envisioned and talked to—in a way such as this—we are alive and our presence becomes more consciously known to all humans.

To begin, I will address this issue. Yetis, along with other so-called mythological creatures, interact with humans on many different levels. There are those who believe we are physical, and it is true that we do sometimes take physical form.

The yeti you addressed is a yeti of the emotional and mental realms— a figure that your unique makeup has chosen to represent a way of interacting between your selves. The yeti was holding experience for you in such a manner so as to entice you to explore further. In answer to your question, therefore, it was partly your makeup that brought forth the yeti and partly your knowledge with legend that made this form available. It is in this sense that the yeti is a useful mythology that fits with what you are attempting to learn.

I took a quick breath. Although I was hearing what the Spirit of Yeti was saying, his words were oddly formed, almost as if he were speaking a different language.

Now, I call myself Spirit of Yeti, but I am more precisely Spirit of the Lost, of the Forgotten. I correspond to the energetic reality that underlies your perception of the yeti. In shapeshifting terms, I am the energy of things that have been hidden away but still need to be found. I can shift my shape into any form that is appropriate—a monster, a lost child, a fog, or a barren landscape. I can be experienced in any shape that fits the interrelation of where an individual is in his or her quest and how that individual wishes to proceed.

Sometimes words are prisons, barriers. Let us engage feelings as we proceed.

"Yes," I readily agreed. For while this communication was coming through the words I had so desired, something else was happening. It was a strange sensation, as if the words I was hearing were struck from a gong, as if the ideas behind those words were circular sound waves that reverberated with multiple rings of meaning. I had never experienced anything like it—thus, perhaps, the impression of hearing a different language. But Spirit Yeti (who was not exactly a spirit or a yeti after all) pressed on.

As the yeti explained to you, when there is deep trauma to the body, mind, or spirit, there is the option of shielding that trauma from consciousness. Some humans (and other animals as well) choose to work through the issue—the teaching, the lesson, the experience—soon after the event. Others are not able to for a variety of reasons, mostly due to the development of their consciousness. This is not to say that the event must be reasoned through or analyzed—far from it. In fact, in most cases, analysis and such is a means of distancing the event; a means of defense. For example, let us imagine you rationalize or analyze an event—perhaps your mind will thus think it is finished. However, it is only your feelings that will truly tell you if you are free of an event or not. If your mind insists on choosing one way, your body will make you aware in another.

It is in this sense that your perception of yetis comes into play. The event you recall, that of being abandoned, was too much for part of you to hold. So, this was shielded from you by an energetic whose purpose it is to shield—as you call it, Yeti.

Now, let us speak of the mythological yeti. The story presented to you was that the monks of Tibet—for purposes of guarding their temple—created the yeti. We might also see this as a form of energy created to guard one's gates of consciousness. The yeti is the guardian, a manifested form of energy that allows in what is considered safe and holds out that which is not considered safe.

In your story, the yetis are abandoned. There is war, internal strife—which is to say, a chaos of sorts within the temple of your being. This would represent trauma, would it not?

"That seems to fit." Although I didn't fully understand the fit, I was curiously reassured by the "rings of meaning" that were now intersecting and merging together with colorful ripples and waves.

And so, in the midst of trauma, the original job of the yeti (to protect and serve as guardian) is lost. Abandoned. For you, the yeti was abandoned. In other scenarios, the yeti might be sent off or accused for doing something terrible and thus banished. But, in the mythology of the psyche, there is always this separation. The yeti guardian leaves.

And yet there is longing. Something is not complete because the yeti's job is to be at the temple, at the interface of consciousness. The yeti is a creation of the temple monk—which is to say, the spiritual overlord or 'higher' self. But if the yeti is sent off by the self's inner strife, then what shall the yeti do? The yeti attempts to come back in some way. One way is by helping the self. By holding all that which the self abandons. In this way, the yeti held the story/image/experience of the abandoned baby for you.

The yeti's forgetting of certain particulars echoes your 'life' as the abandoned baby. Your yeti's manner of forgetting is insightful for you, though not necessarily universally true. Some yetis know exactly where lost or forgotten things are buried. They may show their monk-master freely—or for a price. There are many variations of this. Your yeti was speaking from hurt: 'Oh, I'm not sure where your memories are, because you abandoned me.' Do you see how this turns in on itself?

The rings of meaning were now separating and tumbling about, bouncing against each other like bumper cars. This was definitely the strangest conversation I had ever had with an animal, spirit-being, or— what was this voice anyway?

You are talking with an energy that resides below pattern level. Do you understand what I mean by this?

I paused to consider. "I understand that you are not really the yeti or even Spirit of Yeti so much as you are the energetic that underlies the pattern of this—which you say is the energy of that which is lost and needs to be found. Is that it?"

That is close. Tell me: what do you think it means for the yeti to drop down small white dogs? What does it mean: 'If you take care of them, they will be good to you'?

I paused again. "Maybe it has to do with our own creations. That if we are caring with our thoughts, our manifestations, our words, with all that we put out, they will come back to us—not as fearful monsters, but as loving returned creations."

Thoughts are things. This is also the lesson of the yeti. The monks created the yetis from thought, but then abandoned them (or cast them out). And so the yetis troubled the villagers for centuries because these thoughts were not honored: 'Oh they are only thought creations, only yetis.'

It is very true as you put it: You must embrace all of your thoughts, all of your creations, all of your yetis. This is part of your journey: to embrace the yeti and know that the yeti, too, is who you are.

EMBRACING THE YETI

We fell into a quiet pause then; a silence that yawned open wide, and I felt my thoughts stretching in unpredictable ways.

It occurred to me that the yeti was not only a guardian of lost selves, but a great example of a legendary lost "self." I saw why the monks (or, our own higher selves) would fashion the imposing yeti monster as a guardian: to prevent less-evolved selves or aspects of consciousness from entering the temple before they were ready. And I thought of the troubled villagers—our frenzied, scattered thoughts that fail to go deep, to honor the teaching of our own personal yeti.

Such clever crafting at work here—that my yeti should so carefully share his story of creation and abandonment, and that I should so easily forget or abandon him—as if mirroring his very same tale! And yet it was Yeti's reappearance, so many years later, that ushered in a remembering of my own lost selves, a reclaiming of that which was so lost I didn't even know of its existence. Round and round we come again: knock, knock, knocking at the temple door!

Perhaps the underlying pattern of encountering a legendary lost creature arises from a desire to find our own lost selves, a yearning to recover those hidden, emotional energy-holds in the time-space continuum of our larger self. And yet to do so we must have the key—the properly attuned state of consciousness with which to pass through the doorway. There the great yeti stands guard, fiercely protecting the delicate, dangerous treasures of our deep inner world as he nonetheless continues to guide us, encouraging our longing to become more consciously whole.

I thought of those colorful rings of meaning—the gonged vibrations behind the words of Spirit Yeti, whose mystery held "the energy of things that have been hidden away but still need to be found." And I realized once again that the clues to our remembering are so expertly held within our own stories—be they customs or legends, current events or daydreams, collective tales or personal mythologies. Those forgotten pieces of self are deftly contained, cleverly concealed, safely hidden away until we can find the key: the proper attunement of consciousness that allows us to unlock the story, recover the secrets that we ourselves have hidden, and, thus, re-member who we are.

Is there anything else? I wondered.

Only that the temple is within, said Spirit Yeti. *Just as it has always been. Just as the monk and yeti reside within.* And as he began to walk toward a distant mountain, I saw that he had become an old man clothed in robes—perhaps a wandering Taoist or Tibetan monk, with very long white hair, some of it bundled atop his head. A thin white beard flowed from his chin and a yellow butterfly danced between his hand and face, fluttering back and forth.

The shifting of shape is the outer form, the illusion, he called as he turned to face me. *The real shapeshifting is done within. This is something you will feel one day and know to be true.* And, with a smile, he became a yeti once again.

16

———

The Circle of Projections

The yeti had a profound effect upon my shapeshifting adventures. I still felt his presence from time to time—great hairy paw upon my shoulder, calm eyes watchful and discerning. I welcomed him not only as a symbol of encouragement for finding other lost selves, but as inspiration and helpful guidance as well.

As I continued to ponder all that Spirit Yeti had conveyed, I realized I was becoming more comfortable in "feeling into" and working with connective associations that didn't necessarily make sense to my rational mind. I better understood what Raven had shared about that flow of being that "centers not so much on meaning as overall cohesion and deeper knowing on a symbolic level."

I revisited the notion that had been simmering ever since my Rabbit experiences—that we are sending each other coded messages and reminders across times and lives in just this fashion: storing symbolic pieces of ourselves within the stories of our lives, stashing clues rich with meaning in the scaffolding of our life or, perhaps, in the lifestories of alternate selves living in different times and lands, different cultures and situations.

The yeti adventure had pushed this idea one step further, showing me that some of these messages and clues are not only mirrored keys or reflective clues of who we are, but actual portals that allow meetings between our many selves.

I remembered conversations with Zak about the connection portal—a quickly moving, energetic flow that looked like a shimmering round tube—and felt a deeper sense of what this implied. For not only was it a visual representation of *how* to connect with animals, plants, forces of nature, and other aspects of self but, more than that, it was a vehicle—a means of moving into the energy of connection itself.

I realized, too, that it is through these portals that we shift our normally contained shapes of consciousness beyond the constraints of who we think we are. Traveling between dimensions—visiting different times and places, different bodies and lives—we consciously expand ourselves, opening to a deeper type of meeting.

THE MEETING PLACE

Let us talk about the meeting place—that point in shapeshifting where seemingly different beings meet and merge, said Barney one morning as I was pondering exactly where this meeting of selves might occur.

As he spoke, I realized that not only was Barney present, but the entire group. And, a funny thing was happening: I felt a pressure upon my back, gentle but persistent.

We are attempting to merge with you right now and you offer some resistance, said Barney. *Let us focus on experience this morning. Let us use some visualization to peer into your wall of resistance. What do you see?*

As I "looked" into the pressure on my back, I saw an image of many dogs with their noses pressed up against a wide glass door. With a snicker—what kind of a meeting place was this?—I related what was happening:

"When I open the door, these dogs—who are of all sizes and shapes and breeds—run into the house. It is my house, I suppose. And now a horse and other creatures are coming in, too." I found that as I breathed inward, I began to expand and accommodate more of the vision. It was strangely fun, as if each breath was an invitation to ever more animals—monkeys nimbly scampering, snakes sliding inward, lines of ants and spiders, flies and bees and butterflies filling my house.

As you open and breathe in what is flowing through you, you begin to participate more fully in the action of living, commented Barney.

There was such a rush of movement—more animals, as well as clouds and mountains and flower-beings all crowding into the room— and it occurred to me once again how our imagination truly is an image-nation, a grand nation of images. And now even the room was shifting, turning itself inside out so that the house became a wide, open meadow.

"We are all here," I reported. "Many animals, many voices. One being . . . So, these are all aspects of me?"

Yes, said Barney. *These are not animals themselves, but the projections you hold of animals—the aspects of you that you 'behold' in your projections onto animals. This is an example of the seeing through of karmic illusions—though we use that term lightly. You are recalling your projections back to you. You are reclaiming them so as to reconfigure them. In a manner of speaking, it is to update your reality as you refashion and send variations of ever new projected versions of reality outward. This is the meeting place between thinking reality is 'out there' and realizing reality is 'in here.'*

I had to ponder that for a moment. As I did, a series of thoughts popped to mind. First, I was reminded of the monks and yetis. Did not their story exemplify a similar pattern—creations of thought-forms sent outward, only to ultimately return to the inner temple? But was this manifesting and revisioning an ongoing process? This made me think of scientists, creating theories of reality, only to "recall" these theories years, decades, or centuries later, revision them, and send out new theories. And *this* led me to envision a parade of selves—a similarly ongoing presentation to the world of who we think we might be, through successive revisions of our persona.

As you recall your projections, you reclaim that which you have created in order to view it again with greater clarity, affirmed Barney. *This may occur on many levels—artistically, scientifically, symbolically, emotionally, objectively, and so on.*

The meeting is about inner cohesion: about reclaiming those aspects that on the surface seem different from you while reacquainting yourself (and your selves) with essential oneness. It can be a type of shadow work—recalling that which was lost and decided to hide in the dark. As you soften your resistance to this, you begin to open the relationship between 'outer' and 'inner' worlds.

In terms of spiritual evolution, the meeting place allows you to greet disparate aspects of yourself so as to bring the members back together—to re-member. It is in this 'place' that shapeshifting may also occur.

In a sense, this meeting place is the glue of shapeshifting, for it is what allows the merging of consciousness to occur. You need not shapeshift to experience this, of course, though this meeting is an essential element in the shapeshifting process—as well as in the transformation of every being as spiritual progression occurs.

As for mergence, this is a unique aspect of shapeshifting. On the surface, we could say that conscious mergence is necessary for shapeshifting to occur. To 'become' or ride along with another being, for example, you need to open to some degree of merging with the body or consciousness of another. At deeper levels, however, we are always merging—through auras, thoughts, words, physical closeness. Even in reading a book you are merging with another being, though there is a time lag between the person's penning of the manuscript and the publication of the book and the individual's reading of the words—but do not fail to see this as a type of mergence as well!

We are all in various stages of mergence with many, many beings. We are one vast interconnected whole, constantly shifting our shapes, constantly shifting our mergence in and out of ideas, thoughts, relationships, et cetera.

In this sense, shapeshifting is an ever-present process. We are all engaged all the time with shapeshifting. Our focus—the focus of our group and this book—is to open this to a more conscious level. To be more aware of all that we are doing so as to have clearer awareness of our abilities and—on it goes—so as to open that awareness to even greater clarity! It is a skill we are speaking of: a continual learning curve that rises and falls, narrows and widens according to one's focus of consciousness.

MERGENCE

Perhaps you would like to experience this sense of mergence, now, with our group? asked Barney. *Perhaps you will explain it to others, 'seat it' in this book with words so that others can follow with feelings and find the merging place of their own—which is, of course, all of ours.*

In agreement, and without too much thought of what this might entail—for already I felt a looming wave of thoughts, questions, and ideas—I closed my eyes and dove deep . . .

Breathing in and out, slow and steady, I sense a circular gathering of many beings. I do not see specific forms so much as feel the presence of beings who are very focused, very aware. There is a sensation—a buzz of energy connecting us in this circle, this group. It moves from one being to another, *through* one being to another—faster now, growing in intensity, until we are no longer separate entities, but connected in group consciousness. And now, in this larger body of joined consciousness, we swoop our focus first to the space within our circle, and then to the space without. Back and forth we go; in and out of the circle, and back again. And suddenly—in a spine-tingly moment of heightened presence—I *feel* our awareness as the conscious membrane between the two. Somehow, we know ourselves both as the space within the circle and the space without. We are the delicious meeting place that not only mediates between worlds but *is* both worlds—central space and outer space, known as one.

The sensation has a timeless quality, and yet I feel myself falling back, flipping around to a sense of loosely joined yet individual awareness. I am looking inward now, back to the circle, in which I see a "screen of life." It is similar to what several animals have shared about reviewing their life after death; similar also to the after-death experiences described in *The Tibetan Book of the Dead*. But I am reminded of these things ever so fleetingly, as mere Post-it notes of memory. Much more, my focus—my presence—is on this screen. It is like watching a greatly enhanced movie in which at any moment you can actually feel and sense and know all that is seen and tasted and heard and felt and known through the being on the screen— who is none other than you!

I realize too, however, that the screen itself is a blank; that what is shown upon the screen is our own individual stories— that the others are seeing their stories, each of us viewing projections of assorted selves, numerous lives. And I understand that, just as the "conscious membrane" is an aware, merged meeting space of inner and outer knowing, where I stand now—what I feel now—is similarly an in-between kind of place that allows for a special knowing of selves.

It is a sweet spot of consciousness, a place in which I am both "in" and "out." As with the joined consciousness swooping in and out of the circle, I similarly direct my awareness in and out—into the life on the screen of consciousness, and out again. And I find that "in and out" is a movement that brings recognition. In—to the fullness of individual lifestory awareness, and out—to a larger energetic presence that observes pattern and teachings and the subtle, perfect placement of life lessons and memories and more.

"This is what you mean by mergence?" I said to Barney at last, not so much a question as an expression of wonderment.

The mergence we speak of is an awakening to one's role in creating reality and recalling those creations so as to refashion a more conscious

reality. It is done time and again, over and over, many times in each life.
To be aware of the whole of the pattern is our aim, through the experience
of mergence.

KARMIC ILLUSIONS

As with so many of Barney's guided adventures in experience, it took
me some time to soak in all that had happened.

The sensation of venturing in and out of group space, bouncing in
and out of lifescreens, and finding that sweet spot of awareness that
spans both "in" and "out" reminded me of a term Barney had once
used: *the circle of projections.* He had remarked that each place along
the circle represents a different phase of one's life; as such, what we see
at one point of the circle may be viewed as something entirely different
at another point. That is, our experience of reality is dependent upon
where we are fixated on the circle of our life's projections. Shapeshifting,
Barney claimed, was a means of studying various projections along the
circle as well as instrumental in going beyond the circle.

I wondered if my merging experience, in and out of the group circle,
was itself an example of a recalled projection: an experiential refashion-
ing of my perception of the circle of projections metaphor. As Barney
was fond of doing, we were revisiting an idea from another point along
the circle so as to see it in a new way.

This made me think of karmic illusions—those projections within
our life that force us (or help us, depending upon our projected view
along the circle) to "see again." In this sense, karmic illusions are specialized holds of energy—psychic knots that pop up repeatedly to tug
at our individual awareness. They are karmic in that they are related
to our unique series of lifestories, and illusions because they are projections, rigidly held as "real" at certain points of our circle.

If karma is our larger, overall holding pattern—a soul-based map of
our fears and challenges, obstacles and desires—karmic illusions are the
spiritual clues we hold (and sometimes hide) for ourselves. Reflections

of their presence emerge as the problems, frustrations, dramas, and intense emotions that play out in our lives.

Although our first inclination may be to deal with, plow through, cover up, dispose of, or otherwise move past these irritations as soon as possible, what is really offered here is passage to deeper understanding. These manifest events—personalized configurations of our karmic illusions come to visit—are potential meeting places, ways to contact forgotten layers of consciousness, means of becoming more aware of our own circle of projections. As such, they are not something to be rid of; rather—like our friend the yeti—they present us with invitations to deeper exploration and discovery, gateways to the secret pathways between our selves.

But it's a tricky balance, isn't it? So easy to lose oneself in the "reality" of the lifescreen drama. How actual and genuine everything seems within the lifescreen! No wonder our karmic illusions are so all-absorbing, for they are made for us—by us.

One of the first steps in meeting with the illusory nature of one's self could be called a meeting of one's karmic illusions, commented Barney as he listened to my thoughts. *It is an area of shadow, wherein one looks at that which is still unresolved. Here one confronts what has been hidden and/or detained deep within the psyche—those central motivating fears or holds or prejudices that block energetic opening. This is a clearer understanding of karma than the idea of reward and punishment. Karmic illusions are your own diversions—those you choose to hold.*

For example, say you see a girl walking with an Afghan hound . . .

I jolted upright. "Is this a real example or 'just an example' example?"

Is there ever such a thing as 'just an example' example?

I laughed, intensely amused and impressed by Barney's ability to identify key events that so perfectly fit what we were discussing. I had indeed seen a girl walking an Afghan hound only a few days before. I was struck by the sight and wondered why I find such haunting beauty in these dogs. But this was merely a passing notion and I had soon forgotten it.

Go on, Barney nudged, and I knew what he had in mind. He may as well have said, *Fetch!*

Lowering my eyelids, I opened to what might lie beneath this surface image and feeling. Soon, my inner vision flashed back to a much younger me:

I am thirteen years old, walking on a sidewalk in the small town where I live. I pass a movie theatre and drug store, a bakery and restaurant. On the other side is a busy road, flanked by parking meters and cars. As I glance over, I notice an elegant woman sitting in one of the parked cars. She sits erect and still, almost eerily so, with bright, silky blonde hair hanging down straight, framing the sides of her face. As I pass by, I hear a laugh high in the center of my head that pierces through the rumbling sounds of traffic. An electric tingling ripples down my back and arms.

Even though I am embarrassed to do so, I feel an overwhelming need to go back. Turning around, I casually peek into the car window and suddenly jump back in shock. The woman has an enormous nose! The effect is so surprising that I do a cartoon double take. And then I see: this is not a woman at all—it is an Afghan hound! Laughter peals out of me so abruptly and noisily that I hunker down and clamp my hand to my mouth. This is when the dog turns, ever so calmly, and looks me straight in the eyes.

It is one of those moments that you can't really explain. And yet, my heart thumps wildly, my body buzzing and vibrating like crazy, as if all my molecules are flying apart and then slamming back together again. For a moment, I am outside of myself but inside too, in a larger, different way. I *know* something. And although this knowing—this strange something that I feel but can't make sense of—will be lost to my thirteen-year-old interpretation of reality, in that moment, there is an opening.

My body shudders as I revert to the smaller version of my teenage self. I raise my hand to the dog in a self-conscious wave and start to walk away; faster now, a part of me trying to out-run the experience. But even as I do so, passing stores and cars, the sidewalk sparkling in the sunlight, I realize: my reality has changed.

A FLUID AND MALLEABLE WAY OF THINKING

"Whoa!" My heart was racing and for a few moments I had no words as I felt the enormous potential of transformation held in that keyhole of time. I had forgotten the incident for so long and yet there I was, actually present, though in a much fuller, more inclusive way.

With a delicate shift of focus, I could feel myself stretch around the circle of projections, positioning myself in numerous times and selves. I felt myself tapping into a flow that opened the portal between "here" and "there," "then" and "now." What was most exciting, though, was the highly charged vibration I felt as this connected portal awoke something between these selves. I felt us harmonizing in common attunement—as if a tuning fork was struck, causing us all to vibrate at the same frequency, connecting us in a larger flow of connection. That flow was thrumming, potent and alive—similar in feel and quality to the highly charged energy that had linked me with the others in the ring of joined consciousness.

As I laughed in amazement, I felt a tug on the circle, an echo that was not just sound but movement and even more—a kind of advanced energy sonar that facilitated immediate knowing between these selves. And in that moment of experiential recognition, I realized that the laugh I was laughing now was the very same laugh that had been heard "back then" by my younger self. I felt a shiver that was also the tingling of her skin—a physical connection in simultaneity. In the circle of joined consciousness, this was a concurrent *now*.

"Whoa!" I said again, basking in the pulse of some kind of integration that was beyond what I could put into words.

How to explain what had happened? Was it a shapeshift? A recalling of projections? A meeting of selves? All of the above? With the many escalating experiences into merged consciousness, group focus swooping in and out of circles, conscious membranes and connection portals, my perception of defined terms within the ever-fluxing boundaries of reality was clearly undergoing extensive renovation.

When studying multidimensionality, one needs to call upon a very fluid and malleable way of thinking, Barney noted kindly.

I nodded in mute agreement.

And that is why such events and perceptions are so important. They help us to deepen, to bring all aspects of self into a more conscious present. Thus, you help to enlighten all aspects of yourself. You elevate your consciousness by bringing, for example, 'past versions' of yourself into a more conscious appreciation of who you really are.

In this example, it is about awakening other selves within your time frame as Dawn. It is calling them to be present in you, all of you—the baby, child, teenager, young adult, older adult, old woman: all are present and available in whatever age you are upon the circle.

I rubbed my head. "So, this experience is not so much about going back or forward in time. Rather, it's like awakening to an ever present presence in the now."

That is a nice way of putting it. And now you may use this metaphor to understand how you awaken to other selves in the same way.

As you enter the fluid nature of time (as opposed to straight, chronological time), you enter a different mode of being—and, a different reality. I mean this quite literally. As you shift into another state of consciousness, you become another being. By your new presence, you bring a new element into the opening and so you create a new reality.

In many ways, this is what shapeshifting lessons are all about: a means of discovering where and how and why reality works for you—all of you, which is all of us—humankind, animal kind, consciousness-at-large kind.

As you evolve and open on the multidimensional level, you may also become aware of alternate selves. If you choose to continue in this direction, you will become more aware of these 'others'—who are none other than you! What each of you does in your life can then be shared—mutually accessed, as if on a website, and used (downloaded) by all to enhance experiences. Moreover, you all begin to become more aware of the others in any instance of now. Your skills and awareness are exponentially awakened. The channel between spiritual being and human being is also exponentially awakened. And this is when the fun begins!

17

———

Ever Becoming

Perhaps we might begin to complete a circle, Barney suggested one morning. *I would like to share some information as I prepare to incarnate into another body.*

I instantly jolted to attention. Part of me was very comfortable with Barney the spirit dog as guide, helper, and friend; I wasn't sure how I felt as I considered the idea of a "new" Barney.

I am not yet born but have been making preparations for my life, he began, all businesslike. *However, let us first review some of the information I shared about my death:*

As Barney the dog, I was working with a conscious form of dying. I was aware of my death and had many experiences transitioning out-of-body to other states of existence. I went back and forth—sometimes in one state, sometimes in another, and, quite often, aware of many states simultaneously. This broadened my abilities to be aware both of spirit in-body and spirit out-of-body.

Now, just as when you incarnate you tend to forget what it is like to be in a spirit body, when you are spirit without a body, there is some 'forgetting' of what it is to be physical. Zak allowed me to use his body for short periods of time after my death. This was very helpful to me, as I was able to reacquaint myself with the feeling of physicality from another perspective.

I am again transitioning some of my energy via incarnating into another life. Still, part of my energy as Barney will always be available to you and the group. That is one thing humans don't always understand or make room for in their categories: our individual presence—each of us—is eternal. So, just as you may contact my personal energetic presence through your meeting-form of 'Barney the dog,' you may also know me as 'Barney the guide' of this group. And, you may continue to tune in to me in other ways—through many of my 'other' selves. This is as open as you care to be.

For example, you wonder if we will meet in human form and my answer is yes, should we desire. As we all evolve to a more conscious level, these 'meetings' become ever more interesting, filled with joy and amusement—and creativity!

Many of the beings in our group are consciously aware of their alternate selves. I, too, have other selves 'living' at present. However, it is the aspect of Barney the dog who will become a new person—let us call him Hahmend, a close approximation of his name—and it is from that aspect that we will learn more of the nature of incarnation.

To begin: I am now reviewing possibilities and working with some special beings helping me make various decisions.

I realized that these 'special beings' must be Barney's guides. I was again surprised, for it hadn't occurred to me that just as I have Barney as a guide, he might have one as well.

You are correct, he said. *These beings are unseen to you as present because, for you, there is something disconcerting about seeing your guide's guide. However, it is important to know that we all have guides and helpers, those who make our paths clearer at times.*

Fortunately, you do not hold a desire for 'Barney' to return to you. I would like to note this as a mark of advancement in the inner knowing that all is here now, that there is no need to cling to things or people or events, since all is truly available. Thus, I am pleased to talk with you about my choices for incarnation and some of the energetics involved in my shifting forms. Let us keep in mind, however, that this is simply one approach—and, that we are using the lens of time to view this particular unfolding of form.

BARNEY'S NEXT LIFE

I have chosen the human form, to be part of a nomadic family living in a mountainous region that borders a desert and a temperate area. As I locate my life entry (my parents, place of birth, and basic life agenda), I step into the developing being. That is, part of my presence helps to gradually ground spirit into the body, while other parts of me make contact with spirit-beings who will help to play a role in my awakening as Hahmend. These connections are not as literally set out or realized as you might think in human terms—rather, it is a touching of spirit, a note, a reminder, sometimes a forewarning or greeting. It serves to coalesce those of us who wish to open our connected consciousness in a particular way.

I also meet with my physical mother and others in the immediate family. Because I will have a physical obstacle, it is important for me to ground some information into the family before I arrive. This will allow for certain events and circumstances to emerge in particular ways.

Much of my life will be concerned with traveling short distances and helping others in often unnoticed yet potent ways. As a young male, I will work with sheep and other animals, including dogs. I will have an affinity for animals—quite natural, as I have been an animal so many times before. I have chosen a body that has what you might call a deformity or handicap, especially in the area of speech.

This is a good point at which to explain why some beings choose these restrictions—or opportunities. For myself, it is to better concentrate on inner work. Without the need for traditional education as a child, I will have larger amounts of time and energy to focus my connection with the earth and more subtle arenas. Many humans do not realize the tremendous amount of energy you use in growing your intellect, learning to differentiate, to categorize, and so on. You build your illusion of separation so completely that you make it very difficult to release later. And yet, intellect is a very powerful tool, which is why so many humans choose to develop this capacity.

Part of my choice to incarnate in this form corresponds to a need for a being of my abilities in this time and location. Think of it as certain beings with particular skills consulting a list of openings where help is requested, and in areas in which we are proficient. In addition, there are some personal challenges that will be advantageous to me. I will continue my work with conscious dying and will be able to help several beings in their transition and in understanding the nature of death in a clearer fashion.

Although I wanted to continue, Barney ended our talk there. As he promised to share further, he encouraged me to first engage others and learn more about their experiences in moving between death and life. Specifically, he suggested focusing on *the transition from living in physicality to conscious awareness on the 'other side,' as it is sometimes termed. In truth there is no other side, but let us use that as a useful fiction as we attempt to bring these 'sides' closer together in understanding.* What follows are three variations on this theme.

HELPERS IN AND OUT OF INCARNATION

I once spoke with a guide dog who told me about his mentor—a spirit-based being who helped guide dogs adjust to their very specialized lives with humans. In a later conversation with this mentor, he explained that because canine instinct was so much a part of a dog's software program, maintaining focus and remembering purpose throughout incarnation could be difficult. Thus, the need for a mentor or guide arose.

I was curious, of course. How did he get his "job" as a mentor? And how, exactly, did he help dogs to remember their purpose? As I related my work with shapeshifting and learning from other points of view, the mentor agreed to answer some of my questions and address the issue of working with physical beings from a spirit-based perspective.

I am one of many who work in this way, he began. *You might think of me as a translator who helps to facilitate clearer communication between the physical and the spiritual. I work on the emotional and mental levels as well, but the first main task I have is to ground the spiritual 'goal' into the physical being.*

You might call me an elemental, as you understand the term, for I work with the physical body of the dog as well as with the soul or essence of this being as it attempts to manifest and learn through a canine life with a human.

Some dogs are easier to work with than others. Just as you may find that when your focus lessens, I am not as present to you as when you tap into a deeper connection; this is how I work with the beings in my group. In truth, I am always present; it is a matter of their ability to tune in to my presence and for us to connect in that way.

Most of my job focuses on the initial stages: helping the spirit-being to situate itself in the body so as to facilitate communication. In a sense it's like getting a special 'translator device' hooked up and ready to go.

In later stages, I am available as a guide or sounding board, but mostly in a narrow focus of the job. That is, while the dog's expanded self may work on other issues, my main directive is to remind the dog to focus on connection with its human.

As to how I came to this position, you may have guessed that I have been a guide dog many times. I have been other animals as well, mostly those working in tandem with humans. I have been a plow horse, an ox, a duck; I have spent some time in the bird world also, mostly as a song-bird—in the wild and in a cage, bringing happiness to humans. I have also been a human and have worked with animals, mainly by offering food and shelter—helping in small ways, which helps to raise the consciousness of all those around us.

After my last life as a guide dog, I took this position as an energetic helper or facilitator. I have a light body, which can assume any shape. I mostly appear as a large dog to my charges—often, a large white German shepherd.

I was willing to fill the position of help when it was needed. It takes a certain level of consciousness and commitment. It is not so much a thinking move but a feeling move that landed me here. Do you understand?

I was reminded of what Barney had said about beings with special abilities consulting a list of openings. "You saw something that needed to be done, and so you chose it?"

Exactly, and that is the place of freedom from which beings take the position of guide dogs. Most guide dogs are called service dogs for a good reason—they choose to fulfill a service. Of course, they also learn a tremendous amount and this fulfills a spiritual purpose. And, many benefit—not only dogs and humans. It is a very specialized study; not all beings are immediately accepted for this type of incarnation.

Some beings become guide dogs numerous times so as to continue honing their skills. It may interest you to know that many guide dogs also incarnate as show dogs or in the entertainment industry, which is another means of honing one's skill and working at translation abilities between human and animal.

Now, let us shift gears and address the specifics of how we work to integrate a guide dog's purpose through incarnation. Instinct and instinctual desires are parts of any incarnation program. You might relate it to buying a car: you can only do certain things with the vehicle and are limited by certain restrictions. Though this is not to say you can't make modifications . . .

I smiled as I saw an image of Chitty Chitty Bang Bang (from the children's book and film) as a humorous example of a junk car being transformed into a multipurpose flying, sailing, driving machine.

Yes, continued the mentor, *that is similar to what can be done with bodies. Some modifications may be made, though it is the spiritual essence—the part of the soul that incarnates—that has a desire to learn and experience certain things. I work with this initial meeting of soul and body, working to modify the 'vehicle' so that optimum performance can be had.*

This occurs in many ways: as a 'spiritual download;' through tapping in to memories and personal histories; via reminders on the emotional and physical levels—in all sorts of ways, even from training and voice commands and bonding with humans. Generally speaking, once we modify a vehicle/body, things are fairly well set. Then the life is aimed at fine-tuning, making deeper connections and refining modes of feeling.

My work is generally done within the being's first few years. After that, you might call it independent study, though occasionally I am asked for advice, a reminder or refresher.

I thanked the mentor as we finished our conversation, just as he thanked me for "bringing our words more clearly to humans." It was a pleasure, I told him, and he responded by sharing an image of himself: a white German shepherd who appeared to be smiling.

GOLDEN LUCK JOY: THE TEACHINGS OF LIU TU

Closer to home, one of my favorite fish was dying—a goldfish who lived with several others in a large aquarium. As I moved him to a smaller bowl, he related that since he was not quite ready to die, he would tell me something about his death process to share with humans.

Death proceeds from one's consciousness; that is always the starting point, he began, noting that although he was still connected to his body, he could already feel an expansion. Especially, he said, as I sat near him and connected in this way. *Death can expand all of us,* he affirmed, *even those who are not dying, as we open to the experience.*

First, I would like to tell everyone that being a fish is a wonderful thing. I love being a fish. I know many humans don't think this is a significant life, though I can share my experience that fish are very wise creatures. We have excellent observational skills. Perhaps you think we are not too smart because you can catch us with hooks and worms, or with nets. But fish see this in a different way than humans do. As we see it, you pick apart so many details whereas we come and go with the flow. We understand more than many animals about the nature of recycling;

we understand that by you catching and eating us we become a part of you. We love this ever-becoming! Many of us become fish over and over again because the existence of a water-based life is joyful and what Dawn calls 'fun.'

I laughed as I wrote down his words. For a few moments, we were silent and joined in a lovely, heartfelt way. I felt his passing desire to be a bigger water creature, perhaps an eel or something long and wiggly in the ocean. He flashed images of lives as a salt-water fish in an aquarium and, once, in a public aquarium where lots of people admired him. He was also a snake, kept as a pet, but found that life tiresome and dearly missed the water for, as he shared, *I am primarily a water creature.*

I have had many lives in the waters. I have access to these memories now because I am already partially out of my body. I have been eaten as just a grub, a not fully formed anything. I have also been the eater. I have been many aspects of animals in lakes and ponds and rivers, and in the ocean as well. I have been snatched into the sky at death, taken by a bird—and thus I became part of the bird world. I have been eaten by animals of the land. And I have been taken by my own brothers and sisters of the water.

My message of death is one of recycling—recycling the old so that it becomes part of the new. After my body is dead, my spirit has left; I would like myself to be used in that way, to become a part of something living.

From my perspective, death is a stepping-up of everything into another realm, and a re-becoming of form. My experience of death occurs on many levels. On one level, I go to the bottom of the tank, the lake, the ocean, and allow my body to become again. I am plant, fish, soil, muck, ever re-becoming. In this existence I've asked Dawn to bury my body near a plant, so that I may flower and enjoy this house I've come to see as a home, as well as remind her that we are all re-becoming. This is my fish teaching of wisdom.

On other levels, I am already in the multicolored world of etheric dimensions. Swimming in water is a flying of the spirit—and so, I fly in the ethers as I swim. I convey this to you with words of poetry:

Multicolor bubbles, floating upward;
Turning with my golden tail;
Circles,
Bubbles,
Dancing Joy.

This is already who I am, who I've always been, who I am ever becoming.

Goldfish speak of joy and luck to humans. The ancient Chinese understood us well. Eat fish with joy and remember our wisdom and luck as we become one with you. If you ever need direction or wisdom, tune in to fish. We have a sense of the world that is deep and soulful. I bring wisdom and luck to each of you as I expand into the beyond. I am: Liu Tu, Goldfish of Golden Luck Joy.

MAX'S STORY OF BECOMING

I want to tell you a story about shapeshifting, said my big black Lab, Max, one bright morning as I sat down at my computer. *One that you can add to your book.*

Max was resting comfortably on the floor, just a few feet away from me. As I looked over, he raised his head and let loose with a loud woof. This is typical Max, for he loves to be vocal. Although I have often initiated conversations with Max in hopes of curtailing some of his barking, these talks have never quite worked out the way I'd planned.

While you might think a lot of barking would mean he has a lot to say, Max is not much of an in-depth communicator. When you ask him a question, he answers plainly: yes or no. When asked for longer explanations, he more often than not just walks away. This is why I am often surprised—and honored—when Max comes to share a story with me.

Although to my ear Max's manner of communicating has an amusing, childlike quality, the subjects he speaks of are consistently in deep alliance with the topics I am contemplating. This makes me suspect that Max is a much wiser teacher than he lets on.

This is a true story about me, Max, and about before I used to be the big black dog that I am today, he began. *Here is my story:*

Once upon a time I used to be a little gold fish. Not a goldfish, but a little gold fish who swam in the ocean. I was eaten by a bigger fish and I was scared. But other fish in the belly of this great fish told me not to be afraid. We all swam within the belly of the bigger fish for a while, and then we began to jump out of our bodies and become part of this greater fish. We were like little voices or pieces of ourselves, but at the same time part of the bigger fish. We came to know things from this greater fish. So, now we were also the Great Fish!

We absorbed life and we were absorbed. Soon we became the Great Fish, just as the Great Fish had become from other beings himself—just as we all had! This was an understanding I did not have then, but much later.

Soon, this fish died and was eaten by other fish. And the essence of all of us had choices: to stay with the consciousness of our new fish becoming, or to pop into another existence. It is always like this—pieces of us staying, pieces going and becoming new things. Even if you stay, you become a new thing. I became greater and greater things. Or, you could say, I put my consciousness into other greater things. I directed my consciousness to evolve into greater and greater beings—meaning, larger and larger animals. I was a seal, a whale, an eel, a dolphin-fish, and many other larger fish and marine mammals.

One time I was a salmon who was eaten nearly fully alive by a bear. What an experience! I went directly into the bear and was so amazed by 'bearness' that I stayed and became part of bear. And, you see, when my salmon essence became part of bear, I became part of bear; and so, too, did salmon wisdom become part of bear. This is why it is more important than you realize to pay attention to what you eat, because what you eat is part of what is becoming you and part of what you become!

I loved being bear and I stayed with 'bearness' for many, many lives. Sometimes bear would die and I would choose to become another bear

Good old Max

right away. I also became a bear in other ways, like in the spirit world, in the sense of the way human shamans talk about Bear Spirit. When an ordinary bear dies, part of his 'bearness' also goes to the greater spirit, and sometimes I took this ride and became part of the Great Bear Spirit. I also did this with Salmon Spirit, Seal Spirit, and Whale Spirit. Some of these greater spirits have connections to other worlds (planets) and dimensions, and there are bear spirit presences on other worlds (as well as other animal spirit presences) and I also became part of them.

Right now I am spread over several worlds. One is here with you in the big black dog of Maxness, but another part of me is still largely bear and that is why I like to bark, because it is like the bear's roar and that is still a big part of who I am. So, that is my story of why Max the bear-dog likes to roar!

"That's a great story, Max," I said, holding out my hands to cradle his great black head. "Thank you so much for sharing that with me!"

You are welcome, he said, nudging my hands for a bit of jaw and ear rubbing. *And you are welcome to share it with others. I have thought about telling you this story and now I am happy to tell you for you to write it down.*

I smiled as I watched Max turn around a few times, making his familiar, ready-to-rest circle. Plopping to the ground, he put down his head with a sigh, closed his eyes and took up his position as Office Guardian. Good old Max, I thought. Max the fish, the salmon, the seal, the whale, the bear; Max the great, roaring, barking, dreaming dog, moving gracefully in the interconnected flow of us all, ever becoming.

18

—·—

Beyond the Mirror

For several months, I continued to explore the topic of conscious dying and incarnation with many different animals and beings. Some, like Liu Tu the goldfish, shared awareness of transition as they were leaving their bodies. Others, like Max, shared insights of recalled lives from a physical viewpoint. And still others—like the guide dog mentor—offered unique spirit-based perspectives of their work with beings both in and out of incarnation.

As you delve deeper into the mysteries of life and death and the nexus between the two—which are not really two but one—you begin to move into a much more direct relationship between spirit and manifestation, Barney told me one morning. *In fact, you might begin to see that the screens of life (or death) that you previously saw have now become openings.*

It was one of those curious statements that seem to come true in the exact moment they are heard, for I suddenly experienced precisely what Barney conveyed. While in the past, I had seen the screens of life as somewhat flat displays that one could nonetheless "enter" to feel-sense-experience a life, and "come out" of to observe, I now perceived the screens as full-blown tunnels—actual passageways through dimensions.

This is another instance of an opening of the time/space modality, said Barney. *With this perspective, you move beyond the veil and may observe a direct breathing between spirit and manifested body.*

"Direct breathing between spirit and body," I repeated, for the phrase struck me, sliding inside of me and blossoming in awareness as yet another instance of an inner knowing once dimly perceived, now awakened.

The thrust here is to be clear within the self so as to expand that energy both in oneself and others, Barney continued. *Some of us are even 'spies' in the sense of looking for weaknesses in the veil wherein the breath of spirit might enter more fully.*

In my life as Hahmend, I will be working in such a manner—with a much more direct and open relationship with spirit. As Barney, I held awareness of a spiritual level and could tap into that, though it was not always in my conscious awareness. Working with the consciousness of a dog is very different than working with the consciousness of a human. In some ways, Barney the dog's lifestyle was a preparation for working in the life configuration of a nomadic herder with communication difficulties who fixes his focus on opening others in energetic relationship with death and dying. It was thus important that some of my 'files' from Barney were brought through to consciousness to be seeded in Hahmend, and that the awareness be available to him within his life at certain times.

TRANSITIONS AND TIME

Let us talk more about the transitioning process, Barney pressed on. *But first, let us be clear that I am using a manner of explanation that is symbolic, not literal. Further, it is important to understand that there are many ways to explain avenues of transition and I will do my best to enumerate several. Also, the issue of time must be taken into account.*

You believe in your version of time so deeply that it is difficult to release, and so this structure becomes part of your (human) thinking process. By trying on new variations of time, however, you expand your ability to be more consciously aware.

For example, overlapping time is focused upon simultaneity of time: it is as if you are engaging two or more segments of time in an overlapping fashion. One version, as you've experienced, is to hold different layers of one's selves—child, teenage, and elder self—at the same 'time,' in the same conscious awareness.

Another variation is termed windows of time. A window can be closed or open; it is a special framework you may view through—inside to outside, between rooms or walls. Whereas overlapping time is about simultaneity, windows of time are more like portals that allow one to link or travel in between time frames. Windows of time may also refer to a specific period in which a certain event may occur. That is, a window of time allows you to see things in a fixed way. This is useful for humans who need some structure within which to complete a particular task. Some spirit guides are very keen on using windows of time for this reason.

Let us remember that time is a software program through which you experience your conscious awareness. The 'time' that you know is simply a program—a manner of holding reality so that you can make sense of it. From some aspects of spirit, time is nonexistent; from other levels, time is much more fluid than you understand it.

Let us use a position of fluid time—meaning that we will use the mode or container of time to express certain ideas and sequences, though we will also appreciate a larger construct of time and not such a literal (chronological) interpretation as you are used to—in understanding more about conscious transition. Agreed?

I nodded eagerly.

Within a fluid understanding of time, let us use the helpful concept of time overlaps. When I was the Barney-dog, I used bodily shaking and staring into space as a means of overlapping some of my consciousness into my transition. In preparation for conscious death, I was attempting to link my consciousness (the sum total experiences of Barney the dog) into the spirit body that I would reassume as guide in our group. You must understand, however, that the guide of this group has always been, and always will be—whenever that specific mode of being is engaged.

Barney the dog was attempting to 'download' conscious information into Barney the guide—in a sense, opening a channel so that information could flow both ways. This is close to understanding what conscious death is about: it is about providing an open channel of communication—an actual opening of the multidimensional portal. And, as one aspect opens, it becomes easier and more available for other aspects to open to it. Call it the 'hundredth monkey' theory* on the multidimensional-self level.

I smiled at the small joke as Barney continued.

Now, as I begin another incarnation, I am able to use this channel— to make use of the knowledge of how to do this, as well as make use of the actual channel itself—and create a flow into another being. I am speaking of conscious dying here. This is not typically what all beings do.

As an aside, let us recall a more typical incarnation. This may involve, on opening unto death, a remembering and reviewing of what was done in that life, some 'time' integrating and renewing one's energy, followed by planning for another excursion into the physical. Upon birth, there is a shutting down or forgetting as there is focus on learning the ways of the new body and world so as to experience more of oneself through this particular form.

Many beings of earth reincarnate over and over into this world. It is as if that is their only focus: Earth. No other options exist. This is not to say they don't, however, for as one opens in consciousness, one sees many other possibilities: other planets, galaxies, dimensions; other realities of being. That is another story, however.

Let us stick to Earth, while keeping in mind that these other possibilities do exist. Again, there are many threads here and to even talk about this is necessarily to categorize it in ways that are not entirely accurate.

Questions?

Although we were moving along at a pretty quick pace, I was

---

*The "hundredth monkey" refers to a critical number of beings achieving a new awareness; at that turning point, the theory goes, the awareness is no longer limited to the conscious domain of those specific individuals but becomes part of group consciousness, thus more readily understood, accessible, and available to all.

curious about something. "Can you explain more about the link between conscious death and what might be termed conscious birth? In other words, how much will you remember in your next life?"

A good question! And you are correct to link the two, for the whole purpose of conscious death is to move through realities with intact conscious awareness. Again, I wish to remind you that the 'consciousness' I am speaking of as a segue between lives is different than what you understand as consciousness in your daily life.

The consciousness of which I speak is much more concerned with a multidimensional outlook on reality. This is more a matter of bringing all selves to consciousness—in other words, not so much a knowing of 'first I was this person and then this and then that.' Rather, it is an appreciation of the fluid nature of time and a simultaneous 'holding' of one's selves within the conscious vehicle. In a sense, it is to bring the 'higher self' consciousness of spirit into one's physical existence.

"And this is what some people mean by ascension—not so much bringing one's body into death but spiritualizing the physical, here and now?"

Yes, it is about bringing spiritual awareness within one's physical/ mental/emotional being, about expanding that spiritual dimension into what is normally known at present, in this time frame. Again, it is somewhat difficult to convey this, since your language holds these concepts in a certain way. As an aside, it is helpful to keep in mind that your language is by its nature rather prejudicial in that it assumes certain realities and, thus, also creates certain realities.

Barney paused and I felt a small detour coming on.

Do you know that another way into the multidimensional is by studying and learning various languages? he asked. *As long as an individual is willing to go beyond literal understanding, beyond always translating a different language into one's native tongue—as long as an individual is willing to enter and appreciate the unique reality created by each language, that individual has a foothold in the multidimensional.*

In some ways animal communication serves in this way as well. By communicating with animals, you open to a very different understanding of the world. Some humans will choose not to believe you for this very reason—it is too different than their ordinary reality. As you know, change does not come easily to the ego.

Shapeshifting is also important for this reason. We have covered this previously, but it is significant enough to restate: by shifting into another body, by sharing consciousness or an alternate perspective, one is able to better appreciate the various modes of reality that exist simultaneously. Reality is truly a very individual experience at this point. And yet, what marvelous realities can be created, both individually and in group process! Additionally, all individual realities contribute to the greater reality, whether you are consciously aware of this fact or not.

HAHMEND

To return to your question: how conscious will I be in the life of the shepherd nomad named Hahmend? Some individuals hold open an awakened consciousness through birth. There are stories and legends of babies speaking with full self-knowledge, and indeed such a thing is possible. Usually this is not the case, however, and awakened beings often choose to 'forget' for a period of time so as not to alarm others. Most often a baby speaks only for very specific purposes, as in the case of Buddha or certain Tibetan and Buddhist monks who choose to carry on linkages in this particular way. Other cultures have similar signs that are used by incoming beings as a means of alerting the community to their specialized role.

As for myself, as Hahmend, I will initially hold a veil of forgetting. There will be openings of awareness as I grow as a child. These are designed to help me remember, and all of them have been 'planted' by me. This touches upon the overlapping nature of time. From one perspective, you could say that Barney in spirit preprograms the next life so that Hahmend remembers at certain points. There are variations on this— other helpers may appear in spirit form, through animals or humans, or as sudden rememberings, dreams, déjà vus, et cetera, in order to open the vehicle of Hahmend. It is important to understand that the remembering is already present. In fact, it requires energy to hold the veil of forgetfulness intact.

Hahmend will have the additional benefit of not requiring speech in the traditional mode. His telepathic abilities will be engaged early, as will his emotional body. He will be sensitive to feelings—to what you would term auras *and other energetic realities. As he will not be expected to communicate with others to a large degree, he is free to explore himself in a deeper way. He is given the gift of freedom to be exempt from consensus reality. As a 'misfit,' he is able to work in other ways that, energetically speaking, are actually quite valuable and necessary to the community at large.*

If Hahmend chooses, he will awaken fully to his other lives. This is a matter of choice and it will be interesting to see if and how he chooses to do this. In the background, we will all be present. We always are—just as all of your Dawns are always present with you, just as all people's 'selves' are always present with them. It is up to the individual's conscious focus as to how much of this—and how clearly—the individual vehicle chooses to see.

As one continues to experience more of one's selves, one also begins to open to other selves. The truth is we are all one. This is said over and over, yet saying this and understanding it with your mental body is very different than experiencing this in physical consciousness. As one awakens to this, however, the spiritual self is more deeply integrated into the physical. This corresponds to the notions of heaven on earth, and ascension, and enlightenment—all to varying degrees. One awakens to a greater perception, deeper appreciation, and more conscious holding of one's presence in reality—to one's presence as a creator of reality. And this is truly an awesome unfolding.

CREATIVE INCARNATIONS

Let us review that shapeshifting entails a central focus wherein a grounded 'you' chooses to shift perspectives, Barney began the next morning in a much welcomed summary mode. *Our idea of shapeshifting includes join-ing with other forms of consciousness so that a larger, fuller experience of various worldviews, thought processes, emotional processes, feelings of physical being, and many other aspects may be explored. In other words, the central grounded you merges with another in order to experience that 'other's' being. You then return to your 'home-being' in order to process the information and learn what it means for you in the course of your life and evolution.*

Another form of shapeshifting centers on bringing together various aspects of the larger you. This version allows you to begin working with your other 'selves'—learning to see through their eyes, to understand their life-frames (as situated in different times, in different bodies) so as to bet-ter understand your own.

Now, let us recall that there are many creative ways in which a spirit-being may choose to incarnate. For example, some may choose a set of incarnations in an array of time and space coordinates. One variation is to incarnate in the same space (place), though at different time periods. This is often why some feel a very strong connection to a particular loca-tion—for many of the other 'selves' of that spirit-being are also residing there, though in different times. A similar mode is to incarnate into the same time period, though at different space coordinates. Think of these beings as concurrent in time though 'holding space' in different locations.

Another version is to begin in the same space/time coordinates though in different—let us call them 'modes of becoming.' That is, spirit-being incarnates into one body, though on multiple space/time flows or rivers of being. At certain points when the being is faced with a choice, one being diverges and follows a particular course, with each being following a dif-ferent course throughout the one life (which then seems to become many lives). Since the beginnings were the same, this allows a variety of experi-ences, a variety of paths to be followed, all in one life (that becomes many lives).

Still another version is to hold incarnations in similar space/time coordinates, though in different forms—such as an animal, a plant, a human, and even a weather condition. This may seem more advanced, but let us remember that shapeshifting is by nature a very changeable art and, in truth, we all use all of the methods described above.

To return to the nut of shapeshifting: Let us imagine for a moment that the goal of some of these various incarnations is to open awareness between the 'selves' of one's larger spirit-being. At times, in order to quicken or intensify an awakening, a spirit-being may choose for two or more aspects of self to meet. The purpose is usually to jog memory, for each to spur the consciousness of the other.

As one awakens, especially in the context of shapeshifting, one begins to learn some control. This allows—and often encourages—the student to consciously meet with different aspects of self. The particular pull of this meeting depends upon the original format used. That is, some will focus on 'past' and 'future' lives since their mode was to incarnate in various times. Some may feel pulled to a particular place, while others may feel pulled to meet with particular individuals, to seek out that 'someone' whom they don't yet know (the concept of 'soulmates' often plays a large role here). And in other versions we meet beings of the animal or plant persuasion, and so on. There are as many possible variations as you can creatively imagine—and more. There is no end to possibility!

Another way to think of this is as one large spiritual being that extends several aspects of itself to experience reality in different ways. Each aspect has a life—a personality with a particular agenda. As each aspect grows in spiritual consciousness, it becomes more aware of the others. The idea for many beings is to network these selves—to plant 'meetings' so that a larger form of conscious awakening, experience, and spiritual evolvement may occur.

That is, in meeting your other selves, you not only come to appreciate different perspectives and understand more about the world around (and within) you, but you also have the choice to evolve coexperientially—both of you (which is to say, all of you)—via this meeting and merging.

It is interesting to note that in earlier times on Earth this was a key role of shapeshifting. It is often especially prevalent in the creation of new worlds, or when evolution occurs at a fast rate. Many animal and plant species engage in shapeshifting in order to better acquaint themselves with diverse species in order to further evolutionary possibilities. Sharing of common resources, knowledge, wisdom, and experience is always available, though some species utilize this more than others do. (Bacteria, for example, are some of the prime shapeshifters on this planet.)

If you choose to explore the gamut of evolutionary possibilities (which most often begins through an exploration of various species), you may acquire the idea that evolution is simply about trying on ever more aspects of self. It is about spirit or essence experiencing itself through various forms, faces, bodies, thoughts, and ideas.

Shapeshifting is about opening to this All, so the All can be experienced. It really doesn't matter what body you wear—though some physical forms have unique abilities for both expressing and understanding the All. And that is why shapeshifting in body is so instructive, for you begin to appreciate the incredible diversity of experiencing life through the limitless ways that life can be experienced.

THE ART OF GREATER LIVING

I sat back with a sigh. Barney had a way of meandering our focus into so many unexpected twisty turns of direction that sometimes I felt the conversation itself was a shapeshift. And yet, as was often his habit, Barney brought it around:

By appreciating and engaging the art of conscious death, one is initiated to some degree into the Art of Greater Living. We use this term loosely, to indicate a step into another dimensional perspective. In truth, there is always another step to 'Greater Living'—meaning a segue, a link, a step into something more expansive—for you, something with greater fun.

I laughed as Barney signed off and gave me some quiet time to integrate. While taking a long walk that afternoon, I realized that *the Art of Greater Living* was a term both Zak and Barney had used previously, though in subtle ways. I now sensed in it the beginnings of a much larger unfolding.

'The Art of Greater Living' is an attention getter, Zak stated matter-of-factly a few days later. *It is a 'hook'—a way to engage your thoughts and ideas on living life in a manner in which you are better able to perceive, receive, and experience deeper, larger, greater, more focused and alive, more challenging and engaging aspects of Who You Are. I speak with everyone here—all who read these words.*

I have previously mentioned the need for small deaths, small releases to lighten up and let loose the baggage that weighs one down. Shapeshifting is a means to accomplishing this, for as you unlock your holds and see from ever more perspectives, you gain a greater knowledge and understanding—and experiencing—of the whole of who we are.

Life on this planet unfolds in a unique manner. There is humor in this unfolding—as well as beauty and patience and love and fear. The manner in which you see your world is dependent upon the manner in which you relate to the world. It is also the manner in which you relate to yourself. Do you relate as a victim? Conqueror? Parent or child? Lover? Healer? Or perhaps a yeti? There are many possibilities, many varieties, many flavors.

Experience with shapeshifting may have shown you that all perspectives are valid. All flavors are wonder-filled. All perspectives offer insights.

The Art of Greater Living is something of a self-study. It is to ask yourself how you might relate more deeply with the world and simultaneously relate more widely with the world. By that I mean to hold a number of focuses, a number of perspectives, and operate in a manner by which you are conscious of the interrelations of all.

With a small grunt, Zak closed his eyes and Barney took over.

What Zak is speaking of is a shift in consciousness—a graduation to another level of working with the world, with oneself and others. Another way of relating with All That Is. As we agree, shapeshifting is a tool, a method by which some may choose to learn and graduate to this next level of living. Or, we might say, expand to this manner of living.

Just as death is a transition from one room to another, this expansion also implies a shift from one state of being to another. As you step into that next room—which we will call the Art of Greater Living—you will be asked to remember, to open to a wider, fuller, more 'conscious' experience of consciousness. One in which you will be aware not only of the many facets of your everyday life (including your subconscious life, dream life, mental and emotional life, and so on), but also of the many other selves who work with you on the soul level as alternate expressions of you.

In merging with another being, you merge with another aspect of yourself, of the One, of which you are an aspect. Zak is right, there is humor in this unfolding. Nothing to 'solve' here—simply ever more facets of You to appreciate.

19

—·—

A New Set of I's

For quite some time, Barney had been encouraging me to connect with the member of our group called Tau. Although I valued Barney's insights and recommendations, I frequently felt resistance to talking with Tau. I wasn't sure exactly why, but a fog of indifference kept me from initiating anything on my own.

Leave it to Barney, then, to promote this meeting one morning by flatly stating, *Tau would like to speak with you and begin a dialogue about different modes of perceiving reality.* And, without any space for a response from me, the dialogue began:

This is Tau. Do you have questions before we begin?

"Um," I stalled. "Maybe you could tell me more about who you are and where you come from?"

It is so very interesting to be allowed to watch your life and follow the manner in which you think your thoughts and perceive the world. As I previously mentioned, this is very different from how I am used to inter-acting with a particular reality.

I exist in the spirit world—that is, the 'I' that is speaking to you now is grounded in the spirit world. However, I am aware of several of my other selves, most of which reside in other galaxies and dimensional worlds. I am aware of five of these selves, though I am told there are quite a few more. I have been with this group before, but was gone for a long absence and have now come back to share information. You might think of me as an anthropologist who goes to study remote cultures, then comes home to lecture about it.

I am involved in the shapeshifting group not only because of my interest in the way you and others perceive reality, but also because of my interest in what you call 'dreams.' This is the manner in which I link into shapeshifting. I have had much travel experience in the dreamworld as a shapeshifter—sometimes as a large black feline, one who travels in the jungles and leaps in the trees. I have assumed other shapes as well, but in what you call South America I work with shamans and journeyers in helping them to achieve information through particular animals. The information is mostly of the outer space variety—I often help with assisting them out of their bodies and up beyond the jungle into the outer reaches of what is known as the cosmos in that vernacular. There, we work with all manner of dream images—though not nighttime dreams as you know them—rather, dreams of a kind that are manifest from the deep psyche's creation into real 'space-time.' Sometimes we travel to preexisting dreamscapes, places that already exist in other dimensions; other times we create or add to dreamscapes; and sometimes we build new worlds, new landscapes, though this is usually only with very accomplished shamans and shapeshifters.

If you hold an image of shamans in the jungle, I can help to link you with them and you may learn more about what I do in these dream journeys. I would also appreciate it and consider it an honor if you would allow me to perceive your world, to be a 'visitor' in your consciousness—if this is acceptable. It would allow us to share information and serve to give you experiential awareness of how it feels to be the host in a shapeshift of this type.

"You are welcome to visit," I agreed.

Thank you then. I will contact you in your future time and we will share more.

FALLING FOR THE ILLUSION

This is Tau, he announced the following morning. I smiled at his polite persistence and had to admit I was enjoying his presence much more than I had expected.

Perhaps you are wondering why we have been paired in our group. In many ways, we are at the same level of development, though each in a different sphere of experience. As such, we have much to share. I would like to share with you some of the ways in which I perceive the world. And perhaps you will do the same. So together, in dialogue and through certain experiences, we can begin to grow, teaching each other and learning from each other. Are you interested?

"Of course," I said. "You know I am."

Very well; I will begin. As mentioned, I am something of an adventurer, especially in relation to learning from other cultures. On Earth you think of this mostly in terms of exploring other human societies, but where I am from, we explore various races from different planets, galaxies, and realities, and from alternate time periods and dimensions as well. This is my specialty. I travel on both the time and space continuum to learn from different beings through a variety of their lives and, sometimes, from a variety of their 'selves.'

Here are some of the basics as I see it: Spirit experiences itself in a grand array of manners. The individuation of spirit—what you might call a soul, or a grouping of selves—might be thought of as a strand of spirit, something like a cosmic DNA coding that chooses to further individuate, to experience a variety of lives and learnings.

The idea that many have on Earth—that there is one soul experiencing life—is a simple version of this. But from my understanding, your person is one instance of your greater being—many alternate selves simultaneously learning and experiencing life. In this there is grand diversity, and your soul can choose any form in which to manifest or incarnate. Many on Earth do not utilize their software to feel this at an experiential level.

Most of the beings I work with do use this software. So, one aspect of what I do is to visit with the alternate selves of the various beings I meet and interview. It is as if I take an objective point of view, as your anthropologists do—though I am of the understanding that as I learn about others, I also learn about myself. I am well aware that by seeing others—by looking within the mirror of my reality—I am better understanding myself.

You might think of it as being a journalist who wants to know more about a specific individual. In addition to interviewing that individual, the journalist might also interview the parents, the siblings, the friends, the lovers, and so on, in order to form a larger picture. This is what I do, though the beings I 'inter-view' realize they are all related in essence— they are all versions of the same being.

A shiver flew up my spine and sudden awareness burst open between my eyes. "It is no coincidence that you are talking to me about this, is it?"

Ah! I wasn't sure you would catch on so quickly.

"You are me?" I stammered. "Is this why you are talking to me? Is it because you are also me?"

None other! I am you within our group, from another time, another dimensional world. I work with all of our other selves. It is my job to bring us together, to unite us and help each of us become more aware of the others.

The reason behind my reluctance to talk with Tau fell into place with a thudding domino effect, suddenly setting off many other realizations. It felt like too much, too quick, and I tried to shake it away. "This is too complicated for my brain," I protested, with full intention of stopping the conversation right there and then.

Breathe deeply, he said kindly and slowly. *We are all working together. Most of us are at the same level. We are ready. As our friend Zak notes, 'When one is ripe, the awakenings occur!' It is at this point that we begin to blend our beings, pool the knowledge, experience, wisdom, feelings—everything that we are—in order to open more fully to our oneness.*

In truth, all of us are one. Everyone—isn't that a funny word? Every One. There was a good deal of humor involved in the creation of your language, you know. Our language! This language of English. Other languages, too.

This is your Dawn. Do you think you were named that by accident? It is part of who you are to awaken in this life, to join forces with, and to begin to become aware of, the totality of your being, our Oneness.

A childish wave of petulance rose to the surface. "How do I know this isn't just crazy talk?" I complained. "It feels like whenever I get to some steady ground, the rug is pulled out once again. Here I was feeling pretty good about you and now—look what has happened!"

Is it so hard to believe that we are one? Isn't that what all the animals tell you anyway?

"Well, yes, many animals do say that." But knowing something—even accepting something—mentally is much different than feeling it deep inside. I felt another shiver of fear.

Fear of what?

"Fear that this is a little crazy." Even as I said this, I heard an ancient echo of my constant refrain.

You do have fear of becoming lost in your mind. Why do you think that is so?

I softened as I realized that Tau was doing his best to talk me through this. "Maybe it is the dark side of the mind?" I ventured. "Maybe because I love thinking and using thoughts to arrive at new perspectives, my shadow side is about becoming lost in that place where thoughts are no longer a tool, but where I am being controlled by thoughts. So, that is the fear."

This is a very core fear. And perhaps you notice it reflected in the world around you—stories of paranoia regarding the government, secret agencies, and such. Do you know why that is?

"I suppose it is a projection of our own inner fear—fear that the world isn't real, that things are not what they seem."

Exactly. It is one of the—let us call it 'challenges'—of living on planet Earth, of incarnating into this world. You forget who you are. Not everyone does, of course, and it is true that some species forget less than others do. But for the most part, my observation is that nearly everyone on planet Earth—all beings—hold a certain veil, a certain degree of 'forgetting.'

However, underneath the forgetting is the core knowing that this way of living is all an illusion. It is a game, a program, a means by which you may experience a particular way of being.

So, if you fall for the illusion, accept the illusion, and base your reality on the illusion, it is indeed very frightening to suddenly realize that it is an illusion.

Tau paused. *Right?* he asked.

"I suppose that is true."

And so there are numerous ways of diverting from this information: make a huge joke of it, deny it, anger yourself, become re-involved with the illusion in a very strong way (often found among those who fight for 'causes'), or—if you are just a little open to the idea—blame yourself and think you are a bit crazy. 'You are hearing voices from animals and other beings, for goodness sake! Who do you think you are?'

I conceded a small laugh.

Keep smiling Dawn, said Tau, this other me. *And your world smiles with you.*

MORE QUESTIONS

My thoughts were churning overtime. I couldn't sleep that night for all the ideas and questions that popped and simmered in my brain.

"When you began your anthropological research, did you have the idea that you would find yourself?" I asked Tau the next morning. "And when did you realize that some of the beings you were talking to were actually aspects or selves of you? Or of us, I guess I should say. Also, how did you, among all our selves, get this job? And what about the others? Is the work we are doing right now—all of us—to become more consciously aware of the others? Do most of the others live in similar dualistic worlds, or is it all different?"

Ah! The wheels are turning. This is good. Your excitement and enthusiasm lends energy to our discussions. For some time we were not able to connect with you for the simple reason that you did not have this lightness—and I mean that both by a physical vibration of light and opening as well as the quality of lightness, mentally and psychologically. At the subconscious levels, you held resistance to this information coming in.

"But something shifted," I said, surprising myself in the realization that something drastic *had* shifted.

When you realize that the real work is done on the inner level, you begin to grasp how your selves work together in this reality. There are first—as Zak notes—a number of deaths: death of old perceptions, death of one's investment in the illusion, and so on. As you release this excess baggage, you effect a change in the nexus of your being. All the inner aspects that held firmly onto that baggage (fashioned from perceptions and belief systems) also begin to shift. Sometimes they simply disappear. Other times, they grow and evolve. And so, a new 'guardian' of that particular space appears to present a new way of being to consciousness.

Let us return to shapeshifting for a moment, to tie this material into a deeper understanding of how we shift our shape—which is also how we shift our selves.

Some people on your planet view shapeshifting as something drugged-up shamans do in the jungle. And while it is true that many shamans hold some very ancient material regarding shapeshifting, and that it is very possible for humans to shift into animals or plants, just as it is for some plants and animals to shift into the human form, I would not emphasize this area. It can be easily misunderstood in sensationalistic terms, when in truth the art and science of shapeshifting is very old. In fact, it comes from other planets and is not entirely dualistically based, as are many teachings on Earth. In this sense, it is special and 'case sensitive' material.

Shapeshifting from the perspective of the soul is based on the under-

standing that spirit uses shapes (bodies of all sorts—not solely physical bodies) to experience reality—whatever that reality may be. Once you loosen up your thinking some, you realize that this is a good deal of fun and involves a great deal of creativity.

When a soul strand seeks to learn, it often creates many, many selves—think of them as feelers or nerve receptors—with which to experience different versions of reality. It—which is to say you, us—plays many games at once. Once you open to some of your alternate expressions, you are expanded; things will never be the same.

In order for this to occur, however, there does need to be a certain maturity in all sectors of your being-hood. We might call it an awakening, an initiation, an unfolding of greater awareness.

Various gatekeepers are vigilant regarding the opening of these gates of experience. Certain awareness must occur, particular experiences and journeys completed. Certain shifts must be enacted until a synthesis occurs—a mode of connection that allows understanding to flow between all. Thus, you expand.

I had been rereading Walt Whitman's *Leaves of Grass*, and a line sprang to mind: "Always a knit of identity . . . always distinction . . . always a breed of life."[1] I felt how the whole of the poem was about this expansion—this coming together and enlargement of so many aspects of being. And how, in that expansion, identification with all begins to unfold.

Yes, affirmed Tau. *Your poet termed it 'a sharing of atoms,' and that is precisely what it is. One sees that we all freely share atoms, cells, thoughts, emotions, and many other aspects of our 'selves' in our creation of understanding who we are.*

The more you relax into this, the clearer it becomes. There is no need to prove anything because everything suddenly becomes so clear. Laughter often accompanies such openings. It is interesting to note that I have found laughter (or forms of laughter) to be nearly universal, whatever the being. As many animals have shown you, cosmic humor is very much alive and well in this corner of the galaxy—and good for us all that it is! Laughter is an underestimated mechanism that helps propel beings forward. Often it shakes loose the shackles of old ideas and constraints. It helps to move you outward, opening your awareness into greater and greater expressions and levels of understanding.

But what about mean-spirited laughter, I wondered. What about those who use laughter to deride or ridicule others?

Trust each situation, said Tau. For you it may not be right, but for others it may be what is needed to propel them out of self-doubt and unhappiness. We are talking general levels here. Do you realize you have a way of picking out small details, as if to disagree?

I laughed. "I do like to look at as many aspects of statements as I can. There is a part of me that looks for loopholes."

It is a part of you that still is skeptical. You are quite right that a certain degree of skepticism is important and necessary as we journey. However, I would caution you that the degree of skepticism necessary is far less than what you deem appropriate. (Many will think you need more skepticism. That is their path. Do not worry so much about what others think.) The new journey is about what Dawn thinks. You are our adventurer, Dawn. You are the one who writes and shares our findings with others. This is part of your job.

SHARING EYES—SHARING I'S

Our conversations and adventures continued nearly daily for many months. I shared my ideas, thoughts, and points of view with Tau, and he reciprocated as we joined in consciousness more deeply. At times we were both amused and confused at how different our perceptions of reality could be.

For example, Tau was fascinated with how I could shift from one "frame" of reality to another so quickly. What for me was the simple act of brushing my teeth or feeding my dogs and then going into my office to work was experienced by him as an abrupt shift of realities that was amazing.

As he explained, *I am most often aware of events in a larger context— rather than shifting from one frame to another to the next, I am aware of all simultaneously. Further, the 'I' in relation to each of these events is more aware of the wholeness and interconnections of events. While I do have the ability to shift to one exclusive event—and that is partly why your world is of such interest to me, because you are specialists at this—I have some fear of getting lost in the one place. In addition, it requires an enormous amount of energy for me to experience life in such a manner.*

That Tau was fearful of getting lost in one place was somehow reassuring to me. I appreciated his many insights and assistance, and I was keen to help him as well. I did this by sharing with him numerous "slices" of my reality: perhaps getting lost in one place wasn't as scary—or real—as he imagined.

For the most part, we shared consciousness in small increments: several minutes of popping in and out of joined perception. For me, it was oddly fun to share in this way. Whereas in the past I had joined my consciousness with the physical body of others—raven, fish, dog— to experience their world, now *I* was the physical body being joined. Although I maintained my usual framework of consciousness, when we joined I was also privy to the ways in which Tau saw, felt, and experienced my world.

One beautiful, blue-skied winter day, while driving a snowmachine, I felt Tau connecting, asking if he might ride along. In the spur of the moment, I agreed. As we followed the trail through a hilly area with many evergreens, I felt his astonishment at the intense quality of these Alaskan earth colors, the shapes and textures of trees, and the snow— magical stuff! How light it is and how easily it melts as it flutters down from the branches, falling upon your cheek or neck! How can anything so light and tiny cover so much ground? And how it sparkles in the sun! How tiny rainbows are reflected off individual snowflakes— another incredible, magical thing!

It was exhilarating to see the world through Tau's eyes: to see again the things I had never fully seen in quite that way. As we ventured farther, onto a flat trail, around a frosty swamp and across some ice-covered lakes, I invited Tau deeper, more fully into my body.

Perhaps this was not a sensible thing to do while speeding at forty-five miles per hour, but the idea occurred in such a trusting, natural way that it felt entirely right. I smiled at his thrill on suddenly feeling the snowmachine through my body. I felt his consciousness spread throughout my cells—into my hands, through my fingers; and my heart pounded with his joy as he gently squeezed the throttle. As I shifted back in consciousness, allowing him more control, I was amazed to discover the very light touch he used when guiding the handles. I suddenly experienced—after years of struggling with steering snowma-chines—that by relaxing my usual heavy-handed grip, I could actually guide the machine much more easily. Tau related that in his world all you need to do is think-image a machine to move or turn; that there is a particular 'lightness' of body and thought used in becoming one with a machine, working with it rather than forcing it.

While this seemed right in theory, I was astonished at how easy it was! By feeling Tau's consciousness through my fingers, I, too, was able to turn the machine 'lightly,' easily and smoothly. I found a new sense of steering with the snowmachine: a kind of joining in movement.

After practicing this several times, Tau showed me another way of being one with the machine. In this version, I was aware of a tunnel-like path of energy through which we were riding. It revealed not just where we had been, but where we were going as well. This wasn't exactly where we planned to go, but where we "had been" in the future—where, in fact, we were actually going. As the skeptical part of me starting bristling up, Tau shared the gentle thought that perhaps we could just enjoy the experience.

Laughing, I felt deeper into the tunnel-path and our movement with and through the land. It reminded me of some sled dogs who once explained how they aligned their bellies with the earth and the musher and the land in a flow of movement. Aha! While I once understood the words, here was the experience itself! The trick (and fun) was to move your body with this flow—to feel into it and let go. It was a kind of dance: merging into the flow, and feeling that movement through you—not just you moving through the trail, but the trail moving through you as well.

Thus I joined Tau in embracing the pure enjoyment of experience: our body merging with the land; the white, hilly trail flanked by dark green evergreens; the cool whips of wind across our body; the flashes of bright blue sky and long brilliant rays of sunshine as we glanced into the horizon; the hum of the machine as we raced through space, moving as one; the joy and ecstasy of Being.

20

—·—

Claiming Presence

As Barney had noted early on, "there is nothing like seeing the world completely from another being's eyes to shock you into the realization that the way you experience the world is unique to you."

For me, this was true. Seeing the world from so many different animal viewpoints had revealed to me, beyond a doubt, that our experience of the world "out there" is exceedingly dependent upon the world "in here"—our own distinctive thoughts, observations, and manners of perception. Sharing views with Tau had confirmed this, along with further nudging me into acquiescing that "out there" and "in here" are much more directly connected than we might care to comprehend.

It is one thing to understand this with the mind, but another thing entirely to experience it, Barney agreed. *That is why I recommend shapeshifting so highly as an art and a science to help you realize that the world you perceive is of your own making. This is truly earth-shattering to many. It is why shapeshifting has been feared, why some consider it the devil's art, why some deride it, and why others try to 'put a handle on it'—to make it into something that can be studied and graphed and quantified.*

Did you know that shapeshifting was originally used on Earth as a form of dance and art—as a means of both understanding and holding knowledge? It was knowledge and movement—or, more precisely, knowledge in movement.

I asked if this was the deeper "science" of shapeshifting.

Correct. Such scientific proofs as you use today do not apply in this same way. The science and art of shapeshifting is much older than that. It quite literally exists as knowledge in movement. As such, it is ever expanding, ever changing. This is the core meaning of its name—the shape (of one's body, consciousness, level of knowledge) was ever shifting. Some still understand this in a particular way when they dance in certain rituals and as preludes to a shapeshifting experience.

'Knowledge in movement' is a means of creating and translating soul work in the world. It is essential to understand this relationship, for it is at the core of shapeshifting, and it is the nexus of how the spiritual world intersects with the physical.

"And how is that?"

Let us recall that the physical body has certain rules and structures that exist as a given. And your spirit must work with this basic software in order to manifest a version of itself on Earth—in order to create a 'glove' for its presence on Earth.

Clearly, there is much work to be done while in-body: developing various skills, learning particular languages, modes of thought, and so on. Each individual uses software in a slightly different way and so accesses the world and processes events in a slightly different way.

As a spiritual/physical interface, however, you eventually become aware that you are not only physical but spiritual, too. At first, you may 'slip out' of physicality in dreams, meditation, numinous experiences, and the like. A little crack forms—a doorway of sorts—and you find you have the conscious ability to exist as a spiritual being as well as a physical being.

From the spiritual perspective, physical bodies are mutable. From the physical point of view, this may or may not be true, depending upon your beliefs. Thus, much of the 'shift' in shapeshifting is centered on deepening one's tone or vibration so as to match the vibration of essence itself. At that plane of being, you can become anything—you can use that vibration to access infinite perspectives—because you are *essence.*

As you become more familiar and comfortable with the multidimensional format, this becomes easier to accomplish. You are more at home in both your body and spiritual presence, and more open to experience other manners of being, other modes of perception.

Now, let us bring this around to Tau and his experience of the world. Tau has experience with unity but not as much with diversity, and this is why he is interested in the way you are able to move 'from one thing to another' with what appears to him to be astonishing speed. Your focus is more on diversity, comparisons, and contradictions—how things are similar and how they are different. Duality again. That is your program; that is the way much of Earth is revealed.

But—as you are beginning to recognize—both diversity and unity can be held in simultaneity. Thus, you come to experience in appreciation both the underlying essence of life as well as the marvelous cascade of diversity.

Barney paused and I felt a wave of encouragement. *Trust the unfolding of what is occurring around you and within you,* he added gently, as if in anticipation of what was to come.

NEW VISTAS OF EXPERIENCE

Joining consciousness with Tau for longer periods of time ushered in further changes in perception. While these shifts sometimes seemed subtle on the surface, they were often deeply transforming. That is, simple perceptions frequently struck me in totally new ways, causing me to observe ever more clearly that it is not so much a matter of what we see as how we see it—or, who we are in consciousness as we see it.

For example, one morning while watching the fish in the aquarium, I noticed a reflection in the tank of the kitchen's bay window, on the other side of the house. The small rectangular images inside the tank perfectly revealed the window's vista of blue-gray sky with low puffed clouds nestling atop white-tipped mountains. This was not so strange, of course; it was simple science, easily explained by reflecting waves of light on glass. And yet the way in which I saw the reflection—call it my *relationship* to this reflection—triggered something within.

I wondered why I had never noticed the window's reflection before. Surely it had been there many times. Perhaps my vision had been so focused on the movement of the fish that I simply didn't apprehend other fields of perspective. I thought these things as I watched the fish glide through the blue-gray sky, their bellies skimming the pointy mountaintops, their bodies moving in and out of the clouds' mirrored reflection: water to air and mist and back to water again. As I softened my gaze, I also saw silvery shadows of the fish: fishy doubles that reflected upon the reflection of the window. And as I released even further my habitual way of seeing, I watched with delight as some of the fish broke away from their reflections, swimming quite deliberately into the dark mountain and gray-skied reflection that was also a doorway.

It's a portal, I exclaimed. And, in that early morning frame of fanciful, open-ended possibilities, I considered: *Why not go inside?*

There is a kind of giddy silliness that accompanies some awakenings, and so it was for me. Journeying into the fluidity of water, accompanied by the cheerful encouragement of the Fish People, was great fun, but gliding through the doorway of the mountain, flying into the brightly reflected, brisk, blue-gray sky was exhilarating. I sailed into alignment with the expansive joy that was so cleverly compacted into Barney's phrase—*knowledge in movement*—and knew it to be perfectly true.

Back in my chair, I felt a thrumming, expansive sense of center. I marveled at how a simple shift in perception can act as such a potent key, how the unlocking of something so vast can be held as such a tiny seed inside us all along. Just like the movement in and out of the circle of projections, I once again saw how going beyond ourselves, we also move more deeply into ourselves, and back again, beyond—a great spiraling orbit of self. And how one moment, when perhaps you least expect it, a door flings wide open, exposing with sudden clarity that "out there" is really, truly, "in here"—that, in fact, there is no door. That out there and in here are simply two perspectives that are also one, indelibly infused in this particular game, on this particular planet, alternate expressions of an underlying essence, an energetic suchness both unified and diverse.

BEYOND REFLECTION: THE DOLPHINS OF DELORA

Several weeks later, while on vacation in Mexico, I made the acquaintance of two young dolphins who were very familiar with the ways of humans. After some initial introductions, they agreed to talk with me further. And that is how, upon my return home, I came to question them about reality and perception and shapeshifting. This, in turn, led to meeting with a larger group who called themselves The Dolphins of Delora.* This collective was formed of dolphin consciousness that was manifest both as physical dolphins and as a spiritual presence of guidance.

As they explained it, *Many of us are engaged in doing 'fun' things—leaping up and flying through the air. These are 'dolphin things,' designed to encourage you to open. By having fun, you open your mind to new ways of being, new possibilities, and new ways of thinking.*

We are about awakening dormant modes of consciousness, about meeting and forming meaningful encounters between dolphins and humans, to help you understand that appearance is also an illusion.

I sensed the group as keenly sensitive and felt a sonar wave of dolphin presence scanning my body consciousness, determining the specific tone of awareness with which to relate.

Our subject today is about the inner world opening to the outer world,

---

*The dolphins noted Delora as the name of both a small coastal town in Greece and a planet "from which we sometimes reside." I later understood Delora to signify a kind of multidimensional meeting and resting spot from which this group of dolphins (and perhaps others) could share and disseminate information.

about establishing a connection between inner and outer, and about using inner resources to create and manifest a new form of reality in the outer world, they began.

It is important to realize that the differentiation of inner world and outer world is part of the nature of duality that is prevalent on this planet. Your brain physiology perceives both an inner and an outer world. For dolphins this is not the case. We perceive levels of awareness in a fluid manner. All is interconnected. There are no doorways, no gateways, no portals—rather, it is simply a matter of shifting one's vibration to that aspect of being where all are present.

Our meeting place is where we are one and have always been one. Our goal in working with humans is to bring this thought to your consciousness so that you may deepen in understanding and connection—not only with fellow animals and humans, the plants and planet, but with the deeper nature of your self.

Dolphins—at least most of us—work with humans in the nature of multidimensionality and holographic thought. We exist on many levels simultaneously, and it is this aspect that is our bridge to human remembering.

As you become more aware of your multidimensional nature, experiencing glimpses into other realities, dimensions, and aspects of being, you may connect yourselves between these various levels. Just as you might engage upon an intercultural or cross-cultural study, this is interdimensional learning and understanding.

THE NATURE OF PROCLIVITY

The Dolphins of Delora were very precise communicators. As they signed off, they announced that they would share more the following day. And, they did:

Our talk today focuses on the nature of proclivity and how our propensities or tendencies affect both the 'outer' experience of reality and the 'inner' shaping of reality.

This is an in-depth subject and requires some background infor-mation. We will begin with the nature of the human race and the dol-phin presence on Earth at this time. Humans were formed as a melding between sky and earth. That is to say, your nature (and base material) is from the earth, but your seeds are from the stars. There is much history connected with this story, but at this time let us simply say that humans are both from the earth and from that which exists beyond the earth. That is your core proclivity: both yearning for earth and yearning to be beyond the earth. That is the nature of your duality—the nature of dual consciousness that pervades every aspect of your life.

Dolphins came in your recent history as an adjunct to your own remem-bering. We came to swim through the waters not only of your oceans, but also of the waters of your dreams and memories. We exist to awaken within you a joyful remembering of your 'past' and 'future.' We come to help you recall the nature of your presence on Earth, the core reason why you entered into incarnation on this particular formation of duality consciousness.

Within the nature of the human proclivity, there must always be an 'other.' Your brain physiology, physical make up, body systems, and ways of life are all infused with duality, and this is what we mean when we say it is the nature of your proclivity.

For dolphins, the core pattern is not one of duality but one of fluidity. Our presence is meant to intersect and interact with your own. We bring the nature of fluidity to your duality so that duality and unity can merge in a manner that has never been apprehended on Earth before (at least not in present human remembering).

The nature of proclivity is a tool—a means or vehicle that one uses to attain a certain level of understanding. At some point, however, proclivity is transcended. Thus, one opens to a new view and comprehension of real-ity. This is the point at which you, as a species, now stand.

Our lesson today is to listen to that which lies beyond you—to honor your proclivities while allowing yourself to extend beyond them. This brings you to a new mode of being: a new manner of living in a new set of proclivities.

MOVING THROUGH REALITY

Today we wish to address the nature of moving through reality in a less encumbered way, began the dolphins once again the following morning. *By this we mean moving through your proclivities to arrive at a clearer perception of yourself and the world which you create, inhabit, and adorn with your experiences and interpretations of experience. That is to say, your comprehension of the world varies according to the degree that you consciously manifest and have knowledge of your manifesting tendencies.*

For example, some humans assign advanced attributes to dolphins. While dolphins as a species do have a very special purpose in working with humans, it would be a mistake to believe that all dolphins, in their mammalian form, have direct knowledge of this. Quite often, humans are necessary to spark a particular dolphin's remembering. This is something humans do not always acknowledge. Many are still stuck in the 'student' aspect of our relationship. It is essential to understand that often you are teachers to dolphins as well—and to the planet. Our relationship is very much about this meeting and interacting.

The paradigm of moving through reality unencumbered by one's 'baggage' corresponds to what you learned about communication with animals: one must be aware of one's own blocks, prejudices, belief systems, and proclivities. The more one clears these on a conscious level, the more one is able to hear all messages, and the less slanted will be the interpretation or translation.

As you struggle to see or hear or be in a new way, a degree of muffling may occur because you are not yet in balance. This is the nature of moving through reality without one's proclivities so close at hand. It feels new and odd and you question yourself because it seems as if you are the only one traveling around in this manner. But as you trust yourself and your experiences, you realize that because it is valid for you, it is valid. Thus you begin to awaken a state of being through which you can creatively manifest at a conscious level and appreciate what this means.

We bring the fluid nature of your memories to you. We bring the fluid nature of remembering to all. As you free yourself, you free the world. That is the level of truth at which we reside.

KNOWING WHO WE ARE

Further talks with the Dolphins of Delora—who also called themselves the Dolphins of Remembering—helped me to amplify what might be called a "fluid" chord of awareness. I understood more clearly what Barney meant by knowledge in movement. I began to feel more often a thrilling openness of body and thoughts—a permeated awareness of life living through me.

Tau and I also continued to play with alternate ways of seeing and being. As aspects of one, we knew great similarity, yet held distinct, unique flavors to our perceptions. And so we bounced back and forth, teaching and learning, each of us adding juicy layers of experience. For instance, Tau shared his version of tapping into the flowing manner in which plants and trees breathe and feel and "see" the world. And, going deeper still, how to become like plants and trees—as sentient, sensory extensions of planet Earth experiencing herself. Through such journeys of consciousness, I felt keener attunement to the larger movement of life-energy—and even something beyond that—infusing all beings.

And yet, I also continued to struggle. Not quite resonating in the sweet spot of balance, I sometimes felt, as the dolphins had termed it, a "degree of muffling."

One morning, while waiting for my computer to finish an update, I gazed at the image on the monitor screen: the close-up face of a leopard. His glance was one of sharp intensity: eyes shining bright green-gold, pupils focused in pinpoint precision. As we stared at each other, I felt the rumble of a familiar shift.

The screen shimmered and the image came alive. Suddenly I saw: the leopard was not only looking at me, but through me, and, through me, seeing himself. An unspoken invitation to likewise look through his eyes was extended—to employ this circular manner of perception to see myself. And so consciousness looped around—leopard seeing leopard through me, me seeing me through leopard . . .

I feel the rhythm of his breathing, his pulsing of life with measured focus. Such a small shift to such remarkable fullness as the deeper presence of Leopard Spirit emerges! Within my framework of consciousness in this moment, this seems entirely plausible and "real." I sense a part of me having asked a question—not necessarily in this moment; not a request formed with words and ideas, but a part of me seeking, still searching for something I don't quite want to see.

And I get—very quickly and very unexpectedly, in a way that I know it is absolutely real, no fooling oneself here: *Your greatest fear is your greatest strength.* Although this is a truth I have heard before and perhaps have even written about, for the first time I feel this deeply.

As Leopard Spirit tells me, *I know who I am.* And that is his power—he *knows* himself in a way that most animals know themselves. They do not judge themselves—faster, slower, fatter, thinner, more beautiful, and so forth. No, they are self-possessed, meaning they are comfortable within their skin or fur or feathers or scales. They *know* the essential suchness of who they are because they live it; they exemplify it in the world to themselves and to all others, all the world.

This is your problem, says Leopard Spirit at last, meaning humanity's problem—which, of course, is my problem, too.

"The problem of not knowing who we are," I say in a merging of consciousness in which I now know that while thoughts are one of humanity's greatest assets, they are often our greatest problem. Why? Because we all so often use our thoughts—our rationalities, our belief systems, our addictions—as diversions from our greatest fear: knowing ourselves. We are afraid of the greatness of who we are.

And for a moment I am jostled by a wave of anger, not just from Leopard Spirit, but from a group of animals. Not a personal anger, as we humans think of anger, but an astonished outrage that we have so much—have gone so far—and yet know so little. Not a chiding or judging anger, but a kind of amazement and frustration because this illusion has gone on for so very long . . .

Sometimes this is why we attack and eat you, said Leopard Spirit. *Sometimes the energy is too much and we attempt to shake you up by confronting you face to face, eyeball to eyeball. There were times when humans engaged animals in these ways and a deeper dance was known. You are indeed becoming alienated, detached from your own deeper emotions. Look at how you kill animals now. Humanely you say. Ha! There is nothing humane in making a technology of killing. Much better to face your prey, look him in the eye, and allow the dance to unfold.*

The Leopard Spirit's words reminded me of a shapeshifting experience I once had with an African lion, who similarly told me that lions *claim their presence*. It was the lion's observation that humans allow fear to control them. *Humans need to learn to eat their fear*, the lion had said. *To claim their presence*. And by claiming one's presence, he maintained, one puts fear in its proper place.[1]

This was intimately connected in my mind with a story about the author J. Allen Boone, who was known to travel into African jungles without a weapon, believing that any animals he encountered would be friendly to him if his thoughts about them were friendly.[2] For a long time, I felt that Boone was foolhardy in this respect. What if he caught a tiger on a bad day, or met a gorilla with a temper? Just because you can talk with animals doesn't necessarily mean you can convince a hungry one not to eat you, after all.

And yet the way the lion had shared his statement: *by claiming one's presence one puts fear in its proper place*—had shifted something in my thinking, causing me to see in a new way. Boone had long observed that "right relations" with the world are only possible outwardly when they have first been made so inwardly, and he lived this truth.[3] Sitting in the jungle without a weapon was much more than mere confidence or bravado for Boone, and it had nothing at all to do with the other animals. Rather, by claiming his *presence*, Boone had found "right relations" within himself. By shifting the shape of his consciousness to a new way of being, he also naturally reshaped his relationship with all others: the lion, the jungle, the world.

THE ULTIMATE MYSTERY OF ALL

It is a simple concept, but difficult for some humans to feel, commented Barney, and I had to agree. But why should it be so complicated to find right relations within ourselves? Why should it be so terribly tricky to remember who we really are?

I'll make this short and concise, said Zak. I glanced down at him, lying comfortably beneath my desk. Rubbing his warm golden fur with my toes, I smiled at old Master Zak, taking it all in, commenting with brevity and levity when needed. I closed my eyes and listened closely:

The deeper you open within yourself, the nearer you arrive—to all: to understanding, to sensing and remembering who you are and what you are here to be.

Above all, that is the task of awakening. Some feel this can be done through love or battle or salvation or ascetic means. What I know is simply a matter of remembering—of awakening. It isn't to say that all of those modes of traveling aren't useful—they are to various personality types. Though at the core of all is the gift of remembering . . . the mystery of remembering. It is a gift you hold throughout your life, and each of us decides when to open this gift, this mystery.

Remembering, like death, is not the end of the line. It is simply a transition to another level of the adventure, allowing another type of unfolding to occur.

What Zak knows

For now, you sense the nearness of the mystery. You touch it daily—you have your fingers upon the box, and yet you allow yourself the indulgence of forgetting. Right now you are very close for you can feel the flutter of forgetting, remembering, forgetting, remembering—like the beat of a hummingbird's wings.

It is this remembering that is the key to the Art of Greater Living. You do not have to go anywhere or find anything. All you need is right here, right now; just as it has always been and will ever be. And that is the Ultimate Mystery of All.

21

———

Here and Now

Each year in the middle of August, when the bright purple fireweed blooms nearly to the apex of its towering, leafy stalks, I remember the day when Barney made his smooth transition from this world.

The anniversary of the death of a loved one is often a significant event for humans, Barney notes on one of these fine summer days. *The human mind loves to calculate and quantify, so most often a death date is a mental reminder of a passing away—though it is much more a memory for the living than for the dead. As you loosen your grasp of this type of relationship with the nature of time and space, however, you may find such dates also losing significance.*

Sitting on the top step of the back deck, I look toward his grave. It is a clear, brilliant day, and three ravens swoop in spirals, calling to each other, high in the sky. In the distance low clouds curl around the mountain bases and a small stretch of inlet water glimmers silvery blue. But Barney's grave marker is gone, nowhere to be seen, swallowed whole by a profusion of wild fireweed.

Let us open to a greater understanding of the nature of death, he suggests in his distinctively calm and gentle manner. *Let us re-member with our greater selves and thus open to a larger understanding of inherent connection with All That Is. At deeper levels, I am always with you, just as we all are with each other, all the 'time.'*

Dawn and Barney

Feel your presence at this place where we are all connected. It is here you will discover the secret of shapeshifting, and of all that we are. Remember that shapeshifting is about meeting—a meeting of consciousness, a meeting of mind, of heart and soul. You need only remember yourself and all will be fine. No matter what you are doing, remembering who you are allows for clarity in the now.

I smile as I feel him sitting next to me, just as we have so often shared a few moments on bright summer days in the past. His fluffy white fur and moist black nose lean into my body and nowhere is now here, our spirits shining vast and clear as the cool blue sky.

What you need is always right here, right now, my good pal Barney reminds me once again. *That is all you need to know.*

A FEW MOMENTS OF NOW

One rainy afternoon not too long ago, I sat at the kitchen table reading a final draft of this manuscript. It was a quiet, unhurried afternoon, and I had been enjoying the pleasant comings and goings of the many animals and spirit-beings who contributed their insights, humor, and wisdom to this book.

It was a nice little reunion: Rabbit Teacher and the Penguin People; the Spirits of the Fish on Land and the Birds of the Wide White Wings; cherished Yeti and coconspirator Tau; the Whale People and Raven People, and Elephant too; the Dream Guides, Jen the cactus, and so many more. Zak and Max lay resting on the floor and Barney's generous presence hovered near. Reading through our adventures, my heart was touched by the many friends who joined me for a remembered laugh, last-minute edit, or simple moment of shared awareness around the table.

Looking back to the beginning, it seemed to have happened a long time ago: discovering a oneness of spirit through such a diverse array of perspectives; recovering clarity in dark areas of fear and emotional holding; uncovering knowledge that has waited for just the right time to blossom into consciousness; and, through it all, experiencing the awe and joy of shared awareness. And yet, reading about it again, it also felt totally new, totally now. Time is funny that way.

As I took a short break, gazing out the window, pondering nothing in particular, I felt myself drift. With a flickered shift of perception, I saw myself sitting at this table on a very early morning, many years before: coming into the kitchen from the hallway to fetch Barney a bowl of water only a few short hours before he died. I saw again the spirit-friends of Barney gathered around this table, where now I sat as one of them. I felt myself present in both these places, both these times—here and there, then and now—but also joined, linked in a free-flowing stream of awareness.

With a small laugh, I felt the palpable truth of what Barney so often shared: that as we begin to live in a more centered moment of being, we see that all is available in the ever-present flow of here and now.

Some awakenings come to us in heart-rushing gasps while others slip in calm as the first pale sliver of morning sky. For me, the highs of amazement were sliding ever more comfortably into the centered familiarity of trust and acceptance, gratitude and amusement. I turned to Zak and Max, snoozing loudly on the hardwood floors. Okay, sometimes amusement reigns supreme.

A pale gray light welled through the window. Still adrift in the relaxed openness of here and now, I was moved by how beautifully it formed a luminous backdrop to the diminutive house spider descending from the light fan upon the ceiling. Rappelling downward, backlit by the gray-white stage, she dangled midair upon her translucent thread, a mere few inches from my nose.

During each book I have written, a spider has approached, offering a message of encouragement or support. Sensing that she brought a similar type of blessing, I was charmed by her timing. Here, in the middle of now, she descends in perfect accord. And as I gaze at the golden light body of Spider, shimmering her vastness through the small house spider, gently suspended from her web in space and time, she begins:

Once again, Spider Energy brings to you a threading together of ideas, thoughts, images, experiences, and openings for all.

We would like to address the idea of the Art of Greater Living as a process of weaving. We are most known for our webs of intricacy and beauty. Many of our webs are photographed in the early morning, still wet with dew. Others are seen with ash or dust settled upon them, so that you can perceive them more clearly. This is what you are attempting to do: to give your readers an image of the web of life. In order to more clearly perceive the web, you have dusted it with some thoughts, ideas, and experiences of your own.

Every individual web is different yet the essence of all webs is one. Webs are a creation of cooperation: the spider and her web-making abilities, the spider and the tree twigs or flower petals or house corners around which she builds her web. All is interrelation and the result of the weaving of the web.

There is a phrase we have plucked from your mind to illustrate the essence of what we mean: the web that has no weaver *is the Oneness that underlies all creation. It is the primal web, the template of this world, the chi or life force that holds all together. It is you and it is I, all of us, the spiders, the mocking birds, the monkeys, the whales. We are all part of this web of life, all of the essence of the web that has no weaver.*

Here we come to the crux of creation. For surely someone, or some energy, must have woven the first web? But this is to become entangled in the notions of time—another web! To truly understand the web that has no weaver, you must pass through the web of time and space and apprehend the All That Is. This, we maintain, is the Art of Greater Living. This is the key to holding the divine within the expression of who you are in this life. This is the gateway through which you transform from a sleeping human to one who is awakened.

We send our greetings to the world of humans, to encourage more web building and beauty in our world. We are the expression of the energy of web weaving, of the original web, the One which holds us all together— the Oneness within us all. We are all part of the web that has no weaver. And, we are all the weavers of that web.

A GRAND, GREAT EXPERIMENT
FULL OF WONDERS AND DELIGHT

The more intimately we acquaint ourselves with the mystery of being, the more finely we attune ourselves to that pulsing hum of oneness that permeates all beings. The more we open to the grand adventure of diversity coursing through our fins and feathers, bones and wings, the more we love and appreciate all forms of life for the vital, magnificent expressions of spirit that we are. It is in just this way that shapeshifting opens us to the core of relationship—and reality—itself.

Consider this an expansion into the limitless possibility of form and a deepening into the larger presence of who you are, said Zak as he joined my thoughts from one of his favored places on the floor.

Did you know that humans are now at a point of evolution where this deepening and expanding may be possible in a new way? That there is an opportunity for the human species to open to the unconscious in a much more conscious way, to embody spirit so as to see this—know this, be this—in a much more profoundly human way?

I nodded in recognition. Many have noted this stepping up of awareness—the sense of an imminent, massive shift in the shape of global consciousness: a grand revolution in planetary evolution.

Earth is ripe for this, agreed Zak with a sweep of his tail. *It is her next transition. And it is happening now.*

It is said that there is no time other than now, and this is indeed so. This is nothing new. What shifts in understanding is not "the now," but conscious awareness of now.

"Yes!" I exclaimed, for Zak's words struck me as exactly so. Now is a feeling state that blossoms inside of us as we discover that every moment, every instance, is a point in which we may open to the fullness of who we are.

The key to deep understanding is experience, he concurred. *Now is not really a 'when'—nor space a 'where.' Nowness is simply a deepening into what already is. It is a feeling that opens connection with all—not only humans, but animals and plants, nature beings and elementals, the stars and planets, other dimensions of reality and other aspects of the evolving You. What I am speaking of is direct experience, a relation of spirit to the essence of presence, a mode of being that is all ways and always—timeless, ever present.*

As Zak paused—for emphasis, perhaps—I turned to look at him. And as our eyes connected, our I's merged. Brown eyes ablaze through mine, he woofed, and I jumped back in delight. *'Be here now' is the gist of who we are!*

How wonderful it is to tumble into harmony with a good friend! Do you feel it, too?

Yes, a feeling into nowness is an expansion of the deeper layers of our being, he continued—not missing a beat. *And, as you move into direct conscious knowledge of how our thoughts create our reality, you apprehend another way of interacting with the world.*

As we dream ourselves awake, we shift not only the shape of our own conscious awareness, but the very nature of reality itself.

As you let go of the container—as you shift to the 'dancer becoming the dance'—you have a taste of what this Be Here Now is like. You simply are, here and now: Being.

Can we open ourselves to such magnificence?

This is when the fun begins—for Earth is suddenly seen for what she is: a grand, great experiment full of wonders and delights. Grounded in the essence of who you are, you may enjoy the illusion for what it is; you may participate to learn more about creation and destruction, about the power of your mind, body, emotions, and further awakening of awareness.

You needn't go anywhere or do anything because you are already here. This is your life—all of you reading this right here, right now—in each moment, ever-present: a life of awakening unto You.

ONE LAST DREAM

One early morning, I awoke from a terrific dream. It was so vivid and powerful that its images and ideas still pulsed through my body as I opened my eyes. It was one of those multileveled dreams—one in which I was 'me' but also a spirit self that was part observer, part participant.

The dream opened with a visual of Earth cut in half—the kind of graphic that elementary science books are fond of using when describing the various layers of our planet. But unlike static images in a textbook, this visual reverberated with activity. What I saw were so many layers of colors and movement: a frenzied red-orange molten center; a dark, dense layer that pulsed—magnetic, strong, and powerful; several grid-like layers, electric and blue, like thin moving fields; and many more. Each layer had a unique consistency, pattern and—yes, consciousness.

There were layers upon layers of water, and I noticed differences in such things as "lower waters" and "upper waters." Indeed, nearer the surface crust there were ever more delineations, and the patterns and colors—swirling blues, ripe greens, jagged browns—were exceedingly varied and ornate.

As I moved closer in perspective, I was aware that each layer was actually many layers, and—closer still—that the divisions between layers were not so much rigid separations as stratums of merging. So, too, were there many voices—many interrelated presences alive and aware, each responsible for sharing its own unique presence, each vibrating with its own flashing pulse that was both a tone and a color and—I saw now—harmonically related to the deeper pulse that beats through every aspect of life on Earth. How exquisite!

I was reminded then of how I connect with large fields of presences, such as the Whale People or the energy of Elephant, the Spirit of Raven or the Birds of the Wide White Wings. For me, these are all variations of group consciousness, held by a unifying force and awareness. While the collective energy of an animal people may sound different in tone than animal spirit energy or an ancient order of animals, all are similarly held by a sentient consciousness, a presence with whom we can all connect and learn from, should we choose to do so.

It is difficult to explain in words but, of course, we must always try. This is what I heard in the dream as I was observing the image of Earth and urging myself to remember when I awoke—for part of me had been *awake* in the dream, quite aware that another part of me was sleeping. Everything I saw, felt, and heard was alive and throbbing; so many insights flooding my awareness that I knew the best I could do was simply experience and hope the gist would be carried through to waking consciousness.

I was then aware of being in a large meeting hall—not a meeting hall as we know it in our human way, but a kind of deep-down-in-the-ocean or far-out-in-space setting that had a vague sci-fi atmosphere. And yet, the vivid details of the room—the very molecules of air that effused through this space—were so crisply vibrant that it felt realer than real. Not only that, but I recalled being here before! I remembered many of the beings sitting around the tall, elegant meeting table, which was unlike any I had known in the waking world. How was it that we did not remember this design? For as I looked closer, I realized the table was remarkably simple, natural, and energetically centering.

This was a meeting of the Council of Earth (also known by other names), and the subject of the discussion was the "Surface People." Many of us were in attendance as listeners and students. I was mildly surprised but fully accepting—as you sometimes are in dreams—to find that I was simultaneously sitting on the Council as a speaker and in the audience as an observer, watching, listening, learning.

The Council was explaining how those called to know about the Council—which now includes you, as the larger memory unfolds—are also called to remember that we are all members. We are called to remember ourselves as we come together again in fuller awareness; called to remember that we are all part of something much greater than we normally suspect.

The Council then shared their main concern for the Surface People—those of us living with our consciousness limited to the surface of the planet, those of us living primarily on the surface of our awareness. And the concern was this: our resistance in awakening to deeper levels. As a key example, they showed this in terms of the political arena. As an observer of the Council, I sensed dismay at the levels of corruption, fraud, fear, and fixation on money and control of power that had diverted so many humans from breaking through to a larger awareness that would allow all of us to genuinely feel our connection not only with the wisdom and delight of our deeper selves and others, but with Earth herself. How could this have happened? And why?

And then, just as a wave of an overwhelming frustration, sadness, and overall disappointment threatened to crash over me, I saw a shimmering movement from the Dolphin People. From their mind-beings, they shared an image of the dolphins on Earth: joyous creatures leaping and arcing over turquoise waves in the ocean. On a large, flat screen which appeared in front of us, we watched the physical dolphins leaping and splashing; in a vertical stance, half in the water and half out, they hopped backward, beckoning us with clicks and nods and those huge beguiling dolphin smiles, until we were all smiling and laughing too. This living film then shifted to other animal scenes: a group of ants aerating soil beneath a flower bed; brightly shining bees buzzing from flower to vibrant flower and back to a golden, gleaming hive; dragonflies glittering the sky with their iridescent wings—and I was awash in the group's responsiveness to the innate beauty and tremendous feeling of gratitude for these small beings who do so much. It was as if our hearts were swelling upward and outward, as if our deeper feelings—the ones we always felt but covered over with so much "stuff"—were suddenly coming to light, as if our inner selves were literally illumined and illuminating through our bodies in this joyous state of being.

We watched the Elephant People—such a proud, strong people!—walking majestically through sun-dappled forest. The Fox People showed us their presence in so many parts of the world and we appreciated their fine, delicate movements, their sensitivity to the cycles of the earth, the contours and varying presence of the land. The Raven People, the Polar Bears, the Iguana People, the Crocodiles—each group showed itself like a bubble of consciousness that any one of us could access simply by attuning ourselves and merging in deeper relationship.

There was so much! Worlds within worlds—all these bright sparks of awareness, movement, vitality—and these words are merely wisps of understanding, for it is not even awareness, movement, or vitality as we pretend to know it in our surface way, but a deep, abiding love and connection for who we are in all our wholeness, with all our mindful, heartfelt connections to countless layers of self and selves, to all peoples—plant, mineral, animal, human, sky, star, and more—of Earth, and beyond.

There is a central pulse of such pleasure for our diverse presence on Earth that runs like a song—truly, like a song—throughout our planet.

And between these worlds within worlds—which I now saw were not really separated at all, but constantly flowing, merging, one into another. I understood not just with my mind, but with my being, that this is how it is all over—even on the surface. Yet when we limit our awareness, the very living of our lives, we see only the separation. We so fear the greatness—the fullness of who we really are—that we resist awakening. And so we scuttle up to the surface of things, using only one thin slice of consciousness, diverting our thoughts with so much activity and noise and busyness, so as to avoid the truth we all know deep inside: the ecstatic awareness of our expansive heart.

ALL YOU NEED TO KNOW

The dream took several hours to unfold, bits of it reconnecting me like long-forgotten spiritual synapses, depths to surface and back again, a little at a time.

The dream takes a myriad of lifetimes to unfold—the adventure-filled stories of our many, many selves sparkling bright. As we remember ourselves, we recall all these songs of being, and more. As members who re-member, we ignite the infinite connections of memory and imagination, experience and transformation. We are the dreamers, dancing the dream awake.

As a small laugh of deeper being burbles up to consciousness, I recall the sensation of simultaneously being on the Earth Council and watching the Council, hoping to learn more. I feel again the vast concern and love from the Council's presence—and, the veiled shadow of a smile that arises as the first light of awakening dawns upon us all.

Do you remember?

How is it we are both something so big and something so small? Such an extraordinary game we Surface People play: pretending not to recognize the truth of belonging that flows constantly through our blood and bones and being, linking us to all Ten Thousand things upon this planet, this galaxy, this Universal One.

Barney

As creators and translators of soul work in this world, how can we not help but smile in deep and cherished recognition at all we see and feel and be? Every moment shimmers with such limitless possibility—aspects of awakening cleverly tucked away, artfully scattered, hidden deep and oh so blatantly shining throughout our daily lives.

For deep down, we know; we know: All of us awakening from the dreamy game, laughing with elation in the Great Belonging, dancing in delight with the All That Is, shining the fullness of who we all—really, most joyfully—are.

My heart shines as it touches yours—as you behold my presence through reading these words, as I behold yours through writing them.

We call to each other because we are one. This is not unusual. This is how it really is.

Are you ready?

What you need is always right here, right now, a Master Teacher of Death and Shapeshifting reminds us once again. *That is all you need to know.*

Notes

CHAPTER 2. FACING FEAR

1. For the full story on the birds, see chapter 3, "Beginning with Birds" in Dawn Baumann Brunke, *Animal Voices: Telepathic Communication in the Web of Life* (Rochester, Vt.: Bear & Company, 2002).

CHAPTER 4. ENDLESS VARIATIONS AND INFINITE PERSPECTIVES

1. Carlos Casteneda, *Tales of Power* (New York: Simon & Schuster, 1974), 35–36.

CHAPTER 5. OPEN DOORWAYS

1. W. Y. Evans-Wentz, *The Tibetan Book of the Dead* (Oxford: Oxford University Press, 1960).

CHAPTER 6. A CONSCIOUS DEATH

1. Astrologers note that whereas big planetary conjunctions most often mark the ending of one cycle and the beginning of another, a Grand Cross is more akin to the balanced midpoint of a cycle. That is, the squared planets hold the tension of an evolutionary crossroads. Such crossroads are key points in our path precisely because this tautly balanced position reveals

the many potential futures that open before us, from which we may choose our path.

Although a planetary Grand Cross is a shared event, we may encounter similar "grand crossroads" within our personal lives. The underlying questions faced at a crossroads—whether planetary or individual—are much the same: Will we move into our future from a place of fear and control, stubbornly refusing to see beyond an "us" versus "them" mentality, thus severely dulling our consciousness and limiting our choices? Or, will we expand our awareness by moving consciously through the shadowlands of fear, deepening ourselves to accept more of who we really are, and celebrating the mutual interconnection of all life?

Although I have expressed this in the "one way or the other" format of a dualistic choice, there actually were, are, and will be infinite choices. Our world still holds a strong focus on dualism, so choices are often seen as "this way or that." Beyond the framework of duality, however, our choices are unlimited.

CHAPTER 7. WHAT HAPPENS NEXT

1. Max's full story can be found in Dawn Baumann Brunke, *Awakening to Animal Voices: A Teen Guide to Telepathic Communication with All Life* (Rochester, Vt.: Bindu Books, 2004), 79–80.

CHAPTER 10. LIMITLESS POSSIBILITIES

1. Walt Whitman, *Leaves of Grass* (New York: Viking Press, 1959), lines 1314–16.

CHAPTER 11. DEEPENING DREAM AWARENESS

1. A reference to Carlos Casteneda's *Tales of Power*.

CHAPTER 15. EMBRACING THE YETI

1. For example, see Alexandra David-Neel, *Magic and Mystery in Tibet* (New York: Dover Publications, 1971). (This book is a translation of the original French version, *Mystiques et magicians du Thibet,* published in 1929.)

CHAPTER 19. A NEW SET OF I'S

1. Walt Whitman, *Leaves of Grass,* line 39.

CHAPTER 20. CLAIMING PRESENCE

1. For more on the lion's sharing, see Dawn Baumann Brunke, *Awakening to Animal Voices*, "A Lesson from Lion," 230–31.
2. J. Allen Boone, *Adventures in Kinship with All Life* (Joshua Tree, Calif.: Tree of Life Publications, 1990), ix. (This book was originally published as *The Language of Silence* [New York: Harper & Row, 1970].)
3. Ibid., 32.

BOOKS OF RELATED INTEREST

Animal Voices
Telepathic Communication in the Web of Life
by Dawn Baumann Brunke

Awakening to Animal Voices
A Teen Guide to Telepathic Communication with All Life
by Dawn Baumann Brunke

How Animals Talk
And Other Pleasant Studies of Birds and Beasts
by William J. Long

Kinship with the Wolf
The Amazing Story of the Woman Who Lives with Wolves
by Tanja Askani

The Heart That Is Loved Never Forgets
Recovering from Loss: When Humans and Animals
Lose Their Companions
by Kaetheryn Walker

Dolphins and Their Power to Heal
by Amanda Cochrane and Karena Callen

Shapeshifting
Techniques for Global and Personal Transformation
by John Perkins

Animals and Psychedelics
The Natural World and the Instinct to Alter Consciousness
by Giorgio Samorini

Inner Traditions • Bear & Company
P.O. Box 388
Rochester, VT 05767
1-800-246-8648
www.InnerTraditions.com

Or contact your local bookseller